GOD *and* MAN *in* WASHINGTON

GOD and MAN
in
WASHINGTON

By Paul Blanshard

BEACON PRESS   BOSTON

Contents

Chapter I

Personal Prologue: The Church-State Battle Front

"God, says the unwritten glossary of American politics, is a word in the last paragraph of a political speech." So wrote Paul Hutchinson, late editor of the *Christian Century,* in an article describing recent religious developments in Washington.

Dr. Hutchinson's cynicism was, as we shall see in this book, quite justified. All Washington eulogies on religion are suspect on the ground that they may be self-serving. Every politician who kneels in public prayer is suspected of having one eye opened toward a press camera.

But this commentary on surface etiquette in the national capital should not divert attention from the underlying realities. As Dr. Hutchinson would have been the first to contend, the furbelows of pious publicity and the unctuous amens of the politicians are only superficial. Beneath them all is a serious national problem which America takes seriously. The relationship between God and man is one of the most important aspects of our national affairs.

Oddly enough, this aspect of American life is one of those most neglected by independent critics. Perhaps their neglect results most often from their natural and sincere reluctance to discuss anything so intensely personal as religious faith. Religion is, as the saying goes, a "delicate" matter; it is so closely bound up with men's personalities that they tend to regard any attack upon their religion as an attack upon themselves. At other times, how-

3

ever, this neglect may result primarily from a desire to escape unpleasant contumely and to gain a reputation for tolerance by keeping silent on controversial issues. In religious matters it is now fashionable to define tolerance as the absence of criticism of any standard religion. All too often, this absence of criticism degenerates into a conspicuous absence of thought.

In any case, men who venture to discuss politics and religion with maturity and candor are as scarce in Washington as are men who venture to discuss the British monarchy with maturity and candor in London. In both cases there are traditional taboos and the pretty clichés which brush aside all responsibility for serious analysis.

Washington Is You

This book is not simply a report on the nation's capital and the developments in that capital. It is a book about the American people, their religion and their government, with the focus on Washington. The thing that I call "Washington" does not exist in isolation. It is only the end product of a national process. There is a constant interaction between the activities of government in the national capital and the politico-religious forces in local communities. Often the national policy is shaded, diluted and distorted by local religious pressure groups. Often the thing that becomes national policy has been partially shaped by a local politico-religious machine whose power flows into Washington through the members of Congress who represent that machine.

An atheist in Topeka may be compelled to help finance the activities of a captive Catholic-public school—a public school operated by Catholic nuns who serve on the public payroll—because the Kansas courts have not been sufficiently alert to the Supreme Court's interpretation of the First Amendment clause prohibiting "the establishment of religion." A Catholic schoolteacher in Indiana may be denied the opportunity of teaching in a public school because a Klan-minded local school board never heard of—or never learned to respect—"the equal protection of the laws" guaranteed by the Fourteenth Amendment. A Protestant civil servant in the District of Columbia may be shunted from the logical line of promotion because the department personnel officer is a we-must-favor-our-own-people brand of Catholic who got his own promotion by virtue of that same gospel. A Jewish parent in Long Island may see his child ostracized and humiliated by the intrusion of Christian proselytism into a public classroom because some local school officials are under sectarian pressure from both Catholics and Protestants.

All these controversial religious issues—and thousands more —flow into the nation's capital as naturally as the great traffic avenues of Washington flow toward Capitol Hill. They are national issues which are the concern of all the people of all faiths. They are *your* concern because *WASHINGTON IS YOU*.

These Senators, Representatives, judges, Presidents, pageboys, lobbyists are people you have sent to Washington, either to govern America or to influence its government. You are paying for them, and they are your servants. If they meet religious issues in American politics with cowardly evasions and foolish platitudes, it is because you have lacked sufficient candor and courage in facing such issues. If they engage in legislative raids on the public treasury in behalf of clerical special privilege, it is because you have been less than alert in defending the American principle of the separation of church and state. If they condone the suppression of religious freedom when the victims are unpopular minorities, it is because you have not been sensitive enough to the rights of the heretic and the citizen of dissident views in your home town.

These are the dangers. But we may also take pride in our national religious picture. As nations go, we have done rather well in working out a plan for the relationship between church and state. We take both our religion and our government seriously, and we can be especially proud of the friendly relationship between them. In fact, the particular American combination of tolerance and church-state separation prescribed by our Constitution has often been rated as our most distinctive contribution to modern statecraft. The churches have thrived on it, and the government has flourished under it. Freedom of thought and freedom of faith have prospered under it. Without too much national vanity we could offer the combination to the world as a worthy example of the way in which democracy and religion may cooperate in a nation of many faiths.

Washington is the political hub of a country that has become not only one of the most powerful nations of the world but also one of the most religiously significant. Part of this religious significance can be traced to our size and wealth, but a great deal of it can also be traced to a sound policy in church-state relations. We have given free play to orthodoxy and to heresy in the market place of ideas, and our national unity has not been destroyed in the process. Our neutral state has escaped clerical domination, and our churches have prospered on the neutrality.

The United States is the leading Protestant nation in the world today, with more Protestants than all of Germany and more generous support for Protestant missions than that of any other nation. The United States has more Jews than any other nation— far more than Israel, which could scarcely survive without their support.[1] Although the American people are only one-fifth Roman Catholic, American Catholicism is rightly regarded as the primary factor in the world-wide expansion of Catholicism. It contributes more money to current Church revenues than all the rest of the world combined; if membership statistics were limited to practicing Catholics, the American Catholic Church would perhaps outnumber the Church in every other nation.

The Struggle on the Frontier

Probably most Americans, if they think about the matter at all, regard the problem of church-state relationship in our country as very simple. *We believe in religious freedom and the separation of church and state*—that capsule sentence includes many a citizen's total thought on church-state issues. It looks elementary, but it needs a whole encyclopedia to explain its ramifications and implications.

What is "religious freedom"? What is "church"? What is "state"? What is "separation"? Who should draw the frontiers between church and state power? There are a hundred different interpretations, and the differences are not merely verbal. They go to the very heart of our philosophy of government, and they involve the whole range of the thing we are fond of calling the American way of life.

One can approach these complex problems from a number of points of view. A sweetness-and-light book could be written about the flow of moral ideas from the churches into government and the counter-flow of government devotion to religious ideals. A philosophical treatise could be written about the underlying theories of Western religion and Western democracy. I have no inclination to write either of these books.

I have chosen rather to attempt a popular survey of the most important interactions between government and religion on the whole national church-state frontier, with emphasis on the current conflicts along that frontier. I believe that unless we can arrive at sound solutions in these controversial areas, our present successful plan of church-state relationship cannot survive.

Although I am writing primarily as a reporter of the Washington scene, I do not hesitate to indulge in editorial comment. As an advocate of the legal separation of church and state and a firm believer in the exercise of moral influence in politics, I write as a participant as well as an observer. It was Cardinal Manning who declared that "Politics are morals on the widest scale." In that sense there can never be a complete divorce between the moral forces of organized religion—or organized anti-religion—and the social programs of government. Religion is eternally relevant to politics, and politics is eternally relevant to religion, and no repetition of evasive disavowals can destroy this vital relationship.

Although religious freedom may be treated as an absolute value, the absolute separation of church and state in the United States is as unthinkable as the absolute union of church and state. The word "absolute" is used as a verbal hand grenade in current controversies about the separation of church and state. In actual practice there are no "absolute" factors in the controversy. Religion and government must live in a state of constant interaction, and somehow society must work out a code of conduct to govern that interaction.

All reasonable men recognize that, somewhere between the extremes of theory, somewhere between the complete union of church and state and their complete divorcement, Americans must find a middle ground of adjustment and understanding that will preserve a free church in a free society and simultaneously protect the liberties of the non-religious.

In spite of the many shortcomings in Washington's techniques in dealing with religion, it is my conviction that the present church-state policy of the American government is, on the whole, quite sound and satisfactory. The difficulty lies in application, not in fundamental policy. I believe that the responsibility of the informed citizen is to help preserve the present policy from further encroachment. In that respect I am, to borrow a horrendous phrase from Canadian politics, a progressive conservative. While asserting my loyalty to the underlying principles of the Constitution respecting church and state, I believe that constant vigilance and constant adjustment are necessary to make those principles effective in a changing world. I have faith that the future relationship of church and state in this country can reasonably be trusted to the men we have chosen for national leadership—if citizens are duly vigilant.

The basic scheme of this book is quite simple. In the chapter on "One Nation Under God," I try to describe the most important background items in the national religion-and-government panorama in Washington. Then, with constant emphasis upon the controversies that rage on the church-state frontier, I discuss the way in which the three great branches of our national government—the Supreme Court, Congress and the Presidency—confront religious issues. Then I close with a brief summary and exhortation in behalf of the neutral state as the best device for securing justice in a pluralistic society.

While some history is sandwiched into the discussion, the story of the past is incidental. Primarily this is a review of living events in contemporary America. It is offered as a possible handbook for the ordinary citizen who wants to know more and do more about preserving our religious liberties and the separation of church and state.

The Headline Issue

Although I consider the section on the Supreme Court to be the most permanently useful portion of this book, it is inevitable that the discussion of Catholicism and the Presidency should be considered the most newsworthy. America is approaching a Presidential campaign in which this issue will vitally concern millions of citizens. The 1960 pre-convention campaign—already in progress for more than two years—and the 1960 election campaign proper may well prove to be the most rigorous tests in our history of the capacity of American voters to analyze a politico-religious issue intelligently. Naturally, as a crusading liberal of forty years' experience in public affairs, I am concerned about bigotry, prejudice and hate in such a campaign. I am equally concerned about the attempt to stifle searching discussion of vital religious-political issues by the bland assumption that such discussion is necessarily based upon bigotry, prejudice and hate.

As I see it, two great potential disasters are involved in a campaign for and against a Catholic contender for the Presidency. They are alternative disasters. The first is the defeat of an able Catholic candidate simply because he has been born a Catholic and bears the Catholic label. The second is the election of a Catholic candidate without facing squarely the question of his relationship to those policies of his Church which threaten our present pluralistic society. Specifically I mean the Church's stand for (1) complete abolition of divorce, (2) complete prohibition of contraceptives, (3) the obligation of the state to support Catholic schools with public funds, (4) Church censorship, (5) discrimination against Protestants, Jews and unbelievers in mixed marriage, and (6) creedal segregation of Catholic children in a separate school system, with theological penalties for parents who refuse their bishops' orders to boycott public schools.

In the chapter on the Presidency, I shall document these six social policies and show that they are not merely incidental features of Catholicism. They are organic parts of the Church's highest law. I shall also discuss the reasons why, whether we like it or not, these policies are bound to enter into any campaign involving a Catholic Presidential candidate.

Of course, the current discussion of Catholicism in the press is centered almost entirely on Disaster One. Almost all public leaders from President Eisenhower down discuss "the religious issue" as if it consisted of nothing but unpleasant complications resulting from religious prejudice. They tend to brush aside Disaster Two as if it were the product of a diseased and bigoted imagination. In the chapter on the Presidency I shall try to point out the shortcomings of such an escapist approach.

My analysis of the Presidential issue is not directed toward any individual. I do not reflect upon the personal qualifications of any Catholic hopeful. Indeed, I confess to a considerable personal admiration for the leading Catholic contender, Senator John F. Kennedy, and I outline the reasons why he should be given due credit for challenging the most reactionary views of his own Church's hierarchy regarding certain church-state policies.

I have tried to preserve in these pages a point of view that is neither secularist nor sectarian, a point of view appropriate for a tolerant liberal democrat who believes in the practice of freedom in a pluralistic society. It is obvious that I do not undertake to discuss the truth or falsehood of any spiritual doctrine or dogmatic creed. This book is a study not in the field of theology but in the field of church-state relationships. It is designed for Protestants, Catholics, Jews and the unchurched, who all, I believe, have a right to share without discrimination in the blessings of a tolerant America.

God, man and the devil all belong in Washington because they are organic expressions of a free culture. It is one of the tasks of citizens in a democracy to decide for themselves which is supernal guidance, which is legitimate human welfare and which is diabolical self-interest.

Chapter II

"One Nation Under God"

The wind was cold and the sky murky on that January day in 1957 when Dwight David Eisenhower appeared on the East Capitol stands to take his second oath of office as President of the United States. Officially the ceremony was the inauguration of a civil President as head of a secular state. No bishop anointed the new chief of state; no pledge was asked or given to support any particular faith. The President, a Presbyterian, had asked his own pastor, the Reverend Dr. Edward L. R. Elson, to pronounce the invocation, but this event was quickly followed by other religious features that were neither Presbyterian nor Protestant. For the first time in American history, four faiths instead of three gained full official recognition.

A white-bearded, head-dressed leader of the Greek Orthodox Church, Archbishop Michael, stepped forward to the loudspeaker and gave a short prayer. After a rendition of "America the Beautiful" came another prayer, this time by Dr. Louis Finkelstein, Chancellor of the Jewish Theological Seminary of New York. Although the published oath for presidents contains no mention of God, both President Eisenhower and Vice President Nixon took their oaths on Protestant Bibles. The performance was ended by a benediction pronounced by the late Edward Cardinal Mooney of Detroit. Even the President's address was as much a sermon as a speech, and the glorious voice of Marian Anderson made "The Star-Spangled Banner" a hymn to the American dream.

Eisenhower at this inauguration is a symbol of what is happen-

ing to religion and to government in Washington. His two administrations have seen an enormous increase in church membership in
the United States and a marked change in the religious climate of
American politics. It is now "the thing to do" for government
officials to be effusively friendly to organized religion. Part of this
trend may be attributed to the President himself, who, although
he had never joined a church until he came to the capital, startled
his hearers at the first inaugural by beginning his address with a
simple prayer. It had been written in longhand at the Statler
Hotel the morning of the ceremony, and the desk on which he
wrote it is now being preserved as historic. In fact, the enthusiasts
of the Republican National Committee had to be warned in 1956
by the White House to discontinue the use of the prayer as a campaign document.

The President wrote: "We pray that our concern shall be for
all people, regardless of station, race or calling—so that all may
work for the good of our beloved country and for Thy glory." [1]

That simple fusion of the concepts of God, man and government may be taken as quite typical of the average American's outlook. It is not new. More than 125 years ago the French writer
Alexis de Tocqueville, a liberal Catholic, coming from a land where
church and state were officially fused, was astonished to find that
the moral fusion of church and state was far more complete in the
United States than it was in Europe with its established churches.
"In the United States," he said, "the sovereign authority is religious. . . . Religion in America takes no direct part in the government of society, but it must nevertheless be regarded as the
foremost of the political institutions of that country. . . . In
France I had almost always seen the spirit of religion and the
spirit of freedom pursuing courses diametrically opposed to each
other; but in America I found they were intimately united, and
that they reigned in common over the same country." [2]

It would be an exaggeration to say that religion "reigns"—
in common or independently—over America today. But there is

no doubt that religious institutions are more widely diffused and more prosperous in our present society than they have ever been before in the history of our country. "We are a religious people whose institutions presuppose a Supreme Being," said Justice William O. Douglas in a Supreme Court decision in 1952.[3] Then he proceeded, speaking for the Court, to permit released-time religious classes which meet outside public school buildings but are informally connected with the public school system. To some extent, that was a constitutional innovation in a country which had stood traditionally for the separation of church and state. It reflected the conviction of many Americans—perhaps even a majority—that somehow religion should be given some recognition, at least on the fringes of the public educational system.

Behind the Supreme Court concession, and perhaps explaining it, was the pressure of growing church power—money power and membership power. Neither Congress nor the Supreme Court can ignore such power. It is estimated that Americans contributed about $3,400,000,000 to religious causes in 1957.[4] This is almost $20 for every man, woman and child in the country, and more than $30 for each church member.

In George Washington's day, about one in every ten persons in the United States belonged to a church;[5] in Lincoln's day, the ratio was about one in five; now nearly 61 per cent of the American people belong to some church or synagogue, and a far larger proportion acknowledge some kind of religious classification.

Although all statistics in the religious field are inexact because there is no independent government census of the various faiths, the Bureau of the Census made elaborate test checks in 1957 that showed the trend in majority sentiment.[6] About 96 per cent of the people, when they were asked "What is your religion?" classified themselves as either Protestants, Catholics or Jews. About 66 per cent chose the Protestant classification; 26 per cent the Catholic; and 3 per cent the Jewish. Only 3 per cent denied religious preference altogether.

The results were hotly challenged—and rightly so—by non-church groups because of the general and ambiguous nature of the question. These groups argued that such a question called for nothing more specific than a burial classification, similar to that used in the Army or in prisons. They claimed that actual church membership figures are the only true index of church strength and that such a yardstick would show that some 68,000,000 Americans are outside all formal religious organizations.[7] But even the severest critics admitted that the trial census probably measured quite accurately the proportionate strength of religious groups in this country.

The unchurched Americans, some 68,000,000, constitute both a statistical and a religious puzzle. Apparently about 61,000,000 of them do not belong to any church but choose to put some kind of religious tag upon themselves when they are asked: "What is your religion?" They are, for the most part, Protestant-oriented; but no one knows whether their loyalties are in any sense sectarian or whether they accept only what H. W. Garrod once called "the religion of all good men."

Meanwhile the official figures seem to show that the United States has become one of the most religious countries in the world, with at least 104,000,000 church members. A 1958 Gallup poll indicated that nearly half of the adult population attended church in a sample week during that year.[8] In membership power the Roman Catholic Church, with nearly 36,000,000 members, is far in the lead among individual denominations. Protestants combined claim about 60,000,000, and they could claim millions more if they used the Catholic system of arithmetic. (The Roman Catholic Church counts all baptized babies as full members; most Protestant churches do not.) Among Protestants, the Baptist grouping—sharply divided between Northern and Southern Baptists—comes first, with a total of about 20,000,000. The Methodists, the largest single Protestant denomination, come next with more than 12,000,000. The Lutherans—also sharply divided—

come third with about 7,500,000. The Presbyterians come fourth with more than 4,000,000, and the Episcopalians are fifth with about 3,000,000.

The 1957 test check by the Bureau of the Census, in which the same method of calculation was applied to all denominations, showed that (in terms of the loosely worded question used in that test) the Baptist-Methodist combination outnumbers the American Catholic total by more than 9,000,000 and the balance of American Protestantism outnumbers the Catholic total by some 17,000,-000. All American Protestants together outnumber American Catholics about 2½ to 1. Or, to put the statistical conclusion differently, America is still by personal preference two-thirds a Protestant country.

The Religious Base of Political Power

How much political meaning do these figures have? At the national level the answer is largely guesswork. If religious statistics have any political significance whatever, the significance is largely regional. Rural America is still so overwhelmingly Protestant that few Catholics or Jews are ever elected to Congress from a farm district. The same can be said for the old South. In that section only Louisiana has any appreciable Catholic strength—about one-third of the population. The Southwest is changing a little from the solidly Protestant nineteenth-century pattern because of the influx of Mexican immigrants; and New England, once the stronghold of Congregationalism, now has more official Catholics than official Protestants in every state. In fact, the Catholic Church claims about 48 per cent of the total population of New England.[9]

Here the religious division is definitely partisan. The Democratic Party in New England tends to be predominantly Catholic while the Republican Party is reluctantly associated with Protestantism. With Catholicism claiming more than half of the babies born in Massachusetts, Connecticut and Rhode Island, the future of the Republican Party in these states seems very bleak.

The religious-political picture is strikingly similar in several large cities and states outside New England. Catholic Church membership outruns total Protestant membership in New York, New Jersey and California.[10] Buffalo has a clear Catholic majority, and Chicago, with nearly 2,000,000 Catholics, has a probable Catholic majority. Catholicism now claims about half of the total population of New York City, where Jews are second and Protestants third in the religious classifications. The exclusion of Protestants from high office in New York City has become almost a scandal. In 1959 only 3 of the 34 heads of city departments were Protestants, and only 11 of 208 judges were Protestants.[11]

This urban strength of Catholicism—and the correlative weakness of urban Protestantism—has naturally produced results in national politics. The results are most evident in the Democratic Party because of its urban strength in the North. In part this is a historical accident. There is no difference whatever between the two great parties nationally in matters of church-state policy. Both give enthusiastic lip service to the American tradition of religious freedom and the separation of church and state, and both avoid all reference to controversial aspects of these subjects whenever possible.

The old Southern wing of the Democratic Party is overwhelmingly Protestant because the Southern region is overwhelmingly Protestant. The South chose the Democratic Party long ago, chiefly because it represented the opposition to the anti-slavery forces in the Republican Party. When the largely proletarian Northern Irish Catholics chose the Democratic Party in the middle of the nineteenth century, it was because they were the underdogs in Northern economic society. Naturally they joined the party of protest and discontent, which happened to be the Democratic Party.

This accidental religious alignment of Protestant strength in the South and Catholic strength in the North creates a constantly embarrassing situation for Democratic leaders. The Northern Democratic liberal, whose political fate largely depends on the approval of Democratic Catholic voters in Northern cities, must never say anything in public that can be interpreted as offensive to the Catholic Church. At the same time, if this Northern liberal wants support from the South for his national ambitions, he must be equally careful not to offend the militantly Protestant South.

Republican leaders have a much easier time. They have no large and differing religious blocs within the party that must be reconciled. Their membership is largely Protestant because the nation is largely Protestant and because they have not had to rely for strength on the post-Civil War waves of European immigration. They have enough Catholic leaders for window-dressing, and they publicize these leaders systematically, but they have relatively few Catholic and Jewish followers. Various studies have revealed that both the Catholic vote and the Jewish vote are overwhelmingly Democratic.[12]

It is easy to read too much meaning into these religious statistics. The significance is largely negative: no religious bloc in our society is large enough to guarantee national political success without the help of other segments in the population. Because there are some 36,000,000 baptized Catholics in our population of 175,000,000, it is commonly assumed in Washington that any politician who is branded "anti-Catholic" is doomed as a national figure. This assumption is probably quite correct, but the correlative fact that an aroused Protestantism can easily doom any Catholic figure in national politics is often overlooked.

The members of the two largest Protestant groupings in the United States, Baptist and Methodist, are, on the whole, militant defenders of the principle of church-state separation. They are also very suspicious of the foreign dictatorial control of the Catholic Church. Their combined membership strength of 32,000,000 is not quite equal to the official membership of the Roman Catholic

Church, only because of the generous mathematical methods used by Catholicism in recording its membership. Actually, these two great Protestant groupings together have more votes than all the Catholic votes in the United States, and there is not much doubt that they would be marshaled effectively at the polls if Baptists and Methodists became convinced that any candidate stood for principles or policies threatening the American tradition of church-state separation.

In this official picture of an officially religious people, the non-believers and the unchurched citizens occupy a very equivocal position. They have no spokesman in Congress, no liaison representative at the White House and no organized lobby or pressure group in Washington to speak for them. They are seldom included in any discussion of the rights of religious groups. They are almost completely excluded from the newspapers, the radio and television, especially if they attempt to say anything negative about any powerful religious organization. They dominate many of the leading universities, but that intellectual domination has no corresponding recognition in Washington.

Even the historical role of the unorthodox in building our free institutions is usually overlooked in the history books. Few people realize, for example, that more than 90 per cent of the American people were outside all churches when the nation was founded and that the presence of this non-church majority was to a considerable extent responsible for the two most unique contributions of our culture to political life—religious freedom and the separation of church and state. The churches themselves might never have given America these blessings. Most of the early colonists who were members of churches were quite intolerant men who preached neither religious freedom for those who disagreed with them nor the disestablishment of the churches. They did not guarantee religious freedom for their Christian opponents, and they denied political rights to unbelievers. They were forced to accept a policy of tolerance and church-state separation not only by the cataclysmic events of the Revolution but also by the pressure of the unchurched.

Catholic, Protestant, Jew—that is the prevailing, tripartite description of the religious composition of America. Occasionally someone remembers to mention the Greek Orthodox as a kind of fourth faith. The "fifth faith" of secular humanism is usually ignored as purely negative or inconsequential. Downright atheism is almost unknown, and the word "atheism" has become such a dreaded label in politics that no Washington figure would dare to call himself an atheist publicly. A Gallup poll in the fall of 1958 showed that four out of five voters in America would refuse to vote for an avowed atheist for President under any circumstances. The same poll indicated that less than one-third of the anti-atheist group would prejudge any Catholic or Jew adversely. A 1955 study indicated that the majority of the American people would not even allow an atheist book to remain in a public library if they could prevent it.[13]

Of course, this lowly status of atheism is partly due to the special association of atheism with Communism. Communists are atheists; Communists are America's No. 1 enemies; ergo, atheists are also America's No. 1 enemies. This simple reasoning is good enough for most Congressmen. "The main issue involved in the world today," proclaimed a Wisconsin Congressman in 1948, "is the great basic issue of atheism as against belief in God; realizing that Lenin himself said that Communism is coextensive with atheism. . . ."[14] As D. W. Brogan of Cambridge has expressed it: " 'There are no atheists in the foxholes,' and America is now in the foxhole that she may have to inhabit for a generation. The consequence of this predicament is that refusal to give lip service, at least, to the American religion is a kind of treason and is punished as it was in the America of a century ago."

This extreme hostility to the absolute unbeliever never seems to extend to any group of people who can use a religious label.

Even an extremist cult may acquire full legal protection and considerable freedom from newspaper criticism. When 250,000 Jehovah's Witnesses jammed two great baseball stadiums in New York in August 1958, the authorities were cooperative and the New York newspapers quite respectful.

Official Godliness

When Eisenhower was first inaugurated in 1953, somebody thought at the last moment that the gigantic inaugural parade, which celebrated almost everything from motherhood to the success of the Republican Party, should also celebrate God. A contrivance called "God's Float" was rushed to completion, but there was considerable embarrassment because of the shortage of appropriate materials. The float could not look Catholic, Protestant or Jewish—at least not *too* Catholic, Protestant or Jewish. It would have to be given some dignified place of honor in the parade. But where? Finally, it was put first, and at the heart of the display was placed a rather innocuous and not-quite-denominational building surrounded with mottoes reading "In God We Trust" and "Freedom of Worship."

That truck may well be taken as a symbol of the new era of religious symbols in Washington politics. The new Capitol Prayer Room for Congressmen, near the Rotunda, is physically the most permanent of these religious symbols. The plan for its construction, originally defeated in the Senate in 1952, was finally sponsored successfully in 1954 by a Southern Baptist Representative and an Episcopalian Senator (Brooks Hays of Arkansas and Mike Monroney of Oklahoma). The new room has been in steady use ever since its opening in March 1955.

Although the Prayer Room is paid for by public taxes, even the atheist *Truthseeker* has remarked that it is "helpful" as a "cooling-off room" for troubled legislators. There has been an honest attempt to make it entirely undenominational, primarily a personal service room for individual members. It is, as its description indicates, a "place for meditation," only seventeen feet square and with only ten chairs. It is not available for any exhibitions or assemblies. If it is offensive to non-Christian members because of some of the accompanying features, they have not yet protested. A stained-glass window, provided by private gifts, shows George Washington kneeling in prayer; and other exhibits of the Washington period indicate, according to the Jesuit magazine *America,* "a clear profession of the general's belief in the divinity of Jesus Christ." The editors felt bound to add: "An undenominational prayer room is not, in itself, an ideal." [15]

Actually, the Jesuit magazine was overoptimistic in its Christian interpretation of the objects in the Prayer Room. A Jewish donor has recently presented two large, seven-pronged candlesticks for display in the room, and they almost dominate the scene. The room has no cross.

The purpose of the Prayer Room has been hailed in verse by a poet, Albert Brighton, whose tribute was inserted in the *Congressional Record.*

> A place of prayer where Congressmen,
>   Great Senators, and men
> Representing God, and people
>   Of our country enter when
> There is cause for meditation,
>   A grave decision to be made.
> Men of wisdom, from our sod
>   Seek greater wisdom from our God.
> Men who link their destinies
>   With Him who knows before
> How distant is our harbor,
>   How peaceful is our shore.
> How pure the hearts professing
>   Their faith in Him to know,
> The things that we have need of,
>   The course our step should go.[16]

The Eisenhower administration has attempted to extend to international circles the concept of prayer as a means of moral guidance for political leaders. Henry Cabot Lodge, Jr., United States ambassador to the United Nations, proposed in 1955 that each United Nations Assembly meeting should be opened with a vocal prayer. A New York Catholic Congressman has renewed the attempt regularly, calling on the U.N. to adopt this practice, but both moves have been defeated.

The recognition of prayer as a ceremonial accompaniment of governmental occasions is as old as the nation. So far as I can discover, no federal court has ever ruled against it. The practice is indirectly recognized in the annual Thanksgiving proclamations of the President, which became a national tradition in spite of the objections of Thomas Jefferson. It has been sanctioned for 170 years by the practice of opening each daily session of the Senate and House with prayer by a salaried chaplain. (The Senate chaplain receives $5,500 a year, and the House chaplain $8,192.) Madison in his *Detached Memoranda* strenuously protested that this service of paid chaplains was unconstitutional. He was probably right in theory under a strict construction of the First Amendment. Some of his legal objections were revived in 1854 by a motley group of objectors ranging from free-thinkers to "Particular Baptists," but they were rejected by Congressional committees and the established practice was continued.[17] Now it seems to be so well established that, if the courts interfered, Congress would doubtless initiate a permissive constitutional amendment.

Usually the chaplains of both houses are orthodox Protestants—most recently Methodists and Presbyterians—who have served local churches as regular pastors for a number of years. Their words, as the *Chicago Sun-Times* once said of one house, "are least heeded of any of the millions of words uttered in the United States Senate." There have been two Roman Catholic Congressional chaplains in our history, but no Greek Orthodox or Jewish chaplains. Two distinguished Unitarians have served—

Jared Sparks, later president of Harvard, and Edward Everett Hale.

One Senate chaplain has become quite famous in recent years, more through his wife's best-selling books than through his own achievements. He was Presbyterian Peter Marshall, famed as *A Man Named Peter,* whose soft Scotch burr and rather daring punch lines lifted his prayers even to the attention of the Senators. Before his untimely death in 1949 he had served only two years, having been maneuvered into the position in a rather embarrassing Republican coup engineered by Senator Wherry of Nebraska, Republican whip, who attended his church. The previous and present Methodist Senate chaplain, Dr. Frederick Brown Harris, was temporarily displaced but returned to his post after Marshall's death.

Marshall, who was far from being intellectually impressive, made Godliness theatrically familiar, using such yeasty phrases in addressing the Deity as "coupon clippers," "meeting deadlines," "our swelled heads" and "original investments." Once he prayed to God and some rather convulsed Senators: "Save us from the sin of worrying, lest stomach ulcers be the badge of our lack of faith."

Marshall could not be charged with hortatory inspiration since every chaplain in these modern days of automation must type out his prayers for the Congressional shorthand reporters in advance. In spite of occasional partisan inferences, the prayers in recent years have rarely been offensively personal or partisan. But this has not always been the case. A chaplain in Andrew Johnson's day prayed publicly that the impeached President "might be humbled and cast down"; another chaplain used the Congressional forum to tell God in angry accents that Abraham Lincoln was going to the theater too often "while Rome was burning."

Today politics in the opening prayers of the Senate and House seems to be permissible only if it is anti-Soviet. In 1958, a Byelorussian archbishop of the Orthodox faith, in praying before the Senate, delivered a short political oration reminding God that this was the "anniversary of the Declaration of Independence of Byelorussia, whose freedom was mercilessly suppressed with brute, godless force." In 1959 an Orthodox Ukrainian priest, praying before the House, rendered similar service for his country. He reminded God that this was the forty-first anniversary of the Ukrainian National Republic and that "Thou alone, O Lord, can grant us and all captive nations everlasting freedom."

The near-Protestant monopoly in the Congressional chaplaincies is balanced a little by quite frequent invitations to Catholic, Jewish and Greek Orthodox clergymen to serve as substitute petitioners. There is keen competition from outside visiting divines for the honor of offering these prayers. Since every legislative day must begin with prayer, and sometimes a legislative day begins late at night, Congress occasionally falls back on its own members for opening prayers. There are two Protestant clergymen in the House, but the favorite pinch-hitter in Congress is Senator Wallace F. Bennett of Utah, who is not only a leader of the Mormon Church but also an author of two books on religion.

The prayers, usually delivered to a very slim audience—sometimes there are no more than six persons in the congregation—are preceded in the House by a short verse of scripture. They express in carefully chosen language very broad moral aspirations. Although they can hardly be offensive to any followers of any Christian faith, they frequently end with such direct commitments to "our Lord and Saviour Jesus Christ" that they must make Jewish and agnostic Congressmen squirm a little.

Political party conventions escape any such slight religious discrimination in arranging their prayers. Great care is used in these conventions to see that every possible shade and sector of sectarian allegiance is given recognition in swift rotation. At the 1956 Democratic convention in Chicago, prayers were delivered in successive sessions by a Catholic cardinal, a Southern Baptist vice president, a Methodist bishop, a Reform Jewish rabbi, a Greek Orthodox bishop, an Episcopal rector and the national president of the United Lutheran Church.

The belief is quite widespread that Catholic Congressmen must stay away from non-Catholic Congressional prayers under the rules of their Church. Frequently they do stay away, but the absence is quite inadvertent. The prayers are held before the first roll call, and there are many Congressional excuses for being a few moments late. In any case, though Catholics are forbidden by their canon law to participate in any *formal* worship service of Protestants or Jews, this prohibition does not prevent attendance at a brief religious ceremonial which is part of a public function.

Recent Protestant Presidents and countless lesser officials have developed a habit of attending both Protestant and non-Protestant functions with great alacrity. They welcome the accompanying flash-bulbs as legitimate public relations and permit themselves to be photographed in private religious postures. An Annual Prayer Breakfast has been conducted under Protestant auspices since 1953 by the International Christian Leadership, Inc., a very conservative private organization. Eisenhower has attended this function on a number of occasions, and on one occasion he appeared publicly at the Catholic Red Mass at St. Matthew's Church, an annual affair promoted for many years by Catholic lawyers.

These personal manifestations of religious faith by high government officials excite no criticism in Washington; quite the contrary. They are treated not as violations of the American principle of church-state separation but as personal expressions of personal religious freedom. They are accepted as evidence not only of political sagacity but also of essential goodness and dependability. It is argued that if a President could not assert his personal belief in God, he could not consider himself a free citizen. He could also cite many precedents in important American documents to support such utterances.

Although the federal Constitution contains no mention of

God, forty-four of the fifty state constitutions bring in some kind of acknowledgment of the Deity, including the new constitution of Alaska. It is to be expected that the President of an overwhelmingly religious country should frequently express the religious convictions of the majority, either directly or indirectly. He is under constant pressure to promote religious faith by his public utterances, and it would be surprising if he did not respond favorably to the pressure. One fundamentalist group chided President Eisenhower in 1958 for omitting a reference to God from man's first message from outer space, a tape recording of the President's voice from an American satellite.

The official promotion of religion enters a more controversial field when public property is used for sectarian celebrations. Should churches be allowed to use public parks for religious mass meetings? For the time being, Washington's answer is *Yes,* provided the use is extended without discrimination to all denominations. On October 5, 1958, more than 100,000 persons gathered at the Washington Monument to celebrate the centennial of the Lourdes apparition of the Virgin Mary, and a great imitation of the Lourdes grotto was built at Catholic expense for the celebration. It occupied the Monument grounds for more than a week. Previously, Billy Graham had used the Capitol steps for a mass meeting, and several local Protestant groups had used one side of the Washington Monument grounds. At the White House Christmas celebrations each year, held between December 22 and New Year's Day, both Catholics and Protestants have some feature programs on the Ellipse grounds between the White House and the Washington Monument.

The record does not show any corresponding free-thought demonstration on public land, but it is likely that such a demonstration would be permitted if the free-thought forces could rally sufficient numbers. In 1947 the American Unitarian Association used the Jefferson Memorial grounds to celebrate the 204th anniversary of Jefferson's birth, proclaiming that "Christianity must abandon its claim to a monopoly of the way to salvation" and advocating "a world fellowship of faiths" free of "spiritual imperialism."

Even more controversial than this religious use of property is the imposition of religious mottoes, pledges and in some cases taxes on the whole national community. I shall discuss the legal implications of such developments later. Here it may be appropriate to list a few of the more controversial features.

In 1956 the phrase "In God We Trust" was adopted as our national motto without floor debate and without a single dissenting vote in either house.[18] The manner of adoption was more significant than the fact of adoption. The measure was originally sponsored by a Protestant, and the favorable Senate report was submitted by a Catholic. All Congressmen involved in the enterprise seemed bent on avoiding any public discussion of any controversial issue. No objectors were given a hearing, although written protests by responsible organizations had been filed with the Senate Judiciary Committee months before passage. After the passage of the enabling joint resolution, a brief committee report defending the action was entered in the *Congressional Record* without even being read on the floor. It cited the fact that the new motto had ample precedent in history, as indeed it had. It had been used on coins as early as 1865 and had been made mandatory for all currency in 1955.

There was a little more public discussion in 1954 when eleven different Representatives of varying faiths rushed to introduce resolutions—which were ultimately passed in June of that year—writing the phrase "under God" into the traditional pledge of allegiance to the flag. The House Judiciary subcommittee adopted the idea unanimously after messages had been received from leading Protestant organizations and from Cardinal Mooney. The chief sponsor for the resolution was a Roman Catholic, Representative Louis C. Rabaut of Michigan. The new pledge now reads: "I pledge allegiance to the flag of the United States of America and to the republic for which it stands, one nation under God, indivisible, with liberty and justice for all."

Is the imposition of such a pledge on school children in tax-supported institutions a violation of their constitutional rights? It undoubtedly would be a violation if the pledge were compulsory; decisions by the Supreme Court in the flag salute cases (these will be discussed later) make this quite clear. But Congress was aware of the difficulty, and it has made no attempt to impose the phrase "under God" by force upon unwilling children. When free-thinker Joseph Lewis challenged the pledge in the New York Supreme Court in 1957, arguing that the "guarantee of freedom of religion extends to non-believers as it does to those who choose religion," the New York Court ruled against the plaintiff on the ground that there was no compulsion.[19] Normally a child can refuse to take the pledge of allegiance to the flag altogether, or remain silent during the recitation of that one phrase "one nation under God."

The Supreme Court has not yet answered much more serious questions concerning many peripheral pro-religious activities which involve some tax expenditures. For a number of years the United States Information Agency has had on its payroll two Protestant clergymen, alternating in a post described as Chief of the Religious Section of the United States Information Agency. These ministers have continued publicly to promote a vague, general, pro-Christian outlook in a genteel but quite unmistakably Christian manner. Their office costs the taxpayers very little, and probably their activity is technically constitutional because they are information officers advising the United States government concerning the kind of information about American religious activity which foreign citizens should receive. They help to select the books that are placed in American libraries abroad to inform foreign citizens about America's social conditions, and it is assumed that American religious activity is an important part of those conditions. They serve as liaison officers between American information agencies and the churches of the United States.

More questionable is the gigantic government program for disposing of American surplus goods to the destitute in Europe, Asia and Africa, largely through official sectarian agencies. Catholic, Protestant and Jewish agencies, together with other voluntary agencies, have all participated in this program and have distributed, over a period of six years, surplus and relief goods valued at a total of $670,000,000.[20] Catholic agencies distribute far more goods than all other religious agencies combined, and more than four times as much as CARE.

To many of the millions of needy persons in Formosa, Italy and other foreign countries, the gift and the sectarian giver are one. The packages distributed under this plan bear a clear label saying that they come from all the people of the United States; but when they are given to needy persons by official missionary leaders, the flag and the money of the United States are certainly aiding the promotion of sectarian missionary endeavor. Whether the picture on the label is a picture of the Pope or of Martin Luther, the effect is still the same. American power and prestige are being used in religious promotion—in some places, such as Formosa, with quite scandalous abuses.[21] But thus far, this program has excited almost no opposition in Washington. The churches, of course, contribute a considerable sum from their own revenues, in cash and supplies, to implement the enterprise, and government officials are grateful that they can secure voluntary and honest distributors.

This problem of the distribution of surplus goods through sectarian agencies is a striking illustration of the difficulty which any honest official faces in drawing a constitutional line between church and state. Nominally the government is forbidden to spend any public money for religious promotion; but if a critical and unorthodox taxpayer sought evidence that the federal government is spending his money for religion, he could find quite a formidable list of questionable items. The total sum would certainly run into billions if he included in the list the exemption of churches from local taxation, the distribution of surplus goods and the pay of government chaplains. An angry Minnesota taxpayer did in fact charge, in a 1955 suit, that the United States spent $28,350,000 for the salaries and religious supplies of 993 Catholic, 2,371 Protestant and 102 Jewish chaplains in the armed services, and that the expenditures were unconstitutional since he, as a taxpayer, was being "forced to pay a part of the cost of promulgating religious doctrines" which were abhorrent to him. The suit was thrown out without an examination of the merits of the case on the ground that the taxpayer lacked standing to sue.[22]

All these federal expenditures or exemptions for religion have some legal or traditional excuse. It is said that they are not direct expenditures for sectarian promotion as such, although everybody admits that they come very close to that in some cases. Congress has never passed any general appropriation for religious institutions except those which partake of the nature of personal services for federal or armed services employees. The distribution of government surplus goods through sectarian workers is justified on the ground that the sectarian workers are merely agents in the distribution. The payments to armed services chaplains are defended on the ground that the members of the armed forces are deprived by government directives of their ordinary opportunities for the free choice of religious institutions, and the government must supply religious services as it supplies doctors, dentists and barbers. The argument for tax exemption of churches is that they are exempted as non-profit corporations, not merely as religious institutions, and that many non-religious organizations are given similar favors.

We shall see in the next chapter that there is no completely consistent legal pattern for these borderline phenomena in the no man's land between church and state. There is no such thing in reality as the absolute separation of church and state.

Religion or Religiosity?

On the whole, the new Washington religious boom is as form-less and misty as a politician's peroration. Its devils are all accepted stereotypes; its angels wear no denominational wings; it is purpose-fully vague on all denominational details; it eschews everything controversial; it radiates good will. Countless religious journalists of every denomination have called this new phenomenon religiosity rather than religion. They have declared that it is an attempt to fulfill social needs rather than religious needs. One California clergyman called it "spiritual aspirin": "It doesn't cost much, doesn't do much, and isn't worth much."

The religious allegiance of politicians has occasioned much satire in recent years. The late Elmer Davis has been quoted by Dr. William Lee Miller as saying in 1954: "The greatest demon-stration of the religious character of this administration came on July Fourth, which the President told us all to spend as a day of penance and prayer. Then he himself caught four fish in the morn-ing, played eighteen holes of golf in the afternoon, and spent the evening at the bridge table." [23] In the 1956 Presidential campaign an impudent atheist philosopher from Minneapolis, announcing his candidacy for President on the mythical atheist ticket, pledged: "Just before election, if it doesn't cost too much, I will follow the examples of Eisenhower and Stevenson and join the Presbyterian Church to impress the women voters with my extreme piety, too. This will be a wise move politically for it will split the Presbyterian vote three ways."

Probably government officials are no more hypocritical about religion than other people. They must take into account the im-pression made on religious voters by conspicuous religious faith. They must demonstrate their essential goodness and respectability, and church membership is one of the accepted indices of good character. They cannot be expected to forget the couplet of Arthur Clough:

> The church on Sunday to attend,
> Will serve to make the world thy friend.

Perhaps it is a good thing for America that the religion of Washington politicians stops with this simple identification of goodness and faith. Controversial theology is completely taboo, and all the time-consuming quarrels of doctrine are thus averted. If a national political leader ever says anything for publication about the substantive content of religion, it is likely to remind one of Mark Twain's comment: "You can throw a cart at that sentence and not hit anything." Alexander Miller has published a comment which is applicable to political religion in Washington today: "Faith has obviously got something to do with trust or confidence, but this is about as far as the colloquial use takes us. . . . There is a story of an English M.P. who, after the 1928 debate in the Commons on the Revised Prayer Book, came out of the House muttering that he didn't see what all the fuss was about. 'Surely,' said he, 'we all believe in some kind of something.' " [24]

The "some kind of something" which official Washington accepts is totally non-creedal. It is a faith in faith and moral optimism, not in established dogma. President Eisenhower has been quoted as saying: "Our government makes no sense, unless it is founded in a deeply felt religious faith—and I don't care what it is."

The one essential in this politically acceptable faith is some kind of belief in some kind of God. No one insists on any particular definition of that concept of God, but it is assumed without discussion that the Deity has some positive connection with the Judeo-Christian tradition. If He is not exactly an Americanized God, He is very respectful to Americanism and all that goes with it. The new American Legion building on 17th Street carries in huge block letters the inscription: FOR GOD AND COUNTRY.

There is no suggestion that the two causes might ever be in conflict.

Some religious leaders see danger to orthodoxy in this partial identification with patriotism, and they speak of the possible peril of subordinating the church and its faith to a secular state. They even ask: Is American democracy becoming a substitute religion? Is nationalism replacing faith?

I see no need for clerical anxiety, at least for Christian anxiety. Jews have some basis for complaint because the increased ceremonial promotion of religion in Washington tends to be pro-Christian. But the official neutralism of Washington in all dogmatic matters is a friendly and cooperative neutralism which is quite charitable to all faiths. Although it has a pro-Protestant coloration because of America's Protestant past, it is not hostile to Catholicism, nor is it consciously and deliberately hostile to Judaism. The noted French critic André Siegfried once made a comment about the secure position of religion in American life which may well be applied to political religion in Washington: "Neither Protestantism nor Catholicism is threatened from without by aggressive disbelief, for the agnostics, though numerous, maintain the Protestant vocabulary and the Protestant outlook on moral problems. They like its background, and they're not hostile in any way."

America has no political movement corresponding to European anti-clericalism, and the average American sees no clash between loyalty to his God and loyalty to his nation. One reason for this attitude is that God has not been used in American history to put a clerical class in power above the nation: no church has successfully challenged the power of the national state. The American feels no antagonism between state and religion. He may even have become a little blind in this matter. He has come to believe too uncritically the milk-and-honey propaganda of uncritical tolerance, and he fails to appreciate the dangers of clerical encroachment upon American democracy. He takes the separation of church and state a little too much for granted.

The American is able to take this relatively carefree attitude toward church-state problems partly because there is no single, all-powerful church. There are 267 religious denominations in the United States, 82 of which have memberships of over 50,000. In that religious pluralism there is safety for the neutral state—and also safety for the small church, which might be persecuted by any single, dominant church. The American politician is not bound to accept any particular item of any particular creed in order to be described as religious. He therefore tends to reduce his creed to an absolute minimum and to include in that creed a general amiability toward all faiths. The details of religion, he believes, can be left to the preachers and the priests.

The Local Mosaic

In early times, when Washington was a small city, the federal government participated directly in local church affairs by holding religious services in the old chamber of the House, with the House chaplain as preacher. Occasionally guest preachers were brought in from outside the area, and later the Senate chamber was also used in this manner.

This practice was particularly popular during the administration of Jefferson, who, although he was not a church member, was probably more interested in religion than any of our other Presidents.[25] He actually extracted a whole book from the New Testament, *The Life and Morals of Jesus of Nazareth,* frequently described as "The Jefferson Bible." Although he was intellectually a Unitarian, he was scrupulously impartial in bringing to the Capitol preachers of all standard Christian denominations. According to Canon Stokes, these visiting dignitaries helped to draw great crowds to the House chamber and were more popular than the regular Congressional chaplains. Congressman Abijah Bigelow of Massachusetts remarked that the regular chaplains were "miserable preachers, I mean not to say that they are bad men, but their discourses are much below mediocrity." [26]

Occasionally, when less mediocre men filled the House pulpit, they tended to get the government deeply involved in doctrinal quarrels. The appointment of Unitarian Jared Sparks as chaplain to the House in 1821 touched off a great commotion in the Washington press. The Episcopal clergyman at St. John's, attacking the appointment of so unorthodox a chaplain as Sparks, preached what John Quincy Adams called a "sermon of coarse invective upon the House, who he said, by this act had voted Christ out of doors." An orthodox New York Congressman tried in vain to get a substitute chaplain appointed. On another occasion, John England, Roman Catholic Bishop of Charleston, was welcomed for one Sunday and handled delicate subjects with great skill. He puzzled his Catholic hearers and pleased his non-Catholic admirers by flatly repudiating the infallibility of the Pope. (This was before the doctrine had become binding upon all Catholics.)

Today a sectarian church meeting in the Senate or House chambers would be as unthinkable as a meeting of the Communist Party. The resultant theological quarrels would be regarded with unmixed horror by the chairmen of both the Republican and the Democratic National Committees.

Greater Washington—the area which includes two counties in Maryland, two in Virginia and the city of Alexandria, with a total population of about 2,000,000 inhabitants—is overwhelmingly Protestant and about three-fourths white. The unofficial reckoning puts Jews at 5 per cent, Roman Catholics at 13 per cent and nearly all the rest "Protestant preference." Among white residents the Methodists are easily first; but when all races are included, the Baptists come first and the Methodists second.

Probably it is fair to describe the Protestant Washington majority as predominantly conservative in both theology and morals. For the most part they are devout Trinitarians and avowed enemies of gambling and "loose" Sundays. The influence of the South is quite apparent, but Unitarianism has burgeoned with surprising strength in recent years, and there are strong Jewish congregations.

One special reason for Protestant predominance in Washington is that the inner city is now the only major city in the United States with a Negro majority (about 53 per cent). Three-fourths of the children in Washington's public schools are Negroes.[27] With some exceptions, both white Protestants and white Catholics are building up in the suburbs essentially white enclaves without benefit of formal segregation laws. Some day, probably quite soon, there will be a desegregation explosion in these restricted suburbs, and American Protestantism will be faced with one of its most critical moral challenges.

Despite the strong and official Catholic opposition to segregation, few Washington Negroes have deserted their traditional Protestant churches for Catholicism. In fact, in the nation as a whole less than one Negro in forty is Roman Catholic.[28] In the Washington area, not only do Negroes remain Protestants but most of them choose to continue in their own voluntarily segregated Protestant churches. In this voluntary segregation they have the tacit support of their own Negro preachers.

There is much irony in this confused picture of race and religion in the capital. An officially desegregated city is moving toward a new type of unofficial segregation in spite of law and religious pronouncements. At the city-wide high school championship football game in 1958, the public "desegregated" high schools were represented by an all-Negro team from Eastern High School, while the Catholic "desegregated" high schools were represented by an all-white team from St. John's. Most white members of the middle class, despite their announced principles and the Constitution, are fleeing to the suburbs to escape predominantly Negro public schools, and the public schools of the inner city have achieved a new type of voluntary segregation based upon residence, fear, prejudice and real estate agreements.

On the whole, the Catholic record on desegregation is better than the Protestant record, partly because Catholicism has so few Negro adherents that desegregation is not a serious problem. But the Washington story seems to prove that family and social status are more powerful than official religion in reaching a solution. The predominantly Protestant white population of the District did not discontinue racial segregation in the public schools until the Supreme Court had handed down its 1954 decision. Now, six years later, there is still a great gap between the world of white society and the world of the District's Negro majority. In the moral reckoning of history, Washington Protestantism must accept the primary responsibility for this condition.

The Council of Churches National Capital Area—the new name of the Protestant Federation—has done much to promote interracial good will, but it never officially advocated desegregation in the schools until the Supreme Court had spoken. Even today the Washington Y.M.C.A. is virtually a segregated institution. The Y.W.C.A. has a much better record as an outstanding pioneer in racial adjustments. It was one of the first organizations in the region to open its cafeteria without discrimination.

Underlying the nominal and official Protestant acceptance of desegregation is a profound racial and political anxiety. Will Washington become a Negro capital? If self-government comes to the District with its Negro majority, will the capital have a chief executive as reckless as the New York Negro Baptist Adam Clayton Powell? The specter of such a racial leader as mayor of Washington undoubtedly helps to perpetuate the laws which deprive Washington's 500,000 potential voters of their right to vote.

Liberal Protestants, Jews and Catholics in the capital are willing to accept self-government under Negro leadership, but Southern white Protestants in Congress are not. Early in 1959, Senator Joseph Clark of Pennsylvania, a Unitarian and a thorough liberal in the field of race relations, resigned his post on the Senate's District of Columbia Committee in despair, confessing that all his work for District self-government was being blocked by House members from the deep South who are "opposed to home rule because they are afraid this would give Washington a Negro mayor." [29]

Washington as a Religious Capital

In recent years Washington has become increasingly important as a headquarters city for American churches. At least fourteen great religious denominations either have established headquarters here or are planning to do so in the near future.

Of all these headquarters the most important is that of the Roman Catholic Church. Catholicism has recognized the national capital as a natural center of Catholic power and has acted accordingly. Although the Washington archdiocese of the Church claims only 245,000 members, about 13 per cent of the population of Greater Washington, these figures understate the significance of Washington Catholicism. There is a great concentration of Catholic institutions in the capital. Among the six colleges and forty-two seminaries in Washington is the only national pontifical university in the United States, the Catholic University of America, operated directly by the Catholic bishops. It is the theological fountainhead of American Catholicism, and on its campus is being built the National Shrine of the Immaculate Conception, which will be the largest Catholic church in the United States and the seventh largest in the world.

Washington is also the headquarters of the National Catholic Welfare Conference, the organized bishops of the United States, with a staff of more than 200 employees. Here the American bishops—about 220 strong—meet annually to coordinate their plans and to issue their annual pronouncements. This N.C.W.C.

headquarters on Massachusetts Avenue is the nerve center of American Catholicism and presents a powerful united front to the nation. It is much better equipped, through its legal and publicity departments, than any other religious organization in the capital to express and dramatize its point of view on any matter of legislation or policy. It keeps Catholic members throughout the United States reasonably well informed about government policies affecting religion through a press service reaching 23,000,000 readers of American Catholic publications. Nothing in American Protestantism approaches this organization in scope and activity.

In Washington also, in a palatial residence on Massachusetts Avenue, is the Apostolic Delegate of the Church to the United States. Technically he is a purely religious representative who has no official connection with the State Department, since the United States does not grant diplomatic recognition to the Vatican. In practice he gets a great deal of quiet unofficial recognition as a representative of one of the most powerful political organizations in the world. His residence is called a "legation" by the Washington newspapers, and it is that in effect.

The post of Apostolic Delegate has acquired particular significance because the Vatican does not permit American Catholicism to have its own primate. The Delegate thus comes nearest to being the supreme representative of the Pope in this country. He is always an Italian professional diplomat, and in the past he has been regularly rewarded with a cardinal's biretta for his labors. The present Delegate, Archbishop Egidio Vagnozzi, served under Pope John XXIII when the Pope was Papal Nuncio in Paris. He has already had ten years of Washington semi-diplomatic experience.

The strength of Catholicism in the capital is based not on geographical location or numerical supremacy but on its centralized, hierarchical control. It speaks with one voice. When the Catholic bishops state "the Catholic position" on atheistic Communism, birth control, relaxed immigration laws, tax appropriations for private schools or the recognition of Communist China, every

Congressman knows that that is the Catholic position. On the whole, the Catholic bishops have used this power with great discretion. In fact, they so rarely make a definite pronouncement on a definite piece of legislation that the Catholic program cannot be discovered even by piecing together all the official Catholic pronouncements throughout American history. For the complete program one must go to the Catholic press itself. While each Catholic newspaper is controlled (and often owned) by the head of each diocese, all are supplied with uniformly partisan news from the National Catholic Welfare Conference headquarters in Washington.

Protestant power in Washington is relatively diffuse and disorganized. Only twice during this century has American Protestantism been as fully mobilized as the Catholic Church to influence legislation: in 1919 Protestantism was largely responsible for securing prohibition, and in 1951 an aroused Protestantism defeated the proposal to send an ambassador to the Vatican.

The basic reason for this relative weakness is fragmentation. No organization has the moral right to speak for all American Protestantism. The National Council of the Churches of Christ, nominally representing 38,000,000 members in affiliated bodies, is not a fusion of the churches but a council with very limited powers. It moves with the speed of a loose-jointed elephant. Although its Washington leadership is able, it must consult the wishes of so many heterogeneous organizations that it cannot act decisively on most matters of legislative policy. Its beautiful Washington headquarters on Capitol Hill has a staff of only three executives and three secretaries. It has no national Protestant news service corresponding to the prolific news services of the National Catholic Welfare Conference, and its legislative summaries are simply flat-faced descriptions of the legislative scene, with no attempt to set forth an approved Protestant position. The Council's national headquarters remain in New York, in the impressive new building on Morningside Heights.

One reason, of course, for the Council's relative weakness in

Washington is that several of America's largest Protestant groups are not affiliated, and some of these are actively hostile. The second largest Protestant denomination in the country, the Southern Baptist Convention, remains out of the Council; and a small fundamentalist wing of Protestantism, the American Council of Christian Churches, carries on a running attack against the National Council. Also outside of the Council is the National Association of Evangelicals, which represents directly over 2,000,000 members and claims to speak for "more than 10,000,000 Bible-believing Christians." The N.A.E. abjures any broad social reform program and is temperately fundamentalist in its point of view.[30] At the other end of the theological spectrum, outside all national Protestant councils, is the Unitarian Church.

In spite of all these difficulties, the National Council of Churches has gone on record for a broad social program; if its power could match the nobility of its aims, it would be a great force in Washington affairs. In the 1956 national conventions of the Republican and Democratic Parties, the Council came forward with aims that were quite comprehensive. It favored federal aid to education, with safeguards against federal control; it supported the Supreme Court's decision on segregation; it advocated a rather vague attack on housing evils; it asked for civil liberties for all religious and racial minorities; and it championed the separation of church and state. It expressed concern over some of the wild procedures of Congressional investigating committees and asked for continuing support of the United Nations. It supported reciprocal trade agreements and favored an increase in technical foreign aid. It flatly opposed "a system of permanent universal military training." [31]

Some of the weakness of the National Council of Churches is partially offset by the vigorous national representation of single Protestant denominations. Northern and Southern Baptists have joined to support a Washington office. Methodist influence is represented not only by a large Methodist headquarters on Capitol Hill but also by the vigorous leadership of the chairman of the Council of Bishops of the Methodist Church, G. Bromley Oxnam. For many years he has been a liberal spokesman for social welfare, racial justice and the separation of church and state. He has been largely responsible for the growth of American University, a Methodist institution, whose new School of Foreign Relations is challenging the Catholic monopoly in this field previously held by Georgetown University.

Many vigorous but unofficial Protestant organizations also exert moral influence upon the government. One of the most efficient is an agency organized by Quakers, the Friends Committee on National Legislation, which has fought valiantly for many years against things militaristic and in behalf of conscientious objectors. Another important group, officially outside Protestantism, is Protestants and Other Americans United for Separation of Church and State (P.O.A.U.). This national organization, headed by three former presidents of America's three largest Protestant denominations, has specialized in defending the wall of separation between church and state against Catholic encroachments.

The influence of American Judaism in Washington is very difficult to assess for a number of reasons. A religious bloc with only 3 per cent of the population cannot hope to rival Protestant or Catholic blocs in political power. Moreover, Judaism is divided into three segments—Orthodox, Conservative and Reform. They do not always agree on legislative programs, and they have no single office or lobbyist in Washington representing all American Judaism. New York remains the primary capital of Jewish life and enterprise, and most Jewish activity in Washington is directed from New York.

Yet Judaism as a social force is immensely significant in Washington, and some of the most important work being done in protecting the separation of church and state in the United States is being done by Jewish organizations. In New York the American Jewish Congress (which has many branches throughout the country) has taken a lead; the American Jewish Committee is less militant but equally powerful. In Washington itself, B'nai B'rith, with its Anti-Defamation League, operates from its own headquarters. Judaism's total influence in the capital is distinctly libertarian, strongly favorable to the American policy of the separation of church and state, hostile to racial segregation and favorable to increased immigration. Naturally enough, Judaism has a profound interest in American aid to Israel, and Zionism is a considerable political force.

Outside all these religious and quasi-religious organizations, but cooperating with many of them, is the American Civil Liberties Union. A.C.L.U. is a consistently militant defender of church-state separation. Whenever a legal defender of the First Amendment is needed at a Congressional hearing or a Supreme Court argument, its lawyers are likely to appear.

God and the Press

The whole problem of the relation of religion and government in Washington has been transformed since the days when Thomas Jefferson mounted his horse on Sunday mornings and rode over to the House chamber to hear a sermon. Those were the days of personal contact; this is the day of mechanized publicity. The sermon itself has lost standing as a factor in creating public opinion, and the congregational assembly has been replaced as a vehicle for the transmission of fact and opinion. It is probably accurate to say that not all the religious interest groups in Washington combined can affect public opinion by personal contact as much as one national magazine or television program.

In the goldfish bowl of Washington politics, the power of the press is rising, not only through such devices as the Presidential press conference but also through the intensive coverage of every government activity by a corps of about 1,000 magazine, newspaper, television and radio correspondents. As a subject for that coverage, organized religion plays a rather sorry role. It occupies a subcellar far below business, labor, foreign affairs and agriculture.

The great national newspapers such as the *New York Times,* and the national news weeklies such as *Time* and *Newsweek*, do not have full-time religious reporters stationed in Washington. Their religious news desks are located at central headquarters, and most of their policies in publicizing religion are determined there. These policies may be described as cautiously affirmative and persistently uncritical. It is an unwritten rule of virtually every news desk of every leading newspaper and magazine, and a specifically written rule for television and radio, that religious controversy is to be eschewed if possible. The television networks give free time for bland and affirmative publicity, with one-half of this time reserved for Protestants, one-third for Catholics and one-sixth for Jews.[32] If some church happens to assert itself pugnaciously in a recognized area of secular behavior, it may receive a newspaper headline. Otherwise no readers are to be "offended."

The cynical and very hard-headed Washington correspondents of the great dailies and weeklies are never permitted to reveal their intelligent cynicism in discussing organized religion. As a result of this enforced partiality, their attitude toward religious news is not unlike their attitude toward the woman's page. Feminine and religious interests are linked as personal, sentimental and unrealistic, a little beneath the dignity of adult male intelligence.

America, of course, has no anti-clerical press of general circulation and no magazine which even attempts to attain the skeptical gusto of the old *American Mercury* when it was edited by H. L. Mencken. Nor has America, unlike Europe, any popular sectarian daily newspapers designed to emphasize religious values and religious discussion. Catholicism operates its great press service primarily for the Catholic weeklies. Although it still has four American daily papers, they are all foreign-language papers completely unknown to the English-speaking public. Protestantism has no national newspaper at all. Even the *Christian Science Monitor* can scarcely be described as a religious organ. Although it is owned by the Mother Church, it has gained great national influence through its independent and scholarly journalism. The Jesuit weekly *America* and the Protestant weekly *The Christian Century* publish a great deal of intelligent analytical material about Washington affairs. With their limited circulation, however, they cannot compensate the public for the innocuous and uncritical handling of religious issues by most of the great dailies and weeklies.

The nearest approach to a comprehensive religious press organization in the capital is the Religious News Service, owned by the National Conference of Christians and Jews, which furnishes items—not only from Washington but from most of the leading cities of the nation—for daily and weekly papers. Its factual material is usually sound, and it even ventures occasionally to discuss controversial issues quite frankly.

Perhaps one should not be too critical of those editors who pursue a policy of avoiding all religious controversy. Any editor who speaks up candidly in opposition to the policies of any particular sect is almost sure to encounter savage counter-attacks. The *Washington Post,* one of the few newspapers in America which still ventures to analyze religious problems with some candor, asked in a 1958 editorial on John Foster Dulles and "atheistic Communism": "Isn't it time to end this offensive business of self-righteously invoking the Deity as a crutch in American diplomacy? . . . what a refreshing change it would be if American policy were strong enough to stand on its merits without leaning either on supplications to God or condemnation of Godlessness to prove the point!" The Brooklyn *Tablet,* official organ of the Catholic diocese of Brooklyn, promptly responded with a typically sectarian headline over a news story sent out by the National Catholic Welfare Conference: "Oppose Asking God's Aid for United States: Washington Post and Herald Would Go Along with Communist Strategy." [33]

Chapter III

God, Man and the Supreme Court

I come now to the United States Supreme Court, and I enter its halls very respectfully not only because respectful conduct is obligatory in this marble mansion—especially for lawyers—but also because this Court has become in recent years one of the world's foremost defenders of individual liberty. Bright cynics like Fred Rodell of the Yale Law School ridicule "that holy hunk of The Law known as Constitutional Law" and say that "The Law, as a matter of fact, is all things to all lawyers . . . because the principles on which it is built are so vague and abstract and irrelevant that it is possible to find in those principles a justification and prohibitions of every human action or activity under the sun. . . . the last bunch of judges which gets a shot at the solution of any specific problem has the decisive word." [1]

One can agree that this bit of Rodell cynicism has much truth in it and yet regard this particular Supreme Court with genuine homage. Working with the imperfections of a vague Constitution and many conflicting and ambiguous statutes, it has yet found justifications in history for maintaining American liberties. It has spoken decisive words calculated to preserve the essence of both religious freedom and the separation of church and state.

This Court is the nearest approach in Washington to a strictly neutral agency of government which, in spite of its neutrality, must meet religious issues squarely. It does everything possible to preserve that neutrality without evasion. It does not indulge in any of the sectarian flourishes that have become an accepted part

47

of the routine of Congress and the Presidency. There are no religious mottoes in evidence inside or outside the Supreme Court building, no religious symbols on the walls. At the opening of each session, when nine solemn justices in their black robes march abreast through the three portals in the great red velvet curtain, no formal prayers are offered and no sectarian gestures are permitted. The atmosphere, outside and inside the building, is more Greek than Judeo-Christian. The great marble Corinthian pillars rising on each of the four corners of the three-story chamber symbolize Athens rather than Jerusalem. Above the curving, polished mahogany bench where the justices sit, Greek figures are carved in bas-relief.

As the justices march in for the opening of a session, a Crier, garbed elegantly in a Prince Albert coat, rises and proclaims:

The Honorable, the Chief Justice and the Associate Justices of the Supreme Court of the United States.

Oyez! Oyez! Oyez!

All persons having business before the Honorable, the Supreme Court of the United States, are admonished to draw near and give their attention, for the Court is now sitting.

God save the United States and this Honorable Court.

Then everybody sits down, and the Court goes to business.

This Court is so aloof from all religious classifications that even the religious affiliations of particular justices are rarely mentioned in the press. Most of the justices do not even list their religion in the biographical data they submit to *Who's Who*. In 1958 when a Unitarian (Burton) resigned and was succeeded by an Episcopalian (Stewart), neither man's religion was listed in newspaper biographies. Only when a Jew or a Catholic is appointed does this religious variation from the Protestant norm seem important enough to note.

The only thing remotely involving any religious commitment by the justices is the final ejaculation of the oath of allegiance which is prescribed for all Congressmen and justices under the

United States Code: "So help me God." [2] There is no doubt that if a Supreme Court justice refused to add this exclamation to his oath, on grounds of principle, he would be accepted as a justice anyway, since he could not be coerced into repeating such words without violating Article VI of the Constitution.

As of late 1959 the Court had one Jew, Felix Frankfurter; one Catholic, William J. Brennan, Jr.; and seven Protestants. Although the Court has always been overwhelmingly Protestant in personal composition—only nine of its ninety-three justices have been non-Protestant—there has been no Protestant monopoly since Roger B. Taney, a Catholic, was made Chief Justice by Andrew Jackson in 1836. Taney sat on the Supreme Court bench for twenty-eight years. One other Catholic, Edward Douglass White, has occupied the chair of Chief Justice, and four other Catholics have sat as Associate Justices—Joseph McKenna, Pierce Butler, Frank Murphy and now William J. Brennan. During about twenty-five years of our history, two of the Court's nine judicial chairs have been occupied by Catholics. Only three Justices of Jewish extraction have ever served—Louis D. Brandeis, Benjamin Cardozo and Felix Frankfurter.[3]

In general these justices are extremely careful not to be identified as a group with any institution or ceremony that smacks of denominational promotion. As individuals some of them occasionally speak to church groups, always maintaining the lofty tone of legal dignity and non-partisanship that is imposed on all justices by the American tradition. Once a year they, or some of them, seem to depart a little from this non-sectarian independence by attending the famous Red Mass at Washington's St. Matthew's Cathedral, which has been sponsored by a committee of Catholic lawyers since 1938. Since Presidents and Congressmen also attend this Red Mass, the Court is in good company. Nevertheless, it has become such an obvious piece of denominational promotion that the propriety of Supreme Court attendance has been questioned.[4]

Public Pressures and Personal Integrity

Two facts about the moral independence of this Court should be noted before we discuss its policies on church and state. The government has given its Supreme Court Justices the kind of security that makes moral independence possible. If they are less prone than Presidents and Congressmen to bend before the fickle winds of public opinion, if they come nearest of all Washington officials to the lofty concept of super-representation advocated by Edmund Burke, it is partly because their jobs, their social station and their old age are safe. A Supreme Court justice is appointed for life, and only the most notorious crime could lead to impeachment or removal. Each justice serves without regard to age limit and, if he wishes, may retire at seventy at $35,000 a year.

Let no one think, however, that Supreme Court justices are immune to indirect pressures of public opinion. They read the newspapers and the law journals, and if the opinions of leading editors and bar associations are overwhelmingly critical of a Court decision, that decision is quite likely to be reinterpreted out of existence. As of late 1959 the Court is encountering well-organized attacks on its policies in at least three areas—racial equality, security clearances and the separation of church and state—and its present position is threatened by these attacks. This same type of adverse criticism induced the Court to reverse itself within a space of three years on the question of a compulsory flag salute for the children of Jehovah's Witnesses.

Occasionally the Court may even note the lengthened shadow of an army of the unemployed. In the dark days of the 1930s, after the Court had declared the National Industrial Recovery Act unconstitutional in 1935 and Roosevelt had retaliated with his Court-packing scheme in 1937, Chief Justice Hughes led an adroit retreat from a philosophy of economic conservatism and so made possible the phenomenon known as the New Deal. The same nine justices were on the Court in 1935, when the N.R.A. was declared unconstitutional, and in 1937, when the Wagner Act was declared constitutional.[5] Of course, the precedents were carefully observed, and the justices discovered technical distinctions on which to hang a variation in principle. But the fact was that public opinion induced a change of outlook which amounted to a new interpretation of the Constitution. A Washington scribe wisecracked: "A switch in time saves nine." Justice Cardozo stated the principle more elegantly: "When the social needs demand one settlement rather than another, there are times when we must bend symmetry, ignore history and sacrifice custom in the pursuit of other and larger ends."[6]

The other fact worth noting about the moral independence of this Court is that never in its long history has the religious affiliation of any justice been shown to have determined his decision in a single case. It is, of course, almost impossible to separate and identify religious influences in a complex judicial mind. Also, very few cases presented to the Court have specifically involved subject matter covered by religious directives. Yet it can safely be said that the justices have voted not as Protestants, Jews or Catholics but as American jurists.

One reason for this record is that American Protestantism, which has supplied nearly all the judges in the past, has never sought to impose upon its members any directives that would conflict with the Constitution or their professional duty. Having no history of ecclesiastical courts, American Protestantism has no church code for the conduct of civil judges. Catholicism has, but the Catholic Church has not ventured to enforce this code with Catholic justices of the United States Supreme Court. Justice Frankfurter declared in a 1943 dissent: "As judges we are neither Jew nor Gentile, neither Catholic nor agnostic. We owe equal attachment to the Constitution and are equally bound by our judicial obligations. . . ."[7]

There is also no correlation between the justices' religion and their location in the liberal-conservative spectrum. The most dangerously reactionary judges in the past have been Protestants, but only because 90 per cent of all the judges have been Protestants; some of the most aggressively progressive judges have been Protestants also. The two great dissenters of earlier years were Holmes and Brandeis. Holmes was married by the Episcopalian Phillips Brooks, but he was buried from a Unitarian church. The two most persistent dissenters of the last decade have been Black and Douglas, a Baptist and a Congregationalist.

Justice Brennan, a Catholic, might be expected to rule against Communists in free-speech cases with more severity than other justices because of the implacable hostility of his Church to all Communist organizations. His record in such matters has been, if anything, left of center—so charitable, in fact, that the more conservative newspapers of his denomination have criticized him for extreme liberalism. No denominational influence was discernible in the Court's two most famous rulings on racial segregation in the schools, in 1954 and 1958. Catholic, Protestant and Jewish justices united to condemn segregation by unanimous vote. In the two most important book censorship cases in recent years, the decisions against the books were written by a Catholic and a Jewish justice, respectively, and approved by a Protestant majority.[8]

Perhaps one decision in the history of the Court is open to the strong suspicion that it followed primarily denominational principles. That was the 1927 dissent of Pierce Butler, reactionary Minnesota Catholic, from a decision approving eugenic sterilization for the feeble-minded, which is now permitted under certain safeguards in some twenty-seven states. The plaintiff, Carrie Buck, confined in a state institution in Virginia, was a feeble-minded eighteen-year-old daughter of a feeble-minded mother, who had given birth to a feeble-minded child. Butler was the only dissenter who stood out against the famous dictum of Justice Holmes: "Three generations of imbeciles are enough." [9] His Church makes it a mortal sin for any Catholic judge to carry out or assist in carrying out a eugenic sterilization law. He voted with his Church, but who can say that it was his Catholicism and not a sincere personal conviction that dictated his choice? He refused to file any dissenting opinion.

On many occasions in the past, Protestant and Catholic Supreme Court justices have written or concurred in decisions that seemed to oppose the drift of ecclesiastical opinion in their own churches. Frank Murphy was an outspoken defender of the rights of Jehovah's Witnesses, the most fanatical anti-Catholic sect in the country. In 1899 a Court composed of seven Protestants and two Catholics handed down a decision in the case of *Bradfield v. Roberts* which did serious damage to the American policy of church-state separation by permitting public money to be used even for denominational hospitals with a narrow denominational medical code.[10] The decision in this case was written by a Protestant, Rufus Peckham. Similarly, the 1930 decision of Justice Charles Evans Hughes making it possible for Louisiana to spend public funds for parochial school textbooks was unanimously approved by seven Protestants, one Catholic and one Jew.[11]

In 1948 the Court decided, in the famous McCollum case, to exclude classes in religion from all public schools as unconstitutional. The only Catholic judge on the Court at that time, Frank Murphy, voted with the majority against the noisy reproaches of his own Church's hierarchy, while the only dissenter was a Protestant, Stanley Reed. Reed became a hero in the Catholic law journals, while the Catholic bishops mourned over the amazing departure of Justice Murphy from the principles of his Church.[12]

Probably the most serious blow to the concept of church-state separation in education dealt by the Court in recent years was the prevailing opinion in the Zorach "released-time" case in 1952.[13] In permitting released-time classes in religion outside of public classrooms, the Court used such broad and sentimental phrases about cooperation between church and state that the language has been exploited indiscriminately to justify more serious encroachments upon the concept of separation. But the decision was not Catholic-written or Catholic-inspired. In fact, there was no Catholic on the Supreme Court when the decision was handed down, and the words were those of one of America's most liberal Protestant jurists, William O. Douglas.

Why the Supreme Court Is Important

A visiting student from Great Britain or the Continent might be quite astonished to discover that the Supreme Court is by far the most important government agency in Washington dealing with the principles of church and state, far more important than Congress or the President. The principal reason for this special importance is that legislative control over religious matters has been left to the states, and their mistakes are subject to review in Washington not by Congress or the executive but by the Supreme Court. These mistakes—and they are legion—often remain uncorrected at the local level and pile up in a confused mass of semi-contradictory practices and decisions. When a citizen's rights are too obviously curtailed, he comes (if he can afford an appeal) to the Supreme Court, the one agency in America with the power to straighten out the local legislative and judicial tangle. He cannot always reach the Court, even when he has a just cause, but he can try.

Europe has no parallel to this pre-eminence of an independent judiciary in dealing with local church-state issues because Europe handles such matters by national legislation. Nearly all European nations outside the Iron Curtain have some form of partial church establishment or special church recognition, approved by formal legislation. Some European nations have a large body of national law on church matters, with government departments of religion and religious officers in the cabinets. Even such Communist satellites as Hungary continue to pay salaries to preachers and priests and to maintain government religious departments.

The legislative and executive branches of European nations often decide church-state policies directly without reference to courts of review. In 1951, for example, after a long and bitter fight, France approved payments of public money to Catholic parents for parochial school pupils. The question whether such payments violated the clause in the French Constitution defining the nation as a "laic" republic was reviewed not by an independent court but by a carefully loaded and partisan judicial committee. The committee decided the issue in favor of the Catholic Church on purely practical grounds.[14]

The small amount of law on religion in the United States pleased Lord Bryce so much that he commented in his *American Commonwealth:* "In examining the national government and the state governments, we have never once had occasion to advert to any ecclesiastical body or question, because with such matters government has in the United States absolutely nothing to do. Of all the differences between the Old World and the New, this is perhaps the most salient. Half the wars of Europe, half the internal troubles that have vexed European states . . . have arisen from theological differences or from the rival claims of church and state." [15] These rival claims have been reduced to a relative minimum in the United States, partly because, under the Constitution, there is no state church, and no legal favoritism is permitted for any church.

One reason for the importance of the Supreme Court in this area is that the Constitution is vague and sketchy in its clauses about religion. Someone must give definite meaning to such vague phrases, and the Supreme Court has claimed this right of interpretation since 1803. On many occasions during the past century, advocates of church-state separation must have wished for a definite and ringing pronouncement in the Bill of Rights which would parallel, for example, the phrases in Missouri's constitution: ". . . no money shall ever be taken from the public treasury, directly or indirectly, in aid of any church, sect or denomination of religion, or in aid of any priest, preacher, minister or teacher thereof, as such."

Two of our Presidents, Grant and Garfield, felt so keenly the need for more specific prohibitions against the use of tax money for sectarian schools that they advocated a new constitutional amendment to stop any possible financial concession of this type. The Republican platform of 1880 advocated such an amendment, and on at least one occasion Congress came close to approving the proposals.[16]

Yet the old vague generalities remain unchanged, and the Court must create legal principles with a Constitution in which the words "God," "Church" and "separation" do not even appear. The Court must construct a wall of separation between church and state out of those sixteen words of the First Amendment which constitute the ideological base of American policy on the subject: "Congress shall make no law respecting an establishment of religion, or prohibiting the free exercise thereof."

Those words are negative, and they apply only to federal action. They immediately raise the question: What about the "establishment" of religion and its "free exercise" in the *states?* Fortunately for defenders of the principle of church-state separation, this First Amendment of the federal Constitution was promptly echoed in the constitutions and statutes of most of the states. In many cases, the states went far beyond the federal Constitution in maintaining Jefferson's conception of the wall of separation.

In 1868 the Fourteenth Amendment was adopted, and in 1940 the religion clauses were interpreted by the Supreme Court as applying to the states. Only then did federal church-state policy become binding on all local and state governments.[17] That application of the First Amendment to local communities was almost as important as the First Amendment itself. In practice, it means that every local deputy sheriff or prosecutor in the United States must give every individual in a minority group—a Jehovah's Witness, a Mormon, a faith healer, an atheist—all the rights accorded by the federal Constitution to any United States citizen. Local statutes which contradict the federal Constitution as interpreted by the Supreme Court are not enforceable, and local judges must recognize them as invalid under the Supreme Court's interpretation of the First Amendment.

The historic words of the Fourteenth Amendment read:

No state shall make or enforce any law which shall abridge the privileges and immunities of citizens of the United States; nor shall any state deprive any person of life, liberty, or property, without due process of law, nor deny to any person within its jurisdiction the equal protection of the laws.

Of course, "the equal protection of the laws" is itself a very vague phrase, and scores of difficult legal cases have been fought over its potential ambiguities. The Supreme Court justices are very far from total agreement as to its exact meaning when applied to religion. But this uncertainty is not unique. Legal principles covering vast areas of a complex society must necessarily be very general in order to cover a great variety of situations, and the religion clauses of the Constitution are no more ambiguous, for example, than the clauses about interstate commerce or due process.

In many areas Congress is fiercely jealous of the power of the Supreme Court, but not in the area of religious controversy. There Congressmen actually welcome the importance of the Supreme Court and its power as an arbiter. It relieves them from the risk of partisan reprisal to have an impartial agency speaking without passion in so controversial an area.

Religious Freedom—The Zone of Agreement

In theory it is possible to distinguish the Supreme Court's philosophy on religious freedom from its policy on the separation of church and state. In practice this is nearly impossible. Almost every religious case coming to the Court involves both a demand for freedom and a request for some kind of special privilege or establishment. Every lawyer who represents a client before the Court on a religious issue makes valiant efforts to label his client's demand "religious freedom" since freedom is more respectable and more acceptable than special privilege.

In matters of religious freedom per se, the decisions of the Supreme Court are all so close to complete agreement on primary matters of liberty that it is fair to consider the constitutional problem of religious freedom settled. With only a few technical restrictions, any American can organize a church, teach or preach religion, conduct a religious school, found a religious hospital and publish and distribute literature about his faith without being molested. All these religious freedoms must be extended impartially to all churches or religious schools without discrimination.

Those freedoms seem commonplace enough to most Americans; we tend to take them for granted. Yet they represent one of history's greatest cultural achievements. They distinguish the American way of life in matters of religion from that of many other nations which consider themselves democratic.

Many of the so-called religious-freedom cases that have come to the Court have really been quarrels over church status. What is a church? Is it a majority of the members? When an internal fight for control takes place, must our courts recognize majority power? Must the Court weigh theological arguments in deciding between two factions?

The Supreme Court has answered the last question with a

resounding *No*. It will never try to define the meaning of creeds or to weigh the truth or falsehood of any dogma. It has never presumed to define God precisely, and one suspects that if it dared to make the attempt, the justices would be no more successful in reaching agreement than the theologians.

On those few occasions when the justices have had to manufacture a working definition of religion, they have recognized that the word has no narrow limits. Even God is not always a necessary ingredient. The District of Columbia Court of Appeals probably reflected the present Supreme Court's attitude when it granted tax exemption to the Washington Ethical Culture Society as a religious institution in spite of the fact that the Society requires no belief in God for its members. Religion, ruled the District Court in 1957, may include either worship of a ruling power or "devotion to some principle; strict fidelity or faithfulness." [18]

In the famous case of *Watson v. Jones* (1872), which involved a quarrel between two factions of the Presbyterian Church in Kentucky, the Court said: "The law knows no heresy, and is committed to the support of no dogma, the establishment of no sect." [19] This sentiment has been quoted and cited throughout the years as a beacon of theological neutrality.

In matters of morality, the Court also maintains a lofty neutrality if advocates of unconventional conduct confine their advocacy to the orderly dissemination of ideas. When the Court lifted the ban on the film version of *Lady Chatterley's Lover* in 1959 by declaring New York's licensing law unconstitutional in part, Justice Stewart, who wrote the prevailing opinion, conceded that the film might attractively portray "a relationship which is contrary to the moral standards, the religious precepts, and the legal code" of the American people. But, he continued, the Constitution "protects advocacy of the opinion that adultery may sometimes be proper, no less than advocacy of socialism or the single tax." Senator Eastland of Mississippi, chairman of the Senate Judiciary Committee, promptly proposed in the Senate a constitutional amendment to restore "the right of each state to decide on the basis of its own public policy questions of decency and morality."

In matters of institutional power, the Court cannot maintain such neutrality. When a quarrel for the possession of physical property breaks out in a church, someone must decide which faction has title to its physical assets. In such cases the Court follows the charter of the church and not necessarily the conventions of democracy. If the charter is congregational, the congregation rules. If the charter is autocratic, the bishops rule. This policy is something of an innovation, since the courts before 1870 tended to say that any church could be ruled by a majority of its members. What Professor Mark DeWolfe Howe of Harvard has described as "enforced congregationalism" has now been abandoned.[20]

One reason for the abandonment, no doubt, has been the rise in power of the Roman Catholic Church, whose physical property is owned, in the last analysis, by the bishops and the Pope. To accommodate American law to this type of control, the Court has recognized that, in effect, any church can be as dictatorial as it wishes if its rules for dictatorship are clearly expressed. Its power structure need not even be controlled in the United States.

Oddly enough, this recognition of the right of a local church to be controlled in an entirely undemocratic manner by a patriarch from outside the United States was sealed by the Court in a decision in 1952 which gave the direction of a Russian Orthodox cathedral in New York to Moscow church authorities. The New York legislature had tried to keep the control in American hands by passing a special statute. This statute, said the Court, "directly prohibits the free exercise of an ecclesiastical right, the Church's choice of its hierarchy." [21] The Court, in effect, ruled that the right of self-government in a church includes the right of its members to choose no self-government.

This principle was reiterated and enforced in a dramatic case in Pittsburgh in 1958 when Bishop John F. Dearden sold St. Peter's Roman Catholic Church to the Urban Redevelopment Authority for demolition for $1,240,000 without so much as telling the congregation that he was going to make the sale. In the polite but gloomy words of the Pennsylvania Supreme Court: "The bond and agreement were neither reported to the plaintiff [the lay trustees of the church] by the Bishop nor approved by it. . . . The dispositive rule is that plaintiff, as a parish or congregation, has no standing to sue. The Bishop owns the property in trust for the parish, and alone may dispose of it in accordance with the canons of the Roman Catholic Church." In this case the members of the congregation were so angry that they sued the Bishop and the government through the courts, but they lost when the Supreme Court refused to review.

The right of churches to operate private schools was sustained by the Court in a famous case in 1925.[22] Oregon Protestants had developed a powerful movement for public schools which was tinctured with a considerable amount of anti-Catholicism. The Ku Klux Klan was strong in the state at that time. Although no deliberate attempt was made to destroy Catholic schools as such, a law was passed in 1922 requiring children between the ages of eight and sixteen to attend public schools under the state's compulsory education program. The law, if enforced, would have closed nearly all private schools in the state.

When the law was challenged by Catholic nuns and independent private schools, the Court declared it unconstitutional, primarily for reasons that now seem very old-fashioned. It reasoned that the financial interests of the Catholic teaching sisters and the private schools would be injured arbitrarily by taking away their customers. But the Court also inserted a brief plea for the liberty of the parents to control the education of their children, and later decisions have supplied more complete logic to support this liberty. It is now the settled policy of the nation that children may attend private schools if their parents wish, so long as those private schools meet certain minimum educational standards laid down by the state.

If Catholic nuns and their parochial schools constitute the acid test of institutional freedom, Jehovah's Witnesses provide the best test of individual freedom. The Witnesses are militant missionaries, and for many years they have been the Supreme Court's most troublesome religious litigants. They believe that the world is coming to an end quite soon, and that they will assist the Lord in final judgment, and they are quite scornful of the annoying obstructions which some local communities have put in their way. In some years the Witnesses distribute more than 300,000,000 pieces of literature, some of it very inflammatory. It has annoyed so many local prosecutors and policemen that attorneys for the Witnesses have come to the Supreme Court again and again in self-defense. Their victories have probably been the most important ever scored for individual religious liberty.

Perhaps the most important victory won by the Witnesses in the Supreme Court was the 1940 Cantwell decision. A Witness missionary had had the courage—or foolhardiness—to play a phonograph record on a New Haven street attacking Catholicism as "the greatest racket ever employed among men," operating "by means of fraud and deception." [23] There was no disorder, but apparently the Attorney General of Connecticut was very much surprised that the situation remained peaceful. (When he was later reminded from the Supreme Court bench during the argument that Jesus stirred up "a good deal of trouble in Jerusalem," he replied: "As I remember my Bible, something was done about that.")

Jesse Cantwell, the Witness in question, was picked up by New Haven police and convicted under common law of a breach of the peace. The Court hinted that Cantwell might have been convicted of violating a carefully drawn statute about the use of public streets without a license, if Connecticut had had such a statute. But it was not good law to convict a man of a breach of the peace when there had been no breach of the peace. Preaching was not such a breach even when the words were insulting and provocative. In both religion and politics, said Justice Roberts for the Court,

"the tenets of one man may seem the rankest error to his neighbor."
The Constitution "safeguards the free exercise of the chosen form
of religion. Thus the [First] Amendment embraces two concepts—
freedom to believe and freedom to act. The first is absolute. . . ."

Twelve years later—in the famous case of the Italian motion
picture "The Miracle"—the Court, again by a unanimous decision,
applied the same type of reasoning to religious and anti-religious
freedom in films.[24] The decision in "The Miracle" case has become
a kind of charter of religious freedom for radio, stage and television. In effect, the Court found that blasphemy as such was not
a criminal offense, even after Cardinal Spellman had attacked the
film as "a sacrilegious and blasphemous mockery of Christian religious faith" and New York authorities had withdrawn its license
because it contained an unflattering analogy with the Virgin Birth.
"It is not the business of government in our nation," said the Court,
"to suppress real or imagined attacks upon a particular religious
doctrine, whether they appear in publications, speeches, or motion
pictures."

Justice Frankfurter, in a brilliant concurring opinion in this
case, pointed out that at one time or another many of the most
fervently cherished religious doctrines have been considered blasphemous or sacrilegious by some sect or cult. "Blasphemy," he
said, "was the chameleon phrase which meant the criticism of
whatever the ruling authority of the moment established as orthodox
religious doctrine."

This attitude toward dissident religious or anti-religious
thought was demonstrated again in June 1958 when the Court
struck down as unconstitutional an attempt by the state of California to make churches loyal to the government by statute.[25] California had passed a law requiring institutions that were granted
tax exemption to file an oath that they did not advocate the violent
overthrow of the government "nor advocate the support of a foreign
government against the United States in event of hostilities." The
First Unitarian Church of Los Angeles, whose leaders were con-

siderably left of center in their political sympathies, refused to sign on the ground that "its principles, moral and religious . . . compel its members, officers and minister, as a matter of deepest conscience, belief and conviction, to deny power in the state to compel acceptance by it or any other church of this or any other oath of coerced affirmation as to church doctrine, advocacy or beliefs." Several California Methodist churches joined the protest, and Philadelphia's Yearly Meeting of Friends filed a brief as a friend of the court on the Unitarian side.

The Court's only Catholic jurist, William J. Brennan, ruled for the Court, in an 8 to 1 decision, that California's procedure violated the due process clause of the Fourteenth Amendment. The test of loyalty was too fuzzy for practical application. The state must assume the burden of proof in attempting to establish the fact that a church is disloyal before it denies tax exemption on disloyalty grounds. In this case there was no evidence or proof of actual disloyalty.

Although the religious-freedom clause of the First Amendment was not the chief basis of the Court's decision in this case, it clearly might have been if the justices had felt the need of relying upon it. Two justices, Black and Douglas, wrote a strong concurring opinion saying: "There is no power in our Government to make one bend his religious scruples to the requirements of a tax law." During the heated argument in Court, Justice Black leaned forward and shot a fatal question at the beleaguered attorney for Los Angeles County: "Doesn't this give the legislature the right to measure doctrine?"

The brief of the Philadelphia Yearly Meeting of Friends concluded: "If the State can discriminate in regard to taxes among religious groups on the basis of what they are willing to declare as their views in an area where religion and politics meet, the State is itself declaring what is and what is not patriotic religious orthodoxy, and freedom of conscience has ceased to exist."

Religious Freedom—The Zone of Conflict

Although all the justices believe wholeheartedly in religious freedom, there is a wide difference of opinion as to the boundary line in conflicts between religious freedom and civic responsibility. They all agree that the free exercise of religion must be subordinate to the criminal laws, and that the state must reserve the right to define a crime. An old-style Mormon who argued in 1878 that polygamy was "directly enjoined . . . by the All Mighty God in a revelation to Joseph Smith" was informed that his marital program was criminal rather than divine.[26] Several clergymen who have ventured in recent years to handle poisonous moccasins in their bare hands before awestruck congregations have been denied this "religious freedom." [27]

In many other difficult borderline cases, the Court's lines of demarcation between freedom of religion and the duties of citizenship are quite blurred. May cities license all peddlers, including religious ones, and thus assume the right to limit their work? Should children be permitted to refrain from a compulsory flag salute in public schools because of their religion? Should some children be allowed to die from anemia because their parents reject blood transfusions? May towns and villages refuse to permit churches and synagogues to build in residential areas? Are we denying religious freedom to Jews and Seventh Day Adventists when we enforce Sunday closing laws?

Not a word in the federal Constitution answers these questions specifically. The Court has had to answer them as best it could by elaborate and sometimes rather artificial interpretations of such words as "due process," "free exercise," "equal protection" and "establishment of religion." In the last analysis, many decisions have been based primarily on each judge's personal convictions about the degree of seriousness of the specific offense.

In general the Court is much more tolerant of rebel religious thought than of rebel religious action. It refused in 1958 to free a Pennsylvania farmer from his obligation to limit his wheat fields under the A.A.A., even though he claimed that the limit on production was contrary to Scripture.[28] In another case, it found that a state may, if it wishes, respect the objection of Christian Science parents to the vaccination of their children, but that the parents have no constitutional right to exemption if their children attend public schools where smallpox among Christian Science children may endanger other lives. Said the Court in this standard case on Christian Science: "There are manifest restraints to which every person is necessarily subject for the common good. . . ." [29]

Military service is one of these "manifold restraints." The Court has ruled that no American has a constitutional claim to exemption as a matter of right simply because he says that military service would deprive him of religious freedom. Congress has been quite lenient in exempting persons who have religious scruples against military service, but this is a purely optional matter of legislative grace.

The Court has also refused to allow commercial fraud to masquerade as religion, but in this area its decisions have been somewhat confusing. What is the difference between an old miracle and a new one? What is the legal right of priests, preachers and prophets to collect money on the basis of miraculous claims? The justices do not like such questions, and they have tried to escape responsibility for definitive replies. They have realized the impossibility of establishing the truth or falsehood of any alleged miracle by Court action.

In the 1940s a family of imaginative evangelists named Ballard, operating near Los Angeles as the "I Am" movement, gathered in the shekels of the credulous by claiming that at least one of the family (1) shook hands with Jesus, (2) cured persons of incurable diseases and (3) embodied the personalities of George Washington and St. Germaine. After years of tedious litigation, the Court finally approved by a vote of 5 to 4 a line of reasoning that left the situation still confused.[30] The Ballards escaped punishment on a technicality.

The separate opinions in this case covered the whole spectrum from indignant agreement to indignant dissent. Justice Douglas, speaking for the Court, declared that even such religious practitioners as the Ballards should not be held accountable to a jury about the truth of their beliefs. "Men may believe what they cannot prove," he said. Yes, said Justice Stone in dissent, but "I am not prepared to say that the constitutional guaranty of freedom of religion affords immunity from criminal prosecution for the fraudulent procurement of money by false statements as to one's religious experiences. . . ."

The net effect of the two confusing decisions in the Ballard case is that almost anything is permissible in the field of religious evangelism for adults if the evangelist does not too obviously practice medical fraud. Faith healers, on the air and in the tabernacle, may exploit the emotions of the credulous with very little danger of legal restraint. There is no sectarian Federal Trade Commission to label religious fraud, and the Court will not assume the role of religious censor.

Only when medico-religious fanaticism endangers the life of helpless children will the government step in. Several times in recent years, lower courts have intervened when children of Jehovah's Witnesses needed blood transfusions, and the Supreme Court has approved the principle of the intervention. An adult Witness is allowed the freedom to die without any legal intervention; a forty-three-year-old woman died in this way in Haverhill, Massachusetts, in 1958, proclaiming that any use of blood for transfusions is prohibited by Genesis 9:4 and Leviticus 17:14.[31] But a child is saved from such a fate. The legal theory in such cases holds that it is part of "the responsibility of government" to protect children "from neglect, abuse and fraud" and that the state is more competent than any church to define neglect.[32]

The children of Jehovah's Witnesses have served as judicial guinea pigs in many other cases of alleged loss of religious freedom. Should they be compelled to salute the flag in public schools? The Witness parents say *No,* on the ground that the Bible tells men not to bow down to any graven image. The Witnesses will allow their children to stand up when the American flag is saluted in a public school but not to raise the right hand or repeat the pledge of allegiance. This rejection of a national patriotic formula brought them, in the tense days before World War II, into direct conflict with the authorities in many states.

At first the Court supported the local authorities against these Witnesses. When Lillian Gobitis, aged twelve, and Walter Gobitis, aged ten, were ordered out of a public school in Minersville, Pennsylvania, because they would not salute the flag, the Supreme Court reversed 8 to 1 the verdicts of the lower courts, which had found in their favor.[33] Although most of the justices did not admire the restrictive law, they sided with Felix Frankfurter in supporting a community's right to exact a flag salute as part of its program of community obligations. "Conscientious scruples," said Frankfurter, "have not, in the course of the long struggle for religious toleration, relieved the individual from obedience to a general law not aimed at the promotion or restriction of religious beliefs." He argued that the school authorities were within their rights in using a flag salute "to awaken in the child's mind considerations as to the significance of the flag contrary to those implanted by the parent."

Justice (later Chief Justice) Harlan F. Stone spoke out in lonely dissent. He protested "the surrender of the constitutional protection of the liberty of small minorities to the popular will." Whereas Frankfurter had appealed to the community's right to use a symbol of national unity, Stone appealed for "freedom of mind and spirit." He was supported by powerful liberal organizations, including the American Civil Liberties Union, and even by the American Bar Association.

Within three years, three of the Court's most advanced liberals —Black, Douglas and Murphy—changed their minds and, uniting with Stone and two new justices who had been added to the Court, achieved a 6 to 3 reversal. As a result, some Witnesses' children in West Virginia were exempted from the compulsory flag salute and allowed to continue in public schools.[34]

Justice Frankfurter went down fighting to the end, and carried two other justices with him, Roberts and Reed. His most powerful argument was that, in such a difficult case on the elusive border line between individual rights and civic responsibility, a state has a right to resolve doubts in its own way. "So long as no inroads are made upon the actual exercise of religion by the minority, to deny the political power of the majority to enact laws concerned with civil matters, simply because they may offend the conscience of a minority, really means that the consciences of a minority are more sacred and more enshrined in the Constitution than the consciences of the majority."

It might be argued that the compulsory flag salute laws were very foolish laws, but that if the Court felt it wise to declare them unconstitutional it should have relied upon the principle of free speech rather than religious freedom. Whenever a sect is given the right to carve out an important segment of our body of laws and to gain exemption from penalties on the ground that obedience is contrary to its sectarian principles, the power of democratic government is weakened.

The difficulty of drawing a clear line between personal religious rights and community rights is well illustrated by a number of recent cases concerning zoning. When does a community have the right to exclude churches, synagogues and private schools from a residential district? No decent citizen would condone such exclusion if it happened to be based upon anti-Semitism, anti-Catholicism or any other form of religious discrimination. But suppose the community wishes to exclude *all* types of social organizations that create traffic congestion or bring together large assemblies: must this concept of town planning yield to those who demand the right to build religious institutions as a matter of religious freedom?

At present the Supreme Court has not explicitly passed on the merits of such questions. The trend of its opinions, in refusing reversal in several cases "for want of a substantial federal question," indicates that it still believes in the power of local zoning boards to determine the future of town planning. But several state courts have recently handed down decisions which point in another direction and which seem to put the burden of proof on local planning boards to show that churches and church schools would adversely affect the health and safety of residential districts.[35]

Sunday, the In-Between Day

If the Supreme Court has partially evaded the issue of religious freedom versus the welfare state in zoning disputes, it has revealed more adroitness in handling an equally difficult borderline problem —the issue of Sunday laws.

This problem seems to lie about halfway in and halfway out of the area of religious rights. The decision to describe it in religious terms rather than welfare terms (the need for a regular period of rest from labor) is largely a matter of taste. In the nineteenth century, the Court began by treating the Sunday issue in religious terms. Now it has transferred its language and its concepts to the welfare field, and the justices would evidently like to forget the religious implications of Sunday legislation altogether. The transformation in concepts has evoked bitter protests from all orthodox believers in Saturday as a divine Sabbath, but despite this opposition, Sunday seems to be fairly well established in the Court's thinking as a day of rest for the American majority. Its Christian significance is now accepted as only incidental and historical.

The present condition of Sunday laws at the local level is far behind the Supreme Court's modern rationalizations. Fundamentalist barnacles still cling to Sunday statutes in the South: gas stations in some states are closed only during church services on Sunday, and commercial laws thus become an adjunct of pulpit promotion. In the New York City area, a crazy patchwork of state laws and city ordinances in the converging states of New Jersey, New York and Connecticut impose special hardships on the large Jewish population. Some Jews who observe Saturday strictly as a Sabbath and close their shops at sundown on Friday night are demanding the right to keep their shops open on Sunday. Thus far all permissive bills embodying this compensatory practice have been defeated in Albany, chiefly by Catholic opposition.

One of the oddities of the situation is that—in the North, at least—the Catholic Church, which was once the chief opponent of Sunday laws, has now become one of their chief defenders in the commercial sphere. Only ten years ago Canon Stokes was able to say that "the Roman Catholic Church as distinct from Protestantism is not much interested in Sunday laws." Today, while the Protestant-dominated Lord's Day Alliance has declined in power, Catholicism has begun to place new emphasis on a non-commercial Sunday. Both Cardinal Spellman and Cardinal Stritch issued special statements in 1956 championing Sunday laws. Cardinal Cushing, in 1959, severely criticized a three-judge federal court in Massachusetts for declaring the Sunday law of that state unconstitutional in a kosher market case. He said: "Let us ourselves eliminate from Sunday the unrestrained commercialism which the courts, in deference to what they interpret to be our own wishes, are attempting to legalize." [36]

The enforcement of Sunday laws can be viewed either as an unlawful establishment of the Christian religion or as the assertion of religious freedom by the nation's Christian majority, as a denial of religious freedom to the nation's non-Christian minorities or as a legitimate exercise of the nation's police power in behalf of human welfare.

There is no doubt that American courts originally sanctioned such laws on religious grounds, and Congress unabashedly passed some blue laws for religious reasons, usually after impassioned Protestant orations citing Biblical injunctions about "the Sabbath." Three times between 1890 and 1906, Congress voted appropriations to expositions and fairs on condition that they be closed on Sundays—the Chicago World's Fair of 1892, the St. Louis Exposition of 1901 and the Jamestown Exposition of 1906. There was still enough Sunday conformity left in Congress in 1957 to prevent the second inauguration of Eisenhower on January 20, which happened to fall on that day. The President took a private oath on Sunday the twentieth and was formally inaugurated on Monday the twenty-first.

Few nineteenth-century Congressmen seem to have been aware that, as W. E. H. Lecky once pointed out, "Sunday is not the Sabbath, and its obligation does not rest upon the Fourth Commandment. It is a Church holiday, enacted in the earliest days of Christianity in commemoration of a great Christian event."

The confusion between the seventh and the first days of the week was preserved in at least one American court as late as 1898, when some New York appellate judges, reviewing a Buffalo eruption of Sunday baseball, solemnly announced: "Our laws for observance of the Sabbath are founded upon the command of God at Sinai that we should remember the Sabbath Day to keep it holy." [37] Of course, the Jewish Sabbath is the only sabbath that can be traced back to Sinai. As the distinguished Protestant scholar Conrad Moehlman has declared, the identification of Sunday with the Fourth Commandment is "utterly foreign to Moses, Jesus and Paul, to say nothing of the entire Christian Church prior to the 16th century." [38]

The Supreme Court has not endorsed the Buffalo blunder, at least not since 1885. In that year, Soon Hing, a San Francisco non-Christian subject of the Emperor of China, paid $6 for a laundry license and was caught ironing after midnight on Saturday night. Realizing that purely Christian sanctions would not impress a Chinese laundryman, the Court shifted to social and economic principles to sustain the Sunday ordinance. "Laws setting aside Sunday as a day of rest," said Justice Field, "are upheld not for any right of the government to legislate for the promotion of religious observances, but from its right to protect all persons from the physical and moral debasement which comes from uninterrupted labor." [39] This is the principle accepted by the Supreme Court and most state courts today. The policy was sanctified in the notable Friedman case in 1950 involving two New York Orthodox Jewish butchers who were convicted for selling meat on Sunday. They appealed in vain to the Court for a reversal.[40]

If the New York Court of Appeals, which established current Sunday law principles in this case, had chosen to employ journalistic words, it might have said that family "togetherness" on one joint holiday a week is a valuable ingredient in human welfare. In any case, the Supreme Court refuses to upset Sunday blue laws when the only argument is that they interfere with some traditional activities of a Saturday-faithful minority. Three times in 1957 and 1958, the Court turned a deaf ear to appeals from Arkansas, New Jersey and Ohio to upset state Sunday legislation as a violation of religious freedom.[41]

Neither Seventh Day Adventists nor Jews are satisfied with such decisions. They protest with special vigor because even some government departments still impose handicaps on employees who are unwilling to work on Saturday. People, they argue, should be able to choose their own day of rest according to their own faith. For the majority to impose one day and only one day on the minority is, they insist, an unconstitutional denial of personal religious liberty.

The Court is unwilling to accept such arguments, and it is obviously making every endeavor to keep religion out of the whole dispute as much as possible. Its concept of Sunday as a day of rest for the American majority is generally accepted by organized labor, and this has greatly weakened the position of Jews and Seventh Day Adventists. In any case, the whole conflict over Saturday versus Sunday as a preferred day of rest is being resolved indirectly by the rapid extension of the five-day week. If both days should become days of rest in all states, the arguments about the First Day and the Seventh Day would lose much of their meaning.

Separation—The Zone of Agreement

All things considered, the Supreme Court has had a relatively easy time in interpreting the free-exercise-of-religion clause of the First Amendment. The overwhelming majority of Americans believe in religious freedom, and no large pressure group ventures to oppose the concept directly.

It is quite a different matter with the establishment-of-religion clause. Powerful pressure groups are constantly trying to stretch the Court's interpretation of this term to their own advantage, and some of these groups include important churches. The clause has as many legal meanings as the rainbow has variations in color, and each group of special-interest interpreters is ready to fight for its own interpretation, always under the color of religious freedom.

In this area of establishment—and its converse, separation—the zone of agreement is more traditional than logical. Many of our existing practices do not fit in with any consistent legal pattern; some are still recognized as valid only because the Supreme Court has not caught up with them.

Everybody agrees that there should be no single established church, no official national faith and no formal preference for any particular church. Even the Roman Catholic Church—which, as a world-wide power, stands for partial church establishment—does not assert its claims for such status in the United States. But in practice, at the local level, in spite of the Constitution, the non-establishment principle is fractured quite frequently in the public schools by both Catholics and Protestants. In this area, Jews as well as unbelievers have much to complain of.

Some of the establishment practices are accepted by the Court and by the people largely because they were inherited from England in colonial days. Tax exemption of church property, for example, is one of the secure traditions. It was adopted almost automatically by the new states after the Revolution, although Madison opposed the idea. So, later, did Grant, who even suggested in a message to Congress that only graveyards and "possibly" church buildings should be allowed religious exemptions. Congress did not adopt his suggestion.[42]

Today there is local exemption in every state for both churches and church schools, and in most states for rectories and parsonages. Thirty-two states have some reference to tax exemption for religious organizations in their constitutions, and fifteen of them make such exemption mandatory. The Supreme Court set federal limits to this practice in 1885 by deciding that a Catholic church in Washington could not secure exemption on surrounding land "not reasonably needed" for church operation. California was the last state to exempt all religious schools; its 1952 referendum was confirmed by the Supreme Court in 1956.[43]

Is this tax exemption of religious property an illegal subsidy or merely a legitimate extension of government charity? It can be looked at either way. Certainly the Court's reasons for defending the validity of tax exemption are extremely thin, especially in the light of its strong pronouncements in the Everson and McCollum cases and its statement in the Zorach released-time case that "Government may not finance religion. . . ." But Leo Pfeffer, author of the scholarly study *Church, State, and Freedom,* is probably right in suggesting that, if a taxpayer tried to challenge the ancient policy today, the Court might not even allow him to enter its door. In fact, the Court slammed the door shut in 1956 against a challenge of California's 1952 referendum.

Sometimes special privilege acquires sanction by the mere

passage of time, and the courts apply to the privilege that judicial stop sign called *stare decisis* (to stand by former decisions). It is also argued that the non-religious, social service aspects of church activity have an independent claim to exemption. Many welfare and educational enterprises are mingled with religion under the tax umbrella of the word "church," and their welfare aspects cannot be unscrambled from their purely religious aspects.

The real threat to church-state separation involved in the tax exemption of churches is didactic. Tax exemption is almost always used as the first precedent in a chain of reasoning by those who argue that the Constitution permits public money to be used for sectarian schools. The argument almost always ends with the "clincher": "Since you acknowledge that tax exemption of churches is constitutional, it must also be constitutional to subsidize sectarian schools." As we shall see later, there are many missing links in this chain of logic.

Meanwhile churches and clergymen continue to receive a great many special privileges in addition to property tax exemption under both federal and state laws, and the Supreme Court does not forbid the concessions as an illegal establishment of religion under the First Amendment. Donors to churches, under Section 170 of the Internal Revenue Code, may deduct such contributions in their federal income-tax returns up to 30 per cent of net income. Most states exempt gifts to religious organizations from inheritance taxes; it has been estimated that the exemption applies to $200,-000,000 in bequests in a decade.[44] Clergymen can buy tickets on most railroads for one-half of the first-class fare (and so one-half of the federal tax); the general taxpayers and stockholders pay more than their shares to make up the difference. A similar but more restricted concession to clerical air passengers was made in a 1956 amendment to the Civil Aeronautics Act.

Clergymen have been exempted from military service by federal law during both world wars, and the Court has repeatedly sustained the exemption as a constitutional choice within the power of Congress. The Court has unanimously brushed aside the argument that military exemption for clergymen is an illegal establishment of religion, simply contending that "its unsoundness is too apparent to require us to do more." [45] The Court has repeatedly confirmed the exemption of religious conscientious objectors, not as a constitutional right but as a privilege to be conferred by Congress within its general legislative powers.[46] We have already seen the well-established practice of using government funds for the salaries of chaplains in the armed forces, in prisons and in Congress itself.

All of these somewhat questionable borderline practices of semi-establishment for religion are considered within the zone of agreement between church and state largely because they have endured so long without successful challenge. The reasoning behind them partakes more of sentiment than logic. And who shall say that a Supreme Court must be immune to sentiment, especially when it has the sanction of tradition?

Separation—The Zones of Conflict

There are two great zones of disagreement about the meaning of the phrase "establishment of religion" in the First Amendment. One concerns public money spent for sectarian causes; the other concerns the use of public institutions for the promotion of religious ideas. The two zones overlap constantly, of course, and the issues in both are closely bound up with the problems of the free exercise of religion. Still, there are really two issues involved, not one.

The money frontier between church and state is now the line where the heaviest sectarian cannonading is in progress. The justices of the Supreme Court have had great difficulty in building between churches and the public treasury a wall that is satisfactory both to themselves and to any large segment of our population. In general, Jews, most Protestants and the unchurched want a high wall to be erected; most Catholics and some Protestants prefer a low wall that can be easily vaulted.

The key decisions in this field have concerned the use of local public funds for Catholic parochial schools. This issue did not reach the Supreme Court until 1947, partly because the Court waited until the twentieth century to interpret all the protections of the non-establishment clause of the vague First Amendment as applying even on the local level. There is an analogy here between the Court's delayed action on racial segregation and its delayed action on church and state. In both cases, the Constitution has remained unchanged, but the Court has made new law by new and up-to-date interpretations of old phrases.

May public money be constitutionally used for sectarian schools under the establishment clause? The Court's answer, embodied in three famous decisions of the 1940s, is a definite *No* for all direct appropriations for the central expenditures of such schools. No federal or local tax funds may be used for building costs, teachers' salaries or other regular operational expenses. This principle was established in the famous Everson, New Jersey, bus case in 1947, which is probably the most important case in the whole history of American church-state law. The financial reasoning was confirmed by the Court in the McCollum case in 1948 and the Zorach case in 1952.[47]

In the Everson case, a New Jersey town, acting under a state statute, had allowed local tax funds to be used to reimburse Catholic parents for the cost of buses bringing children to parochial schools. A local taxpayer challenged this use of public money as an unconstitutional establishment of religion. The Court took a deep breath and expressed in one vital paragraph those general principles about the money frontier which now constitute American policy on the subject. On these principles the justices were unanimous. The paragraph actually goes far beyond the money frontier; it also sets a boundary between church and state in the promotion of religious ideas. The Court, speaking through Justice Black, said:

The "establishment of religion" clause of the First Amendment means at least this: Neither a state nor the Federal Government can set up a church. Neither can pass laws which aid one religion, aid all religions, or prefer one religion over another. Neither can force nor influence a person to go to or remain away from church against his will or force him to profess a belief or disbelief in any religion. No person can be punished for entertaining or professing religious beliefs or disbeliefs, for church attendance or non-attendance. No tax in any amount, large or small, can be levied to support any religious activities or institutions, whatever they may be called, or whatever form they may adopt to teach or practice religion. Neither a state nor the Federal Government can, openly or secretly, participate in the affairs of any religious organizations or groups and *vice versa*. In the words of Jefferson, the clause against establishment of religion by law was intended to erect "a wall of separation between church and state."

So much for the principles. This ringing pronouncement in favor of separation has blocked all use of tax funds for the central activities of sectarian schools, except in those few isolated centers of the Middle West where public schools have been taken over by Catholic religious orders. These captive schools are educational freaks and will certainly be wiped out when local taxpayers finally bring their existence to the attention of the Supreme Court.

The Court astonished some of its admirers in the Everson case by splitting 5 to 4 in applying its own principles to the borderline case of bus transportation. Was bus transportation at public expense a legitimate service to the child or an illegitimate service to the religious institution? The majority called the service legitimate and evolved a new "child welfare theory" to support it. Admitting that the use of public money for such transportation would help the sectarian schools maintain their attendance, the majority still argued that it was not a contribution to the schools as such but only an aid to "help parents get their children, regardless of their religion, safely and expeditiously to and from accredited schools." It classed such services with police protection.

In spite of this concession, the decision was far more of a victory than a defeat for believers in church-state separation. In effect, it legalized the use of public money in sectarian schools for such health and welfare services as school lunches and medical examinations, which nobody had opposed anyway. It sanctioned the use of public funds for school buses under the strictly limited conditions established by the New Jersey statute. But, by inference and dictum, it set a fairly clear limit to such use of public money, indicating that bus transportation was at the edge of the financial frontier. The warning was clear: thus far and no farther.

The Court also made it clear that its action on buses was purely permissive. The majority said specifically that a state *could* provide such services exclusively for public school pupils *if it wished*. Most of the states—twenty-eight out of fifty in 1959— still refused to supply such services for sectarian schools, and some of those that nominally grant consent actually limit the services very strictly. Catholic authorities usually count only seventeen states as granting the privilege in reality.[48] And states which have strict prohibitions against such a use of public funds have been left undisturbed. The Court has made no attempt to override their present laws providing public funds for public school pupils only, nor has it made any attempt to declare that free bus transportation for sectarian school children is a constitutional right rather than a legislative privilege.[49]

Even this relatively small financial concession to sectarian schools was altogether too much for four of the justices in the Everson case—Jackson, Rutledge, Frankfurter and Burton. They considered the bus appropriation an illegal gift to the sectarian school, not a welfare grant to the child himself. Justice Rutledge wrote a brilliant historical analysis of the background of the First Amendment showing that it was designed to prevent "every form of public aid or support for religion." Jackson's dissent was an equally acute analysis of the position of the Catholic school in Catholicism, showing that the parish school is perhaps the "most vital" part of the Church itself, ordained by Canon Law and controlled entirely by the hierarchy. "The state," he said, "cannot maintain a Church and it can no more tax its citizens to furnish free carriage to those who attend a Church."

The question naturally arose: How much of this definitive new interpretation of the establishment clause of the First Amendment could and should be applied retroactively to all the past cases of public expenditures for religious institutions? Since the Court never answers such a question until a specific case is brought before it, one can only guess at the answer.

Probably the Court under the Everson doctrine would say that public grants to church hospitals are legitimate if distributed without denominational preference, but no one can say whether the justices would approve the use of public money for hospitals that insist on denominational medical codes. That question has never been raised in the highest tribunal since the Court began to handle the religion clauses of the Constitution analytically. Protestant and Jewish hospitals apparently have nothing to fear from the Everson bus ruling; Catholic hospitals might have, since they insist on a Catholic medical and surgical code for patients of all faiths. At present, denominational hospitals are getting many millions each year through the Hill-Burton Act under a Court decision of 1899, whose reasoning Justice Rutledge described in the Everson case opinion as "highly artificial." [50]

One current type of public expenditure for sectarian pupils in some states would seem to be invalidated by the Court's reasoning in the Everson bus case. That is the expenditure of public funds for non-religious textbooks for pupils in sectarian schools. Such expenditures for Louisiana's private school pupils were sanctioned as constitutional in 1930 by a court which did not even consider the application of the First Amendment to the situation.[51] If a textbook case ever reaches the Court again and is discussed on its merits, it is difficult to see how such use of public funds can be approved even under the child welfare theory. A textbook is not an article of health or safety equipment but a basic feature in the educational process itself.

Of course, *any* feature of a school system can be treated as a welfare service to individual children if judges care to stretch the child benefit concept to the point of absurdity. Transportation to Sunday school might be classed as a safety measure; even the teachers' uniforms and the blackboards on the walls might be crammed into that category. This is one reason why defenders of the separation of church and state regard the concession of bus funds in the Everson case as potentially dangerous. The amount of money involved is not large. The critical question is whether the child benefit theory will be stretched under ecclesiastical pressure to cover more than the Court intended.

The Catholic World, in an open letter to President Eisenhower in 1955, gave a dramatic illustration of the way in which the bus concession could be stretched.[52] Its editorial, entitled "Eisenhower and Parochial Schools," asked whether the federal government is "planning to offer any help toward the building of non-public schools" and declared that the "wall of separation said to have been erected by the First Amendment exists only in the mind or rather in the imagination of legal students smoking the opium of secularism." It continued:

It's time to put a stop to such juggling of the meaning of a patently clear Amendment. . . . in the matter of the erecting of new school buildings, it's obvious that American children are entitled to the benefits of public welfare legislation regardless of race, creed or color. That was the decision of the United States Supreme Court in February 1947, upholding a New Jersey statute providing free bus transportation for children attending Catholic schools. American youths, whether Catholic, Protestant or Jewish, have a right to be educated in school buildings that have decent physical facilities. . . . there is nothing sectarian about heating equipment, windows and a roof over children's heads. . . .

When a sober religious journal takes such liberties with a Supreme Court decision, it is apparent that a Supreme Court justice's life is not a happy one. If he makes any concession to either side in a heated religious controversy over public money, his every word may be used as a verbal hand grenade on the sectarian barricades.

Religion in Public Schools

The financial challenge to the First Amendment in the Everson bus case was primarily a Catholic challenge. The religion-in-public-schools challenge was originally Protestant—and still is. Throughout the nation during the nineteenth century, some Protestant encroachments on the neutrality of the public school were condoned over the protests of Catholics, Jews and free-thinkers. These Protestant encroachments were a major factor in persuading the Catholic hierarchy to establish a separate and competing Catholic school system.

Beginning in 1913, a system of religious instruction, chiefly under Protestant auspices, had developed in connection with many public schools. It came to be known as the "released-time" system, operating sometimes in public school buildings and sometimes in outside private buildings. Catholic leaders at first were hostile or indifferent to this system. Later they became its chief advocates and beneficiaries.

The issue of the constitutionality of this plan finally reached the Court in 1948. It was raised by a humanist, Mrs. Vashti McCollum of Illinois. The verdict handed down by the Court in this case was such a sweeping rebuke to all those who attempted to use public classrooms for religious education that it provoked much hostile comment in both Protestant and Catholic circles.

Terry McCollum, ten-year-old son of a professor at the University of Illinois, was compelled to sit alone in a Champaign public school once a week while other students in his class received religious instruction from a Protestant teacher who was brought into the school to teach religion. The class was taught on school time in Terry's regular classroom. There was a separate class in the basement for Catholic pupils.

Terry's mother, Vashti McCollum, objected to this procedure as a taxpayer and a parent on the ground that it was an illegal establishment of religion in a tax-supported institution. She carried her case to the United States Supreme Court at great expense, losing the vote of every judge in every lower court on the way. In the highest Court she won a resounding 8-to-1 victory. The Court, with only Justice Reed dissenting, decided that all definite religious instruction as such should be eliminated from all public classrooms in America. Of course, the decision did not bar an objective treatment of religion in history or literature classes. It only barred the teaching of religion as sectarian promotion.

Both Justice Black, speaking for the Court, and Justice Frankfurter, in a concurring opinion, stressed the affirmative reasons for this decision. "For the First Amendment," said Justice Black, "rests upon the premise that both religion and government can best work to achieve their lofty aims if each is left free from the other within its respective sphere." Said Justice Frankfurter: "Separation means separation, not something less. Jefferson's metaphor in describing the relation between Church and State speaks of a 'wall of separation,' not of a fine line easily overstepped."

Justice Reed, in lonely dissent, declared: "The phrase 'an establishment of religion' may have been intended by Congress to be aimed only at a state church, not at aid to all churches." (This "multiple establishment" theory was and is the official theory of the Catholic Church.)[53] The Court disagreed with Reed and reaffirmed the position that the Constitution prohibits not only preferential aid to any one church but general aid to all churches. The justices were obviously astonished when the counsel for the state of Illinois argued before them that the state had a perfect right to distribute $5,000,000 a year "to religion" so long as all faiths were treated alike.

The McCollum decision established once and for all the rights of unbelievers in public schools. In addition, it put to rest the notion that general non-preferential aid to religion could be considered constitutional.

The reaction in some religious circles was bitter, and a few independent legal experts and law journals joined ecclesiastical leaders in an attack upon the decision.[54] Never in American history had the Catholic bishops spoken out against an American court so directly. The *St. Louis Post-Dispatch* expressed its astonishment by saying that the Catholic attack "must be without precedent in the relations of Church and State in this country." "Lawyers trained in American tradition," said the bishops in a long official statement published in nearly all the newspapers, "will be amazed to find in the McCollum case the majority opinions pay scant attention to logic, history or accepted norms of legal interpretation. . . . There we see clearly the determining influence of secularist theories of public education—and possibly of law. . . . We, therefore, hope and pray that the novel interpretation of the First Amendment recently adopted by the Supreme Court will in due process be revised."

Although twenty-six leading Protestants, speaking not as representatives of their denominations but as individuals, joined the attack on the Court, the major Protestant denominations as such did not criticize the decision, nor did American Judaism.[55] On the whole, Jewish leaders were enthusiastic, since the decision vindicated their effort to keep Christian promotion out of public classrooms attended by Jewish pupils.

In Congress, a few critics attacked the decision in words almost as bitter as those used ten years later against the school desegregation decision. Declaimed Representative Dwight Rogers of Florida: "When an atheist, who is not interested in religious and spiritual values, can interpret and prevent the teachings thereof, then this Nation has forsaken the ideals of our forefathers who landed at Plymouth Rock." [56] The Court's doctrine, said Representative Samuel Hobbs of Alabama, was calculated "to destroy every mark that characterizes this a Nation dedicated to God and to freedom of worship." "It means," he said, "that we have got to surrender our Sunday, and in addition to that Christmas must go." He introduced a joint resolution to repeal the Fourteenth Amendment so that the Court's ruling could not make this "a pagan Nation." Representative John W. McCormack, leading Catholic spokesman on Capitol Hill, commended Mr. Hobbs for making "one of the finest and most philosophical speeches I have ever heard in this Chamber." [57]

The sustained attack on the McCollum decision probably affected the Court's outlook. Otherwise it is difficult to explain a new softness in the Court's line on church-state separation which appeared in 1952. When the next released-time religious instruction case, the Zorach case, reached the Court, six of the nine justices approved as constitutional the New York plan for one hour a week of released-time religious classes outside of public school buildings.

The circumstances in New York differed from the circumstances in Champaign, Illinois, since the Illinois classes were held in a public school building. In making the concession to New York advocates of released time, Justice Douglas, speaking for the majority, used some general phrases about cooperation between church and state that have been widely employed to "prove" that the Court has changed its whole outlook on the separation of church and state. This interpretation is scarcely defensible. The Court still held that "Government may not finance religious groups nor undertake religious instruction nor blend secular and sectarian education nor use sectarian institutions to force one or some religion on any person." But Justice Douglas also commented: "The First Amendment . . . does not say that in every and all respects there shall be a separation of Church and State"; and he added:

When the state encourages religious instruction or cooperates with religious authorities by adjusting the schedule of public events to sectarian needs, it follows the best of our traditions. For it then respects the religious nature of our people and accommodates the public service to their spiritual needs. To hold that it may not would be to find in the Constitution a requirement that the government show a callous indifference to religious groups. That would be preferring those who believe in no religion over those who do believe.

The dissents were caustic. Said Justice Jackson: "This released time program is founded upon abuse of the State's power of coercion, which, for me, determines its unconstitutionality." Justice Black accused the majority of abandoning religious neutrality and indulging in "legal exaltation of the orthodox" to the "derogation of unbelievers."

There the matter rests—or perhaps does *not* rest. The Court has not spoken out on religion in the public schools since then, but the interpretation and misinterpretation of its words by local school boards, attorney generals and churches have plunged many a community into bitter conflict. Many communities have deliberately defied the Supreme Court's ruling, with the connivance of local churches; the defiance has escaped public attention in the storm of excitement over Southern defiance of the Court in racial matters. Eight years after the McCollum decision and three years after the Zorach released-time decision, a survey by the National Council of Churches indicated that one-third of all released-time classes were still being held in public school buildings.[58] The worst violations occur in Protestant-dominated Southern states.

The general, persuasive words of the majority, used as arguments for a very minor concession, have been inflated by clerical and legal imagination in some law journals and in several religious journals, both Protestant and Catholic. In 1958 a Jesuit writer in a book published under the imprimatur of the Archbishop of Washington calmly announced that, as a result of the Zorach released-time decision, "the First Amendment in no way inhibits governmental non-preferential aid to religion." [59] This startling view can fairly be described as wishful thinking. There is no indication that the Court ever intends to adopt it. Even Justice Reed, the sole dissenter in the McCollum case, did not go that far.

The Unanswered Questions

One of the surprising things—at least surprising to laymen—about the Supreme Court is that so many puzzling questions on the relationship between church and state are allowed to remain unanswered. Probably most Americans think of the Court as the ultimate place where every citizen, no matter how humble, can secure a definite answer to any constitutional question as a matter of right, especially if he can afford a proper appeal. Unfortunately, this assumption is very far from the truth. The Supreme Court has repeatedly rejected this so-called right in rather sharp language.[60]

The Court is not obliged to hear all comers. It may refuse to review a case without offering any explanation, even after a litigant has fought his way up through the courts on an important moral issue. The right of a taxpayer to raise issues under the religion clauses of the Constitution seems to be especially uncertain: religious violations often involve little public expenditure, and the Court tends to view with disfavor any challenge which does not involve some money outlay. But even this generalization is clouded in doubt.

The right to sue on a constitutional religious issue varies from state to state according to the precedents of each state, and the United States Supreme Court does not presume to tell the state courts in detail what entrance requirements they should impose upon religious litigants. After a taxpayer has successfully entered the local court to challenge a local practice—for example, a sectarian ceremony in a public school—and has come to the Supreme Court in Washington, he may still find that the nine justices not only refuse to hear him but even refuse to state a definite reason why they refuse to hear him.

Some of the most important constitutional questions about religion ever raised in American courts have been denied an answer by the Supreme Court on the ground that the plaintiff lacked a sufficient monetary interest. This was true in 1928 when a taxpayer challenged the expenditure of federal money for the salaries of chaplains.[61] The Court brushed the plaintiff aside because he lacked a special pecuniary interest in such expenditures. But who has a special pecuniary interest in the salary of a government chaplain? Perhaps if two divorced wives of the same chaplain fought for alimony, the chaplain's right to receive public money could be raised as a spite issue and a side issue. Otherwise, under the Supreme Court's rule, it is difficult to imagine how this important constitutional issue can ever be brought to the Supreme Court.

Even when a special pecuniary interest is involved, an aggrieved plaintiff is not sure of a hearing in the Supreme Court. For three years, beginning in 1956, New York plaintiffs with special financial interests challenged the right of the federal government and of New York City to sell land below cost to Fordham University as an incidental feature of a federal slum clearance and redevelopment project in Lincoln Square. The question of constitutionality was a very close one. Fordham is an organic part of the Catholic Church, entirely owned by the Society of Jesus. Was it an invalid establishment of religion to bestow a financial favor on such an institution as part of a package deal which had many sound welfare aspects? The New York courts approved the project as constitutional. Twice, in 1958 and 1959, the Supreme Court refused certiorari (declined to review), leaving this important issue unresolved.[62] Because of the uncertainty, a new fight against a similar indirect grant to a Jesuit university in St. Louis began in 1959.

The Court, of course, would be swamped with appeals if it raised no barriers whatever against crackpots and grudge litigants. It has had to limit the scope of its reviews in order to permit the justices to live a normal life. In 1956 it wrote only 94 opinions and heard arguments in only 123 cases of the 900 that reached its doors. If it had listened to all of the appellants and written opinions in all their cases, the justices would have had no time for sleep.

Nevertheless, the present situation in regard to ordinary citizens who raise a sound, moral issue under the religion clauses of the First Amendment is disturbing. The Court may reject their pleas by denying certiorari or by saying that the appeal is "dismissed for want of a substantial federal question," or it may grant a motion to dismiss for some other reason. Who can say what the rejection means in terms of the merits of the case except that one side has won and the other side has lost?

The Court has laid down the rule that it will never explain a dismissal, and Congress has given it the power to act in this way. At least four justices must agree before the Court takes up a case, and if some justices protest the rejection and announce their disagreement, they need not state the reason publicly. "This Court," says Justice Frankfurter, "has rigorously insisted that such a denial [of certiorari] carries with it no implication whatever regarding the Court's views on the merits of the case which it has declined to review." [63] The refusal to review creates some kind of a vague presumption, but lawyers are unable to explain exactly how much that presumption means.

Happily, these uncertainties do not apply to the major issues in the field of religious freedom. On these issues the Court has permitted litigants to come before it in spite of the lack of financial interest, and it has treated their claims with real consideration. Anybody in America can worship God in his own way, organize a church, publish religious books or magazines, operate a religious school and preach to his heart's content. If his rights in these areas are challenged by local authority, he may rely upon the Supreme Court for relief. Conversely, nobody can suppress a church or religious school or a religious publication or compel anyone to support such activities directly without facing condemnation by the Court.

The remaining uncertainties on the church-state battle front in the field of establishment are still substantial. Litigation is very expensive, and plaintiffs cannot tell whether even the expenditure of large sums will guarantee them a hearing in Washington. In some remote districts, it is almost as difficult for a plaintiff to bring a local school board to the bar of justice for sectarian intrusion into the public schools as it is for a Negro to bring a prejudiced official of the deep South to the bar of justice.

The practice of Bible-reading and the use of the Lord's Prayer in public schools illustrate the difficulty of getting a decision on the merits of a case before the Supreme Court in Washington. The New York Civil Liberties Union started a Court challenge of the use of the Lord's Prayer as an item of sectarian promotion early in 1959, shortly after Pennsylvania parents had challenged a combination of Bible-reading and the Lord's Prayer in the public schools of that state. Neither phase of the problem has yet been accepted by the Supreme Court for a decision on the merits. Professor Milton Konvitz, an authority in this field, believes that in view of past rejections "it is doubtful if in the foreseeable future the Supreme Court will again permit a Bible-reading case to come before it." [64]

But Professor Konvitz wrote his prediction in 1957. In September 1959, something happened which may change the whole picture and force the Supreme Court to commit itself on both issues. In that month, in a case brought by Unitarian parents in Pennsylvania (*Schempp v. School District of Abington*), a three-man Federal District Court in Pennsylvania decided unanimously that Pennsylvania's law requiring daily Bible-reading and recitation of the Lord's Prayer in public classrooms violates both the First and Fourteenth Amendments. The practice, said the court, "amounts to religious instruction or a promotion of religious education," and its compulsory character "prohibits the free exercise of religion."

Nothing daunted, the legal officials of Abington announced that they would appeal to the United States Supreme Court for a reversal, and it appeared certain that the Supreme Court would have to hear the case. A state whose laws have been declared unconstitutional by a federal court is in a very different position from that of an ordinary litigant. Mr. and Mrs. Edward Schempp, who served as plaintiffs in this case with the support of several national organizations, might have been refused admission to the Supreme Court as appellants for various technical reasons. The officers of a public agency can scarcely be refused.

Most state courts permit Bible-reading but not comment or interpretation. Sixteen states either require Bible-reading or authorize it in public schools; some exclude the Bible altogether as a sectarian book; and some state attorney generals rule out all prayers, including a simple grace before a school lunch.[65] Yet a Tennessee court in 1956 went so far as to permit "simple ceremonies" in public schools combining Bible-reading, Christian hymns and the Lord's Prayer, ruling that even this triple combination was not an establishment of religion under the First Amendment.[66]

So long as this diversity exists on the state level, the exact role of the Supreme Court will remain in dispute. How much power does the Supreme Court hold over local communities? Are the justices, in applying their own detailed interpretations of the Constitution to local governments, usurping some of the functions of Congress and the state legislatures? Are they manufacturing law in the area of religion without justification?

The challenge to the Court's power in religious matters has passed almost unnoticed in the public press because of the much more sensational and far-reaching attack on its power in racial matters. The criticism of the Court is not wholly confined to religious and racial reactionaries. Even so liberal and distinguished a jurist as Judge Learned Hand, in his 1958 Harvard lectures, *The Bill of Rights,* expressed some uneasiness about the role of the Court as a "third legislative chamber." He wondered about the "equivocation" with which some religious prohibitions are being enforced by a Court which is accountable to no one but itself.

Although such questioning coming from such a source must

be treated with profound respect, it should not be stretched to justify the imposition of any curbs upon the Court's powers in interpreting religious rights. Obviously the founding fathers did not *deliberately* intend that any Supreme Court should outline in detail the religious policy to be adopted by American public schools— or their policies on racial desegregation. There were virtually no public schools when the Constitution was written. The founding fathers could not possibly have anticipated all the varied applications of their principles to a complex, twentieth-century society. Madison and Jefferson could not have foreseen all the consequences of the words they chose to employ in attempting to define the frontier between church and state. Yet someone must interpret those words and apply them to the living world—and who is better qualified to do so than the justices of the Supreme Court? They have revealed wisdom and flexibility in adapting ancient concepts to a living society. They have helped mightily to make religious liberty and the separation of church and state successful in operation. In our complex pluralistic society, their continued functioning in their present role seems indispensable.

Chapter IV

God, Man and Congress

Although no Emily Post has yet published a code of religious etiquette for Congress, several rules of decorum in religious matters are almost universally observed by successful Congressmen:

If possible, never allow yourself to be maneuvered into a record vote on any controversial religious issue.

Never show any unfriendliness to any religious sect on the floor of Congress.

Eulogize the principles and performances of religious organizations at every possible opportunity.

Join a church or synagogue, but do not be too partisan or conspicuous in promoting its interest—unless you come from an Irish district.

Behind these rules of Congressional etiquette lies the Law of Adverse Noise. According to this law, the gentle noises of approval coming from voters are measured according to their intensity, not their total volume—and adverse noises should be multiplied by two. In religious matters, the aggrieved sectarian has the longest political memory. A small bloc of very angry Baptists, Catholics or Jews may ruin a good Congressman's political future by actively campaigning against him; an egregiously inept and incompetent Congressman may win their approval because he has never excited their sectarian animosities.

One factor which helps to explain the cautiously friendly and cooperative attitude of all Congressmen toward all churches is the pluralistic nature of Congress itself. A French parliament may be roughly divided into clericals and anti-clericals. An American Congress is always a pluralistic religious body with a vaguely Protestant majority and no very strong sectarian feelings. If sectarianism appears, it is likely to be canceled out by a competing sectarianism.

The numerical balance in Congress does not exactly correspond to the national religious composition, but it comes fairly close. In 1959, in the 86th Congress, the report on religious affiliations by the Library of Congress showed that Congress had 103 Catholics, 13 Jews, 412 Protestants and only 5 members who reported "Not Given." [1] In spite of the recent election of many new Catholic Senators and Representatives—there are now 12 in the Senate and 91 in the House—Catholicism does not have more Congressmen proportionately than its share in the population. Among the Protestants, Methodist Congressmen come first with 99, Presbyterians second, Baptists third and Episcopalians fourth. There are 2 Christian Scientists, both in the House; 9 Mormons, 4 of them in the Senate, 6 Unitarians, and 2 Universalists. The 1 Sikh, Judge Saund of California, lends a slight Asiatic flavor to the denominational mélange. (The admission of Hawaii in August 1959 increased the Congress by 2 Protestant Senators and 1 Protestant Representative.)

The Technique of Accommodation

Congress is now organized in such a way that open discussion of any controversial religious issue can be avoided quite easily. The floor debate is declining in importance; most of the real decisions are made by committees in executive sessions, or by caucuses in the Capitol suites of the majority and minority leaders. Since both of the major political parties are religiously pluralistic, and nearly all Congressmen come from constituencies that are religiously mixed, it is a matter of mutual self-interest to avoid any public decision or discussion involving a clash of creeds. If a legislative decision is unanimous, the unanimity can be recorded, no matter how it was achieved. If there is a serious split on a religious issue, the measure can be buried in committee without a record vote.

This technique of accommodation employed by Congressmen in handling religious issues is not unique. It is part of the process of avoidance and adjustment that every successful politician must master if he wishes to stay in office in a democracy. Since the typical Congressman is a Protestant lawyer fifty-six years of age, he has usually acquired enough sagacity by the time he reaches Washington to apply these principles with skill. His age has taught him the folly of quarreling; his legal training has taught him to speak skillfully on all sides of every question; and his Protestanism, with its vague diversity in creeds, has taught him flexibility.

He finds that it is perfectly safe to introduce bills that favor religious sentiment in general, or that confer minor favors on particular sects. And it is always good practice to insert pro-religious publicity material in the Appendix to the *Congressional Record,* usually in the form of quoted sermons or addresses delivered at religious celebrations. Each Congressman, with unanimous consent, can introduce into the Appendix as many sermons and speeches as he wishes, without cost to himself, provided no single sermon or speech runs more than two printed pages. Hundreds of pages in the *Record*—costing the taxpayers about $81 a page— were used by the members of the 85th Congress to record such momentous events as the anniversary of the canonization of Mother Frances X. Cabrini (introduced by a Baptist Representative); the "forty years of pastoral zeal" of the Right Reverend Monsignor Stephen J. Krasula, pastor of St. John Nepomucene Parish, New York (introduced by a Presbyterian Senator); and an eloquent long poem, "A Nation Needs to Pray," from the *Christian Science Monitor,* written by a cabinet member, Robert B. Anderson, and inserted by a Lutheran Senator.

Congress itself, in these modern days, almost never hears an appeal to religion and the Bible. This is partly because Congress rarely hears any kind of sustained emotional oratory. Unlike the House of Commons, it has ceased to be a primary forensic arena. Its important speeches are sober, factual and often very dull.

Woodrow Wilson, discussing Congress in the 1880s, expressed some anxiety about "the leadership of artful dialecticians, the success of tricks of phrase, the victory of rushing declamation" over sound sense. He remarked sadly: "It is natural that orators should be the leaders of a self-governing people." But there is no need for such anxiety today. In a television age, orators are not the natural leaders of the people—at least not orators of the old school. Few Congressmen go to the trouble of preparing eloquent orations in the grand manner, since their words might be spoken to a virtually empty chamber. If their orations on the floor are not polished, the polishing can be done afterwards; each Congressman may correct and revise his halting phrases up to 9 P.M. of the day they are printed in the *Record*.

Complete sermons and baccalaureate addresses frequently swell out the bulky Appendix, and many are distinctly partisan in tone. A religious address is almost never published if it scores some other faith directly; but "materialistic secularism" and "atheistic Communism" are always fair game, and no holds are barred in discussing them. Protestant "pinks" are favorite targets of Congressional oratory.

A conflict between Protestantism and Catholicism is always avoided in the *Record* or on the floor if avoidance can be accomplished gracefully. A great controversy broke out in Chicago in December 1956 over the television showing of the Protestant film "Martin Luther"; the policies of the Federal Communications Commission were directly involved, and there was a flood of public appeals for a Congressional investigation. Yet not a Congressman could be found who would introduce into the *Record* even a balanced, three-part summary of the issues—from Protestant sources, Catholic sources and the *New York Times*.

In June 1958, Senator Humphrey, always a champion of free speech, calmly set a precedent by inserting in the *Record* a temperate TV discussion among four participants on the NBC program "The Big Issue," in which Catholics and Protestants discussed Catholicism and the Presidency quite candidly. It was "a splendid public service," said the Senator, to bring "this difficult question to public attention in such a dispassionate and helpful way." [2]

Biblical allusions are rapidly disappearing from the floor, and God is rarely mentioned after the opening prayer. A few Southern gentlemen, during the recent debates on racial segregation, have cautioned their hearers that God made the races unequal in quality as well as coloring, and that the Old Testament proves this. They have been duly rebutted, without too much passion, by quotations from the New Testament. In a sense, the segregation controversy is repeating the slavery debate of the 1850s, but now in muted key and with less Biblical sanctimony. Debaters on both sides rely more on reports about juvenile delinquency, lynching and the denial of voting rights than they do upon God and the Bible.

Perhaps the decline in Biblical knowledge is partly responsible for this decline in Biblical dialectics; or perhaps the primary cause is a decline in literal faith in the whole population. Those Southern Protestant Congressmen who occasionally refer to the authority of the Bible seem to do so with some embarrassment, as if they were aware of changed popular tastes in forensic style.

There was more than a touch of irony when, in a 1957 debate with the late Senator Joseph McCarthy, Presbyterian Sam Ervin of North Carolina reported a list of contradictions in the Bible to show that one of McCarthy's intended victims could disagree about a certain fact without being guilty of perjury. Every one of the four Gospels, said Senator Ervin (citing Matthew 27:37, Mark 15:26, Luke 23:38 and John 19:19), reports a different wording for the legend written over the cross on Calvary. Good men and true looked at that cross together, and each reported what he saw differently. With this reminder of "the fallibility of human recollections," Senator McCarthy was completely routed.[3] This is, to the best of my knowledge, the only occasion in this century when higher criticism has been used as an instrument in Congressional debate.

The services rendered to religion by Congressmen include not only generous assignments of free space in the *Congressional Record* but also a great many special pro-religious bills which their sponsors present without any substantial hope of adoption. These bills are in the nature of advertising—advertising for the piety of the Congressman and for the religious cause which has won his temporary support. No matter how nonsensical the bills are, they can be printed with the Congressman's name as sponsor and circulated to those sectarian advocates who enjoy seeing their ideas enshrined in a government document. Frequently these bills are presented with a fine disregard for the First Amendment and the American policy of church-state separation. Sometimes they are so far from any possibility of adoption that they are denied a committee hearing and are promptly lost in the maze of 15,000 to 20,000 defeated measures introduced in a modern Congress.

At least seven bills were introduced in 1957 calling upon the Post Office Department to issue a stamp commemorating the seventy-fifth anniversary of the founding of the Knights of Columbus. The bills never even came to a hearing because the Department has adhered for years to a policy of refusing to issue "religious, fraternal or political" commemorative stamps. In 1954 Postmaster General Arthur E. Summerfield rejected a memorial stamp celebrating the 100th anniversary of the Y.W.C.A., a Jewish Tercentenary stamp and a Catholic Marian Year stamp. This did not prevent Representative Breeding of Kansas from introducing a joint resolution in 1958 calling for a special annual stamp "to commemorate the birth of Jesus Christ in the true spirit of Christmas." It was lost in the legislative shuffle.

Non-denominational, pro-religious legislative proposals have a somewhat better chance of adoption than sectarian ones. After a campaign of several years, conducted by Representative Louis C. Rabaut of Michigan (chief author of the new "under God" phrase in the oath of allegiance to the flag), special "Pray for Peace" cancellation dies were authorized by Congress in 1956 at a cost of $250,000. Postmaster General Summerfield declared that the project "epitomizes the highest aspirations of the American people."

Senator Styles Bridges of New Hampshire has been fond of introducing in recent years a bill for a concurrent resolution to "proclaim our faith in the Word of God." It calls upon Americans to "perpetuate renewed observance throughout the world, by nations and individuals, of the Ten Commandments." Since joint resolutions are only emotionally binding on Congress, it is assumed that if such a resolution did pass Congress no one would attempt to test its constitutionality.

When Bridges introduced his resolution in 1956, there was a moment of embarrassed silence while Senate officials pondered the question of which committee had jurisdiction over the Word of God and the Ten Commandments. Congress, of course, has no standing committee on the relations of church and state or the general extension of moral principles to world society. Finally the Senate sent the resolution to the Committee on Foreign Relations!

Pressure and Silence

There is very little formal pressure on Congressmen by organized religion for specific bills—certainly nothing to approach the insistent buttonholing by the great veterans', business, farm and labor lobbies. In the total picture of Washington lobbying, registered church lobbies are almost unnoticed: there are only seven registered religious lobbyists in a total of 1,000. The great anti-liquor lobby of the prohibition era, which was essentially a Protestant lobby, has faded away to an ancient, straggling color guard of the W.C.T.U.

Organized Protestantism, although it has great moral influence in the capital, has no paid lobbyist for its chief agency, the National Council of Churches. Organized Catholicism had for a time one paid lobbyist for the National Catholic Welfare Conference but now has none. Jewish synagogues as such have no lobbyists at all, although several Jewish welfare groups have representatives. The only substantial religious group that operates directly under the lobbying act is the Friends Committee on National Legislation, with three paid lobbyists and a comprehensive information service. However, it does not act as an organic part of the Friends' denomination.

The present lobbying law, passed as part of the Legislative Reorganization Act in 1946, was never intended to restrain or even to measure accurately religious pressure on Congress.[4] Probably the religious organizations were included in its scope only because complete exemption from registration for religious lobbyists would have seemed like favoritism. There are so many loopholes in the regulations that a church organization can ignore them and still exert a considerable influence on Congress. The law, which requires public registration of all paid lobbyists and public quarterly reports of all expenditures, does not apply to editors or witnesses who merely appear before Congressional hearings, or to organizations having less than a "principal purpose" in the area of specific legislation. The government interprets "principal purpose" very generously in dealing with churches.

These purely formal relations of churches and Congress, therefore, are not the total situation. Informal pressures are much more important than formal lobbying in imposing a point of view on Congress. Personal mail (each Congressman receives tons of it), editorial comment and television and radio propaganda all play a more persuasive role than formal lobbying. Probably the most important lobbyists in Washington are men who are never described as lobbyists—the newspaper, magazine, television and radio correspondents whose words reach through all doors to the Congressman's office and home.

In the field of religion a great deal of the pressure comes from points far distant from Washington. A New York press interview with Cardinal Spellman can alert every non-Catholic as well as Catholic Congressman to the mortal danger of "offending" the Catholic vote. An emotional appeal by a Texas fundamentalist radio preacher has been known to flood Congressmen's offices with thousands of letters for weeks. The denominational press of any large denomination, operating from distant parts of the country, can produce more results in Congress than all the personal contacts made by religious lobbyists during a legislative year.

Protestant churches and Jewish synagogues are handicapped as legislative agents by the absence of a unified Protestant-Jewish point of view on many major issues. The A.F.L.-C.I.O. publishes a score card for all Congressmen, rating them on a scale of 100 according to their votes "for" or "against" labor. (In the 85th Congress, on the basis of sixteen ballots, the A.F.L.-C.I.O. discovered sixty-one "perfect" and eighteen absolute "zero" labor Congressmen.)[5] No large church group would dare to judge the records of Congressmen in this way. All the large church groupings include Democrats and Republicans, economic liberals and economic reactionaries, advocates of reduced armaments and advocates of a preventive war against Moscow. The National Council of Churches recognizes the necessity for a certain legislative neutrality on many questions by refusing to indicate, when it issues a legislative summary, whether it considers one attitude "right" and another "wrong." [6]

The Catholic Church is better organized to express a single opinion and make that opinion effective, but the bishops are very cautious about public and specific directives on individual bills.

Their lobbying is generally indirect, and their primary instrument is the controlled diocesan weekly press, which has much the largest circulation of any religious press in the country. The bishops themselves never appear at Congressional hearings, and priests from the N.C.W.C. rarely appear as often as half a dozen times a year in such public functions.

Professor Luke Ebersole, in his valuable study, *Church Lobbying in the Nation's Capital,* has described how effective Catholic indirect lobbying may be. It is carried on not by registered lobbyists but by priests and members of religious orders who maintain constant personal contact with Catholic members of Congress. These unofficial Catholic representatives are often admitted to the ground floor of the legislative process in a way which must make their Protestant confreres quite envious. The Church's contact with Catholic Congressmen is naturally more frequent and effective with Democrats than with Republicans because nearly all the Catholics in Congress are Democrats. In the Senate, all twelve Catholics are Democrats.

One reason for clerical caution about "right" and "wrong" votes is that the moral aspects of many important issues never come to a clear-cut vote. The central issue in a controversy may be lost in a cloud of amendments and procedural irrelevancies. An adroit Congressman can guide his steps so circumspectly over the legislative eggs and through the legislative labyrinths that at least one of his votes on successive modifications of a major bill can be presented as pleasing to each side. Even the language of the *Congressional Record* in describing a vote can be utterly confusing. On a warm day in August 1958, Vice President Nixon, calling from the chair for a Senate vote, announced:

> The present parliamentary situation is that the question is on the motion of the Senator from Utah (Mr. Bennett) to lay on the table the motion of the Senator from Arkansas (Mr. McClellan) to reconsider the vote by which the motion to lay on the table the amendment of the Senator from Arkansas was rejected.[7]

Sometimes a Congressional committee deliberately conspires with cautious church leaders to suppress a religious controversy that might be embarrassing if it came to public notice. The worst recent example of this type of suppression occurred in the Senate in 1955 when the Hennings Subcommittee on Constitutional Rights canceled public hearings on violations of the religion clauses of the Constitution after it became apparent that the hearings would involve a head-on Protestant-Catholic conflict over birth control, the illegal use of public classrooms for Protestant evangelism and the capture of Midwestern public schools by Catholic religious orders. The cancellation was so sudden that some witnesses, after being guaranteed a hearing, had already arrived in Washington, only to find the doors closed. The culprits—it is difficult to assess the blame accurately because the chairman was ill at the time—were Senator Thomas C. Hennings, Jr., of Missouri, an able and progressive Democrat, and a Presbyterian; Senator Joseph C. O'Mahoney of Wyoming, a Catholic; and Senator William Langer of North Dakota, now deceased, who preferred to withhold any description of his religious affiliation.

The Hennings subcommittee had opened in September before the television cameras in the old Supreme Court room in the Capitol. The "jury" of eleven prominent citizens of all faiths, chosen to hear the evidence and sponsor the inquiry, were assured in no uncertain terms that the subcommittee would explore the whole area of the enforcement of the Bill of Rights. Apparently the three Senators involved did not realize that breaches in the wall of separation between church and state are being made by both Protestants and Catholics in many parts of the country, and that the dramatization of these little-known local battles would attract national attention.

A Protestant clergyman and a Jewish rabbi from Connecticut asked to testify about the suppression of birth control clinics in their state under clerical pressure. The American Jewish Congress wanted to submit proof of sectarian invasions into public schools.

Protestants and Other Americans United for Separation of Church and State had prepared a detailed and documented story of public schools in Indiana which had been taken over by Catholic religious orders, and of public high schools in the South exploited by evangelical Protestant organizations in defiance of Supreme Court rulings.

The disturbed Senators hastily called a secret meeting of the subcommittee, induced three leaders—Catholic, Protestant and Jewish—to share their anxiety and then canceled the religious hearings by telegram "on request." An inept and innocuous private survey, without field investigations, was substituted for the public hearings. Among newspapers, only the *New York Times,* the *Washington Post* and the *Christian Science Monitor* gave reasonable coverage to this astounding performance.

Usually even the religious crackpots are given better treatment than this. Many ludicrous sectarian proposals receive solemn consideration in committee if they do not involve either anti-Semitic overtones or a Protestant-Catholic conflict. For more than ten years, a hardy legislative perennial known as "The Christian Amendment" has made its appearance in Congress, with the sponsorship of several Representatives and Senators. It proposes to add to the Constitution a twenty-third amendment committing America to "the authority and law of Jesus Christ." If adopted by three-fourths of the states, it would establish Christianity as an unofficial state religion.

The Protestant backers of this "Christian Amendment," with their Washington lobbyists, have operated for years an elaborate publicity campaign centered in Pittsburgh, with a journal called *The Christian Patriot* and frequent radio broadcasts. For a time they had the support of Senator Flanders of Vermont, but he withdrew his name when it was used in a questionable manner. The authors of the amendment claim that it would not "establish" any religion officially, but the claim is at best very doubtful. It would actually change the whole neutral policy of government in dealing with religion by committing the nation to a particular theological preference. It was left to scholarly Jewish witnesses at a 1954 hearing to point out this fact. If Christianity becomes our preferred religion, they argued, then every Jewish American will be demoted to second-class citizenship. The Senate Judiciary Committee voted unanimously against the proposed amendment.[8] Since then, the amendment has been regularly reintroduced and regularly buried in committee.

Communism and the Clergy

Senator Hugh Scott of Pennsylvania, former chairman of the Republican National Committee, once wrote a book, *How to Go Into Politics,* in which he quoted some sage advice for all Congressional candidates: "Never get into an argument with a newspaper or a preacher; the newspaper always has the last word with its readers, and the preacher always calls on Heaven as witness that he is right."

Congressmen usually observe this rule in regard to preachers quite faithfully. The one exception is in the area of Communism and national security. Even after the end of the McCarthy era, Congress is still reluctant to listen to any preacher who calls on Heaven to witness that American policy toward Communism is too harsh. Washington tends to accept the assumption that the crusade against Communism is both religious and patriotic, and that any objector, lay or clerical, is neither very religious nor very patriotic if he challenges the all-out policy of last-ditch resistance.

On the whole, there is fundamental agreement among all churches and all political parties on the demerits of Communism. The only disagreements among churchmen on the subject are disagreements on strategy in dealing with Communists here in the United States and in dealing with critical situations that may plunge America into a third world war. Many church leaders, but

Protestants more than Catholics, question McCarthyism at home and "brinkmanship" abroad. Protestantism is also more aggressive than Catholicism in demanding an end to nuclear tests.

There is a distinct difference between Catholic and Protestant pressure exerted on Congress in respect to bargaining with Communism. Catholic pressure tends to be hostile to any gesture of compromise with any Communist-dominated nation unless that nation is making some concessions to the Vatican. Catholicism became much less hostile to Communist-dominated Poland in 1956 after the Polish government made concessions to the Church in the area of religious education. After those agreements, the world was treated to the spectacle of the Catholic Church supporting a Polish National Front ticket 52 per cent of whose candidates were nominees of the Communist Party.[9]

To put it bluntly, Catholicism's policy vis-à-vis Communism is made in Rome by the Pope and the Vatican's Department of State and not by the American bishops. This means in practice that European considerations often outweigh American considerations in arriving at official policy. Since there are more Communists in Italy than in all the Protestant nations of the world combined, the Vatican naturally tends to feel somewhat more desperate about Communism than do Protestant nations.

Twice, in July 1949 and in April 1959, the Popes have forbidden Catholics to support Communist political organizations even when these claim to be tolerant and charitable toward Christianity.[10] Pius XII threatened excommunication even for those who merely read the literature of the Communist front, but conditions in Italy made it impossible for him to carry out the threat. John XXIII renewed the ban on voting or aiding Communist organizations in language which seemed to bar any kind of cooperation at the polls with any Communist front anywhere in the world. (Polish-Vatican relations had degenerated by that time to the point where official friendship no longer seemed profitable to the Church.)

In acting on foreign policy, Congress must take into account the special policies of the Catholic Church concerning Communism and anti-Communism, partly because the Church controls enough votes in the larger cities to destroy the future of Congressmen who can be branded as "pro-Communist." This was particularly evident during the Spanish Civil War, when Franco emerged as victor partly because Catholic pressure on the White House and Congress prevented the shipment of munitions to the Republican government. Many American Catholics were in sympathy with the Republican regime, but the Catholic bishops, controlling the diocesan press, continually underscored their contention that in Catholic eyes the Spanish issue was an issue of God versus atheistic Communism. (There was some truth in this viewpoint, but it was only a part of the truth.)

Roosevelt, said Harold Ickes in a 1938 entry in his diary, "told me that he had discussed the matter with Congressional leaders that morning. . . . He said frankly that to raise the embargo would mean the loss of every Catholic vote next fall. . . . This proves up to the hilt what so many people have been saying, namely, that the Catholic minorities in Great Britain and America have been dictating the international policy with respect to Spain." [11]

Occasionally Catholic anti-Communist pressure on Congress has become very vigorous in recent years. It was a wave of such organized pressure in 1957 that forced the government to cancel its plans to entertain Yugoslavia's Tito, even though President Eisenhower had already extended an invitation to him. Knights of Columbus petitions against the proposed visit were circulated for many months during 1956, and in Congress itself the Catholic majority leader of the House, John W. McCormack, spearheaded the successful anti-Tito drive. Congress and the President were told in countless Catholic editorials and letters that Tito's visit would be an "insult" to American Catholics, not only because of the dictator's Communism but also because of his special record of hostility to Roman Catholics in his home country. Even Anastas

Mikoyan, Soviet Deputy Premier, seemed more acceptable to American Catholicism during his 1959 visit than Tito would have been. Mikoyan's record was that of an all-out cynic opposed to all organized religion; Tito's policy was specifically anti-Roman.

While Protestantism agrees almost unanimously with the major items in the Catholic indictment of Communism, many Protestant leaders insist that there are a few other devils in the world almost as ominous, notably fascism and Nasser. Some Protestants regard the Catholic policy on Communism as a trifle obsessive. As usual, Protestantism is sharply divided on such matters, with the extreme fundamentalists of the American Council of Churches trying to outdo the Catholic press in fervid anti-Communism. These fundamentalists appeared at Washington hearings again and again during the McCarthy era with denunciations of the World Council of Churches and the National Council of Churches as too "pink" to represent American or world Protestantism.

The Washington reign of Senator Joseph McCarthy of Wisconsin, which ended with the Senator's death at the age of forty-seven in 1957, produced a number of open clashes between liberal Protestants and Congress over the government's policy in regard to Communism and progressive thought. The most sensational of these clashes was that between the House Committee on Un-American Activities, headed by Representative Harold Velde of Illinois, and the president of the World Council of Churches, Bishop G. Bromley Oxnam of the Methodist Church, a former president of the Federal Council of Churches.

Long before 1953, Oxnam had been a vigorous social reformer. Like many advanced liberals, he had joined some organizations that were later captured by Communists; and during the period of Soviet-American collaboration which grew out of the Russian-American alliance of World War II, his name appeared on letterheads of some organizations for Soviet-American friendship. A great many distinguished conservative names also appeared on such letterheads during this period.

The House Committee on Un-American Activities, although it operated sans McCarthy, was a typical expression of the McCarthy spirit. For many months, in its offices only a few hundred yards from Oxnam's office on Capitol Hill, it conducted "private investigations" of the Oxnam record without calling in the Bishop for two-way discussions. Committee agents began to dribble to the press, from their "private" files, carefully loaded bits of "evidence" picturing him as a red sympathizer.

After many well-planned leaks of this type, Representative Donald L. Jackson of California, a member of the Velde Committee, launched a sudden attack on the floor of the House declaring that Oxnam "served God on Sunday and the Communist front for the rest of the week." [12] Oxnam could not sue for libel because Jackson spoke from behind the cloak of immunity provided by law for all Congressmen when they speak on the floor of Congress. The House gave Jackson an ovation after his attack on Oxnam, and the newspapers gave the charge national publicity. No one could say that there were any Catholic versus Protestant overtones in this particular clash, since Velde and Jackson were both Protestants.

Oxnam's counter-attack was so vigorous that his appearance before the House Committee on July 21, 1953, may well be considered the turning point in the McCarthy era. Before popping camera-bulbs and a packed chamber in the old House Office Building, he was grilled from early afternoon until midnight. He declared for the record: "I have been actively opposed to Communism all my life," and denounced the Committee's practice of releasing to the press "unverified and unevaluated material designated as 'information.'" The Committee exonerated the Bishop from all charges of membership in the Communist Party, but refused, by a narrow vote along strict party lines, to give his denials reasonable emphasis in the record. The *Washington Post* got hold of the Committee's entire Oxnam file—largely an F.B.I. product—and published it with specific answers by Oxnam on twenty-four points.

Then it published an editorial headed "Malicious Gossip." That heading represented the sober opinion of most fair-minded critics.

At almost the same time as the Oxnam hearing, a much more serious Protestant-Communist publicity scandal developed when Senator McCarthy, acting with exclusive personal authority, hired as chief investigator for his Senate Committee J. B. Matthews, a former fellow traveler of the Communists who had turned against them and become an anti-Communist agent for the Hearst newspapers.[13] Matthews, once a Protestant missionary, had published a sensational article, "Communism and Our Churches," in the July 1953 issue of *American Mercury,* a once-reputable magazine that had fallen into the hands of racist reactionaries. Matthews included some solid evidence in his indictment and then went on to the fantastic charge:

> The largest single group supporting the Communist apparatus in the United States today is composed of Protestant clergymen.
>
> Since the beginning of the First Cold War in April 1948, the Communist Party of this country has placed more and more reliance upon the ranks of the Protestant clergy to provide the party's subversive apparatus with its agents, stooges, dupes, front men, and fellow-travellers.
>
> Clergymen outnumber professors two to one in supporting the Communist front apparatus of the Kremlin conspiracy. . . . The Communist Party has enlisted the support of at least 7,000 Protestant clergymen in the same categories—party members, fellow-travellers, espionage agents, party line adherents, and unwitting dupes.

This last sentence was a masterpiece of McCarthyist literary style. It gave the impression that there were 7,000 Communists among the Protestant ministers of the United States, whereas Matthews could document only 700 as even remotely connected with Communism, and among these the majority had never been Communists but simply idealists who had, along with many Communists, signed the so-called Stockholm Peace Appeal, believing that it would help a desperate world to avoid annihilation by atomic bombs.

In a subsequent television appearance, Matthews was unable to name a single American Protestant clergyman who was an espionage agent. When he was asked: "If testifying under oath tonight, could you name 15 Protestant clergymen who are card-carrying members of the Communist Party?" he replied: "I could not."

Even McCarthy, who was accustomed to stormy weather, was astonished by the repercussions of the Matthews article. When a frontal attack of this character was made on a large segment of the Protestant clergy, scarcely anyone in Congress wanted to be associated with it. The Democratic members of McCarthy's committee resigned in a body, and even the Republican Protestant members —Dirksen of Illinois, Mundt of South Dakota and Potter of Michigan—deserted him on the Matthews issue. McCarthy accepted Matthews' "resignation" as chief investigator after protests from Protestant leaders in all parts of the country. Some Jewish and Catholic protests were added to the chorus, and President Eisenhower stepped into the situation with a public statement deploring the attack and declaring that "The churches of America are citadels of our faith in individual freedom and human dignity."

Another sharp clash of opinion between Congress and American Protestantism over Communist strategy broke out in 1958, this time in regard to Communist China. Congress had on several occasions after 1950 voted *unanimously* against the admission of the Peiping government to the United Nations. This unanimity of both houses on such a controversial issue was considered quite surprising at a time when many of our allies held contrary views. Although Presbyterian John Foster Dulles was once the chairman of the Federal Council's Commission on a Just and Durable Peace, he did not carry American Protestantism along with him in his Far Eastern policy. Many Protestant leaders opposed the use of American matériel in defense of the off-shore Chinese islands of Quemoy and Matsu, and the president of the National Council expressed his "deep concern" over the situation created by this policy in a telegram to President Eisenhower late in 1958.

Then, in November 1958, at Cleveland, an unofficial but very important group in American Protestantism directly challenged the China policy of Congress and the administration. The Fifth World Order Conference of the National Council of Churches, after listening to a speech by Mr. Dulles, adopted unanimously a recommendation by its section on international affairs in favor of the admission of Communist China to the United Nations.[14]

Although the Conference was not the primary voice of organized Protestantism in this country, its views echoed a widespread Protestant feeling and produced immediate repercussions in Congress. Dr. Frederick Brown Harris, chaplain of the Senate, denounced the suggestion as a "Trojan horse trotted out in the name of world understanding" and expressed gratitude that "there is an American Committee of a Million Against the Admission of Red China." Majority Leader McCormack introduced into the House *Record* some scalding words of Archbishop Patrick O'Boyle of Washington about those who advocate "peace at any price." In New York, the Jesuit weekly *America* headed its attack: "Christians Betrayed by Pacifism"; and two of America's most noted Protestants, Norman Vincent Peale and Dan Poling, essentially agreed with the Jesuit criticism. *Christianity Today,* new right-wing Protestant magazine in Washington, castigated the Cleveland resolution and its sponsors and claimed that its own poll of Christian ministers and lay leaders ran 8 to 1 against the Cleveland policy. Representative John Bell Williams, Mississippi Baptist, introduced into the *Congressional Record* a four-page diatribe against the "pink" leaders of the National Council of Churches which was almost as extreme as the attack by J. B. Matthews.[15]

This clash over the wisdom of our policy toward Communism is symptomatic of something deeper and more persistent. Communism is bound to be a crucial issue between Protestantism and Catholicism for years to come. The fact, which is rarely mentioned above a whisper in Washington, is that American Protestantism is not quite so rigid in its attitude toward Soviet power at this point in history as is the Catholic Church. The attitude of Catholicism might shift if more compromise agreements could be worked out between the Vatican and the Soviet Union in eastern Europe, but it is inconceivable that the Catholic Church in its present mood would have permitted the publication of a Cleveland-type resolution by American Catholic laymen and bishops.

This greater flexibility—or moderation—in Protestantism in matters of foreign policy is partly due to its looser and more informal organization. It is democratic down to the grass roots—at least in most American denominations—and this permits a wider divergence of opinion and policy. But aside from a difference in form, there is also a slight difference in primary philosophy on the cold war. In 1955 Dr. Eugene Carson Blake, then president of the National Council, and two other Council leaders rejected "the view that negotiation with the Communists is appeasement. We are convinced that there is no substitute for negotiation except the arbitrament of force, which creates vastly greater problems than it can ever solve. It is true that experience with Communism teaches us that what passes for negotiation only too often is a cover for deceit. Yet this very fact can, by skillful diplomacy, be converted into a means of enlightening world opinion concerning the pitfalls on the way to peace." [16]

It would probably make for better Protestant-Catholic understanding if each group made one minor confession about its own sins before and during the McCarthy era. The Protestant confession of sin would admit that, although the Matthews revelations were inflated beyond all reality, there actually were some Communist sympathizers who infiltrated Protestant pulpits after World War II, and some of them used the Protestant name for genuine subversion of democratic ideals.[17] The Catholic confession of sin would need to be longer and more detailed. It would frankly admit that the Catholic diocesan press of the United States made a hero of McCarthy until almost every other group of responsible citizens had abandoned him because of his misrepresentations and demagoguery. The most fanatical pro-McCarthy propaganda that beat upon the walls of Congress for more than five years was largely Catholic propaganda, and the few Catholic magazines like *America* and *Commonweal* which refused to succumb were drowned out in the pro-McCarthy chorus. The only Catholic bishop in the United States who dared to speak out against McCarthy at the height of his power, Bishop Bernard Sheil of Chicago, was promptly demoted by Cardinal Stritch. He was not promoted to the rank of archbishop until 1959, after the deaths of both Cardinal Stritch and Pius XII. It was not an accident that 4 bishops, 20 monsignori and 75 priests assisted at the McCarthy pontifical requiem mass in Washington's St. Matthew's Cathedral.

Swords and Ploughshares

Congress has always been embarrassed—as who hasn't?—by the apparent necessity of reconciling religion and war. Throughout history the most universally disregarded of the Ten Commandments has been "Thou shalt not kill." Christian clergymen, especially between wars, have a compelling sense of guilt about this fact; as compensation, they rush to support all the standard preventives of conflict. Foreign aid, the League of Nations, the United Nations, the World Court receive virtually unanimous support from all denominations. When the federal government takes some positive step to prevent war, it is sure to receive the enthusiastic blessing of the clergy. Nearly all religious leaders in recent years have favored in principle a ban on nuclear tests.

After war has broken out, the embarrassment about God and war soon evaporates. Almost all churches accept the necessity of defensive war and encourage loyal participation by their members. Each nation's participation becomes "defensive" for the clergy of that nation. The ministers become chaplains in the armed forces, and nationalism becomes an organic part of their faith. The will of the nation and the will of God are rapidly fused.

Although a large segment of the churches questioned the wisdom of Woodrow Wilson's policy in leading the nation into World War I, it took Chaplain Henry Couden of the House only a few days to inform God in an opening prayer that "It is a gigantic undertaking for truth against error, righteousness against evil, liberty against suppression, democracy against autocracy, divine right of men against the divine right of kings." [18] Pink-whiskered J. Hamilton Lewis of Illinois electrified the Senate with an oration on war, God and the sinking of the *Lusitania:* "in that dark night, in the distant seas . . . little children floating with their pale faces upward, where the Christ that has ever welcomed little children could at least beckon their souls to His bosom."

Only a few religious organizations and leaders retain their pacifism in wartime. The Quaker or Friends denomination, with a total membership of 120,000, and a few scattered Protestant sects like the Church of the Brethren, which has some 200,000 members, are the chief advocates of pacifism. The Quakers, who include some of America's most respected citizens, have no consistent pattern of conduct in time of war. They are far from being unanimous in their pacifism; in fact, the majority of American Quakers of military age enlisted in the armed forces in World War II. Former President Hoover, Vice President Nixon and Senator Paul Douglas are Quakers—and there is no pacifism in their records.

Today Congress has only one prominent pacifist, Representative Byron L. Johnson of Colorado, a member of the Fellowship of Reconciliation and the Congregational-Christian Church. A former college professor, he was elected to Congress in 1958 after a stormy campaign in which his pacifism was exploited by his opponent without avail. One other peace advocate in the new Congress, not a complete pacifist, has attracted national attention. He is William H. Meyer, who, in the 1958 election, became the first

Democrat to be elected from the state of Vermont since the Civil War, in spite of the fact that he did not conceal his sympathy with conscientious objectors. Both Johnson and Meyer boldly led off their Congressional careers in February 1959 by opposing the extension of the draft.

These two men are the exceptions that prove the rule. Ordinarily a conventional war record is almost mandatory for a Congressional candidate, especially if he falls in the appropriate age group for fighting. Any past statement that can be interpreted as hostile to "national security" usually guarantees defeat. The majority of the members of both houses of Congress are war veterans and members of the American Legion.[19] An even larger percentage are members of Christian churches, and most of them see no conflict whatever between military policy and religion. In fact, the identification of the Communist enemy with atheism has tended to turn the struggle against Communism into a military-religious crusade.

In such circumstances, it is noteworthy that Congress has become more and more tolerant in recent years toward religious opponents of war and military service. Perhaps that tolerance is a measure of the weakness of the anti-military forces in these days of the cold war. Perhaps the motive behind the policy is more strategic than charitable. During World War I the government learned that harsh treatment for conscientious objectors and pacifists did not pay off. It excited more bitterness than it allayed. Eugene V. Debs in Atlanta was worth far more to war resisters than Debs at liberty.

Before and during World War II, Roosevelt and Congress initiated a much more tolerant and understanding policy for dealing with religious objectors, allowing them reasonable alternative forms of non-combatant service. The government's sagacity was rewarded with almost unanimous sectarian support for the war effort. Today, at Congressional hearings, the Roosevelt policy of the soft answer continues. Committee members rarely engage in arguments about principle with pacifists or opponents of conscription, and a head-on collision between religious and military champions on the floor of Congress has not taken place for several years.

In this age of popularly accepted peacetime conscription, it is difficult to remember that during many periods of our history such conscription has been regarded with horror as the final symbol of government tyranny. Daniel Webster once thundered to a Congressional audience: "Is this, Sir, consistent with the character of a free government? Is this civil liberty? . . . The people of this country . . . have not purchased at vast expense of their own treasures and their own blood a Magna Charta to be slaves."

Even as late as 1924, the spirited opposition of the Federal Council of Churches, with a consequent flood of protests to Congress, induced the government to cancel a specially heralded Mobilization Day. In the late 1920s and early 1930s, polls taken among Protestant ministers showed that the majority not only opposed peacetime conscription but endorsed outright pacifism.[20] In 1930, in the presence of the Chief of the United States Army Chaplains, Dr. Peter Ainslee declared from his pulpit in Washington's First Congregational Church: "There is no more justification for being a chaplain in the Army and Navy than there is for being a chaplain in a speakeasy!"[21] Protestant opinion remained almost pacifist until Hitler's invasion of Poland, and some of Catholicism's most noted leaders were considered isolationists until Pearl Harbor. Then the nation was left with no honorable alternative but to defend itself.

Since then, Congress has adopted a series of extensions of compulsory military service and training by overwhelming majorities. "Christian" opinion has not served as a visible deterrent. Even the all-out drive of many church groups in 1948 against any extension of Selective Service seemed to have little effect.[22] Apparently, peacetime conscription has become a permanent part of the national life, and the present terminal date of 1963 for the draft is commonly accepted in Washington as a marker in the continuing and possibly eternal series.

The 1959 Congressional hearings on the extension of the

draft may be taken as a sample of the relative futility of church pressure on Congress in these military matters. The Catholic Church did not oppose the 1959 extension when the proposal came before the House Armed Services Committee, but Protestant opposition was quite outspoken. A spokesman for the National Council of Churches told the Committee that, while the Council favored adequate military strength to repel aggression, "we are opposed to permanent universal military training" and the extension of the draft.[23] Passionate and well-documented attacks on the wisdom and morality of the draft were made by young Methodist peace advocates, and both the Friends and the Church of the Brethren reminded the House Committee that war was an affront to the will of God.

Then Methodist Chairman Carl Vinson of Georgia, who had listened in polite boredom, removed his cigar, adjourned the Committee hearings and called a secret meeting. In a few moments the draft was extended by a Committee vote of 34 to 1. Without even waiting to give Representatives the opportunity to read the protesting testimony of witnesses at the hearing, the extension was rushed through the House a few days later by a vote of 381 to 20. The measure went through the Senate almost as rapidly. "The draft law," said Mr. Vinson, "is a tribute to the Christian principles of our people."

The speed and abruptness with which the draft was extended in 1959 characterized its extension in 1955 under circumstances almost identical. On both occasions, although the great majority of the members of Congress were members of Protestant organizations affiliated with the National Council of Churches, the specific opposition of that Council to the draft bills seemed to have no effect whatever upon their votes. One reason for this phenomenon is that, in general, Protestants do not consider themselves morally bound by the opinions of national church organizations. Particularly in matters of national legislation, their consciences are their own.

Another reason is that even the best American newspapers frequently ignore the most important Protestant statements of principle—although they rarely ignore the Catholic bishops in this manner. The almost incredible fact is that on January 30, 1959, the largest religious organization in America, the National Council of Churches, supposedly representing some 38,000,000 Americans, publicly opposed the extension of the draft laws before the most important military committee of Congress and accompanied its statement of opposition with a scholarly analysis of the situation, which was duly released to the newspapers. The next morning, even America's two most important and scholarly newspapers, the *New York Times* and the *Washington Post,* did not publish a single line from the Council's statement, and most other American newspapers also kept silent.

Although Congress has virtually ignored Protestant opposition to the draft, it has been quite charitable in respecting the individual consciences of members of small Protestant groups opposed to military service on religious grounds. Congress is equally charitable to clergymen. The law exempts all ordained clergymen and students in divinity schools who have been registered there for at least one year.

In the First World War, a conscientious objector was sure of exemption only if he belonged to a "well-recognized religious sect whose creed or principles forbid members to participate in war." [24] The Quakers, the Mennonites and the Brethren were safe under that rule, but conscientious objectors of other denominations were not. In World War II, Congress broadened the exemption to cover any person "who, by reason of religious training and belief, is conscientiously opposed to participation in war in any form." Such a selectee is not, of course, exempted from service of all kinds but only from military or combat service. He may be assigned, for example, to a work camp or a hospital if he convinces his local draft board that he is a bona fide conscientious objector.

The World War II revision of the law admitted conscientious

Methodists and other members of orthodox denominations, but it left unsolved the difficult problem of interpreting such words as "religious training and belief." What do those words mean? Do they require church membership for exemption? Congress, in the 1948 Service Act, indicated that church membership was not required, and it spelled out the meaning of those words as follows:

> Religious training and belief in this connection means an individual's belief in a relation to a Supreme Being involving duties superior to those arising from any human relation, but does not include essentially political, sociological, or philosophical views or a merely personal moral code.

This wording eliminates the requirement of church membership, but it leaves the conscientious objector who is a believer in God in a different category from that of the humanist objector. Yet the humanist may claim that his conscience forbids killing just as clearly as the orthodox conscience does.

Congress was asked in 1959 by both the American Humanist Association and the American Ethical Union to exempt non-theists who based their attitudes solely on "personal, moral and philosophical conviction." "Millions of people in this country," said one witness at the 1959 hearings, "believe sincerely in spiritual and moral values without being able to say whether the world is ruled by a single 'Being' or whether that 'Being' is 'Supreme.' Their consciences are just as much entitled to respect as the consciences of the orthodox." [25] It was approximately at this moment that Chairman Vinson removed his cigar, adjourned the hearing and rushed through a 34 to 1 vote of approval of the extension of the draft. There is no present indication that Congressmen are sufficiently venturesome to vote a new formula for dealing with non-theistic conscientious objectors.

Congress and the Vatican

Probably the most delicate religious problem that Congress faces today is the problem of American relations with the Vatican. The key fact that distinguishes Catholicism from all American-based religious organizations is that the parent Church is both a church and a state. Moreover, the capital of its centralized government is located abroad. These two circumstances establish the status of the Catholic Church in American law as a *de facto* foreign state, even though our government has not sent an ambassador or minister to that state since the Vatican assumed its present political jurisdiction in the Mussolini-Lateran agreements of 1929.

The State Department has acknowledged the political reality of the Vatican State again and again in recent years.[26] Since the separation of church and state is a basic American policy, and since the Vatican is the most complete union of church and state in the world, it is obvious that the United States government and the Vatican are not wholly compatible. They operate on two different planes of political reality. Throughout history the United States government and the Vatican government have approached each other very gingerly because they represent two extremes in the spectrum of church-state relations.

How can two such governments cooperate without violating the American concept of the separation of church and state? Congress has always regarded that question as somewhat delicate. Primarily, of course, it is a Presidential problem because the President is responsible for foreign relations. But it is also a burning political problem for Congressmen who live in a nation that is 20 per cent Roman Catholic and who have some authority over foreign policy.

When, in the nineteenth century, the Catholic voting bloc in this country was relatively small, Congress was quite blunt and occasionally hostile in dealing with the Vatican. The sins of the Pope were frequently debated in Congress, with frank animosity on both sides, during the decade before the Civil War. The Know-Nothing movement sent 8 Senators and 104 Representatives to Washington in 1854 with the avowed object of destroying papal power in the United States. Forty-three Know-Nothing Congressmen, who were blatantly anti-Catholic, actually held the balance of power between Democrats and Republicans in 1855 and attempted vainly to enact an anti-papal legislative program.[27]

It was during a part of this period—from 1848 to 1868—that the United States sent ministers and chargés d'affaires to the old Papal States. They had careful instructions to keep away from "ecclesiastical questions." Then, in 1867, by a vote of 82 to 18, the House wiped out the appropriation for a legation in Rome because of some discrimination against Protestants and because of Pius IX's alleged leaning toward the Confederate States during the Civil War.[28]

The next time Congress had a chance to express itself on the question of diplomatic relations with the Vatican was in 1951, when President Truman asked the Senate to confirm the nomination of General Mark Clark as a full ambassador to the Vatican. The circumstances which led up to this event were not calculated to make the Senate receptive. In 1939 President Roosevelt had by-passed the Senate, with its constitutional prerogative of confirming all ambassadors and ministers, by appointing the late Myron Taylor as a "personal representative" to the Pope. The Senate was given no opportunity to approve or reject Taylor, although he used the American Embassy in Rome rent-free, most of his work in Rome was done by assistants on the State Department payroll and the Vatican gave him ambassadorial status.[29] The act of appointing Taylor without Congressional debate and approval was an unparalleled piece of Presidential effrontery, a defiance of the financial powers of the House and the confirmatory powers of the Senate.

Taylor held his post in Rome until 1950, under both Roosevelt and Truman, in spite of repeated assurances given by Truman to Protestant leaders that the Taylor mission was an emergency one, not to be renewed. In February 1950, an inspired Vatican dispatch in the *New York Times* declared that "The Vatican would be more than pleased to have the United States government accredit a permanent diplomatic envoy to the Holy See but is not desirous of seeing another personal representative of President Truman appointed." The President waited until the closing days of the Congressional session and suddenly sent in the nomination of General Mark Clark to be a full ambassador to the Vatican. It was too late to discuss the appointment before adjournment. If Clark had been confirmed, he would have become the only full ambassador to the Vatican from a non-Catholic government.

The storm that broke over the White House and Congress might be described as a Protestant typhoon. In spite of support for the nomination by several leading newspapers and Catholic bishops, the opposition was overwhelming. The National Council of Churches led the assault with the greatest unanimity it has ever achieved on any issue, and Truman's own pastor joined in the opposition.[30] Truman suddenly discovered that there was a hitherto undisclosed technical reason why he could not give the general an interim appointment. After more than two months of protest, Clark finally decided that the graceful thing to do was to withdraw his name. Congress heaved a great sigh of relief, since it had been freed from the necessity of a public hearing or a record vote on an "anti-Catholic" issue. As David Lawrence remarked: "Everybody is off the hook."

Two months later, in March 1952, Congress had its chance to rebuke Truman—and indirectly Roosevelt also—for their policies on this question. Representative Prince H. Preston, Jr., of Georgia induced the House Appropriations Committee, by a vote of 19 to 17, to attach a rider to an appropriation bill providing that no funds could be spent for a chief of a diplomatic mission prior to his confirmation by the Senate. That provision would have blocked any interim appointment of a Vatican ambassador.

The two chief spokesmen of the Catholic Church in Congress, John W. McCormack and John J. Rooney, led a spirited attack on the Preston rider. "I intend to make the fight of my life to defeat this amendment," said Rooney. McCormack denounced it in the name of "the unity of our country and the unity of our people in connection with the destruction and inhuman communistic challenge and conspiracy that confronts the world today. As I view the present world situation it is a religious conflict." [31] McCormack and Rooney lost in the House 159 to 82, but when the rider reached the Senate it was finally removed from the appropriation bill under pressure by the chief Catholic spokesman in that body, Senator Pat McCarran of Nevada.

Since then, the Vatican ambassador proposal has been sporadically revived in Congress without any visible results. In 1959, a Catholic Congressman from New York, Victor Anfuso, tried to resuscitate the issue by introducing a resolution calling for the appointment of a full ambassador, but even the newspapers paid little attention and Congress refused to be interested. Most journalists and legislators regard the movement for an ambassador to the Vatican as a lost cause, which is occasionally revived rhetorically for political reasons.

At the present time the policy of Congress is to permit the Catholic Church to be a state or a church in American law according to its own choice of roles. The general theory is that if there is to be any unscrambling of church and state in the Vatican's status under American law, the unscrambling should be done by the courts.

American cardinals are permitted to vote in Vatican elections, and American archbishops are permitted to serve as full-blown political diplomats for the Vatican, in spite of prohibitions against such conduct in the Immigration and Nationality Act of 1952.[32] An appropriation of $964,000 for the repair of the Pope's summer palace at Castel Gandolfo, damaged by American air raids during World War II, was passed unanimously in June 1956 although the State Department declared in writing that there was no legal obligation to make the appropriation.[33] Ordinary church damages in Italy were not liquidated in this way. Even the Church's collaboration with the Franco dictatorship in Spain, one of the most notorious facts in contemporary politics, is almost never mentioned in Congress although it has special religious significance for the American people. American money is keeping Franco's government alive, and that government is openly destroying religious liberty in Spain with Catholic support.

Religion and Judicial Fitness

Occasionally the Senate is caught in a religious controversy when it is called on to examine and confirm Presidential appointees to the Supreme Court. In general, religious questions are not raised directly against any appointee on the basis of creed alone. Much anti-Semitic mail was received when Louis D. Brandeis was appointed in 1916 and when Felix Frankfurter was appointed in 1939. Some anti-Catholic letters were received when Pierce Butler was nominated in 1922. All three of these non-Protestant appointees were confirmed but only after much discussion and some show of bigotry.

The six-month wrangle over the Brandeis confirmation and the one-month wrangle over Frankfurter's confirmation were due almost entirely to alleged radicalism. Professor John P. Frank, in his valuable study of Supreme Court confirmations, quotes a letter opposing Frankfurter: "If we put another Jew on the Court, then the Jew element in the Court will represent 29,000,000 of the population. . . . would you put two Negroes on the Court, or two Chinese?" [34] (Justices do not, of course, represent specific racial or religious groups. Each justice represents all Americans in the nation as a whole.)

Senators sympathetic with the Ku Klux Klan opposed Pierce Butler noisily, but Frank Murphy was spared this type of bigoted opposition. The Catholic question in reverse was raised in the Senate in 1937 when it was rumored that Hugo Black had once been affiliated with the Ku Klux Klan. Both Catholics and non-Catholic liberals were deeply disturbed, and Black was bitterly attacked in many Northern newspapers. Although the rumor of Ku Klux Klan membership was verified after the Senate had confirmed him by a 4 to 1 vote, Black's subsequent record showed that he had completely shaken off any Klan philosophy. In fact, he became one of the Court's most consistent and distinguished champions of a tolerant culture.

The Black incident raises a nice question in Senatorial responsibility. How far should Congress go in holding an appointee responsible for the policies of organizations to which he belongs? The Senate has never had the temerity to apply an organization policy test to membership in the Catholic Church, but the issue was raised obliquely when Justice William J. Brennan appeared before the Senate Judiciary Committee for confirmation as a justice of the Supreme Court in February 1957.[35] The Committee's hearing about his fitness was rendered somewhat ludicrous by the late Senator Joseph McCarthy, who, in one of the last great hysterical outbursts of his career, attacked his fellow Catholic as too friendly to Communism, crying that Brennan had described some Congressional investigations as "reminiscent of Salem witch hunts."

In the general uproar, it was scarcely noticed that one would-be witness had raised a fundamental question about Vatican policy and the American judiciary. This was Charles Smith, a small, white-haired atheist from New York, who came to the hearing with his lawyer and two books—*Morals in Politics and Professions* by Monsignor Francis J. Connell, formerly dean of the School of

Sacred Theology of Catholic University, and *The Moral Obligations of Catholic Civil Judges* by Father John D. Davis, also of Catholic University. Both books had been produced under official imprimatur, and both, particularly the Davis, contained some very definite statements about the moral supremacy of Catholic authority over "unjust" civil laws.

A Catholic judge who followed the teachings in the Davis book conscientiously—and presumably that would be his duty since the work represents the official point of view of the highest authorities of his Church—might be disqualified for serving impartially in many cases involving liberal divorce laws, birth control, eugenic sterilization, religion in public schools and the use of public money for sectarian education. The Davis work instructs Catholic judges that they have a moral duty to penalize Catholics very lightly if they should go on a tax strike against the "injustice" involved in the American system of using tax funds for public schools only.

When atheist Smith asked the right to insert these books into the record at the Brennan hearing, he was shunted to a subcommittee. There he was permitted to raise a general theoretical question about the double allegiance of Catholic judges, but without the documentation of specific instructions to civil judges. Without this documentation, his questions became largely rhetorical. Senator O'Mahoney, a liberal Catholic, very politely presented Smith's one general question to Brennan before the whole Committee. Asked whether, in the event of a "mixed issue" involving both papal decrees and "the laws and precedents of this nation," he would be bound by his religion or by his oath to the nation, Brennan replied with engaging directness that he would unreservedly follow his oath to support the Constitution and laws of his country. The incident was over and the newspaper headline read: BRENNAN PUTS COURT ABOVE HIS RELIGION. (The headline was correct. Brennan has proved to be an intelligent and independent jurist.)

Sin and Social Welfare

The weakness of formal religious lobbies in the capital should not be taken as evidence that churches fail to take a stand on social issues. Frequently their public utterances have great influence on Congress even when no specific bill is at stake. The drift of Christian policy during the past century has been more and more toward a responsible and meaningful social gospel, and both the papal encyclicals of the Catholic Church—beginning with Leo XIII's *Rerum novarum* in 1891—and the repeated statements in behalf of social justice made by the Federal Council of Churches and its successor, the National Council, have had an effect in Washington. American Judaism has also had an important role in promoting social idealism.

It is difficult to realize how far America has moved from the pronouncement of the bishops of the Methodist Church South in 1865: "Know your high calling. Preach Christ and Him crucified. Do not preach politics." Most religious leaders of America today do preach some politics in the sense of promoting moral values in political life, and their right to do so is a basic part of American freedom. Their Christianity (or Judaism) would be a feeble and useless thing unless it attempted to provide some kind of moral guidance in that vast realm known as politics.

It is difficult to identify a single Protestant attitude or a single Catholic attitude on any of the great social and economic issues considered by Congress in recent years. On the whole, the Catholic attitude is easier to identify because of Catholicism's centralized system of control. In general, it may be said that organized Protestantism is still hostile to the liquor traffic, while Catholicism is not; that Catholics condone gambling while Protestants are quite anti-gambling; that Catholics take the lead against supposedly indecent literature and films while Protestants are more cautious about advocating any kind of censorship; that Protestants and Jews favor the right of contraception while officially Catholics do not; that Catholics and most Jews are more eager than Protestants to liberalize the immigration laws; that Catholics and Protestants are about equally progressive (or reactionary) in facing problems of poverty, but that Catholicism is somewhat more pro-labor at the present moment; and that both religious groups are hopelessly divided on racial segregation, although official Catholicism is more clearly committed to the support of the Supreme Court's policy because the Church's official discipline is monolithic. If a proposed family allowance system ever reached the floor of Congress, the Catholic Church would undoubtedly support it in principle, just as it would undoubtedly oppose any uniform divorce law if it tended to liberalize divorce.

There are, of course, so many holes in these generalizations that a statistical scientist could drive a horse and wagon through the openings.

The attitude of Catholicism and Protestantism in the present struggle over segregation in the schools is an example of the difficulty in defining sectarian attitudes and assessing their influence on Congress. To begin with, Congress did not start the trend toward desegregation; the impulse came primarily from outside organizations and from the Supreme Court. Congress did not desegregate the Washington schools until the Supreme Court made it obligatory in the 1954 Brown case. In fact, religious pressure on Congress in behalf of desegregation has been in the nature of a postscript. The *New York Times* in July 1959 estimated that in the North only 10 to 12 per cent of all churches, Protestant and Catholic, are integrated, and that in the entire seventeen Southern states where segregation has some sanction in law, there are not more than 200 integrated churches.[36]

The Catholic Church, through its American bishops and through many pronouncements by the Popes, has condemned racial discrimination in general and racial segregation in particular. It has even gone so far as to condemn laws against miscegenation. In Southern border territory, desegregation in Catholic schools has been accomplished with no great disturbance, although one reason for the smooth transition has been the fact that very few Negroes are Catholics. To the credit of the Catholic Church, desegregation began in the Catholic schools of Washington before Congress began to desegregate the public schools.

The other side of the picture may be seen in Louisiana, the only state of the old South with a substantial number of colored Catholics. There white Catholic lay resistance to integration has been almost as severe as white Protestant resistance in Georgia. Archbishop Joseph Rummel of New Orleans, who ordered desegregation in the Catholic schools of his jurisdiction in 1956 with the support of the Vatican, was forced to suspend the application of his decree indefinitely when he was faced with the almost unanimous opposition of his lay leaders.

Verbally, American Protestantism has supported the Supreme Court in its stand against segregation, and scores of statements can be produced to show this. The Federal Council of Churches made a pronouncement against segregation as unchristian eight years before the Supreme Court's decision.[37] Yet the core of Southern white opposition is largely Protestant, and most of the die-hard Senators and Representatives in Washington who are fighting the new civil rights legislation are conspicuous Protestants. The largest Protestant group in the old South, the Southern Baptist Convention, is seriously divided on the segregation issue, although the Convention voted to accept the Supreme Court's verdict in 1954 and refused to reverse this stand at Louisville in 1959. The most conspicuous Southern "moderate" on the issue in the 85th Congress, Brooks Hays of Arkansas, was president of the Southern Baptist Convention at the time when he was maneuvered out of his seat by Governor Orval Faubus. Faubus was affiliated with the same denomination.

When the Southern Manifesto against civil rights legislation and the Supreme Court was issued by eighty-two Representatives and nineteen Senators in March 1956, all but four of the signers were Protestants.[38] But this fact is almost irrelevant since the only four Catholics in Congress from the deep South, all from Louisiana, also signed it. Regional interests rather than moral philosophy seem to have determined almost all the votes on recent civil rights legislation. If there is a Christian point of view, it has not triumphed over geography and local group pressure.

Such denominational feebleness does not apply to prohibition and its surviving stepchild, the movement to abolish interstate liquor advertising. The original Anti-Saloon League, which conferred prohibition on America from 1920 to 1933, was formed in a Washington Baptist church in 1895, and it was always proud to consider itself a militant arm of American Protestantism. Its chief ally was the Methodist Board of Temperance, Prohibition and Public Morals, and its Baptist allies were almost as zealous. Its chief opponent—aside from the liquor interests and the millions of individual Americans who like their liquor—was always the Catholic Church.

This does not mean that the Catholic Church has had no advocates of temperance; quite the contrary. The Catholic Total Abstinence Union grew side by side with the Protestant temperance societies in the 1880s and 1890s, and the Third Plenary Council of Baltimore of 1884 urged liquor dealers to "choose a more honorable way of making a living." [39] But Catholic policy on liquor has always favored voluntary abstention or voluntary use, not compulsory control by the state.

The Church sees nothing wrong in priests' manufacturing brandy and wine for commercial sale if the profits go to Catholic institutions. The practice is permitted under Canon 142.[40] In fact, the Catholic Church is now one of the chief liquor manufacturers of the United States, according to its own description.

Both the Jesuits and the Christian Brothers, two of the chief religious orders of the Church, engage in the commercial liquor business in California; and the Christian Brothers (De La Salle Institute), advertising themselves as the chief producers of fine wines and brandies in America, sued the federal government for a $490,-000 refund of taxes in 1957 on the ground that the business is an organic part of the Catholic Church and that all property is "church property, subject to the control of the Pope." After exposure of the facts in two Congressional hearings, the Christian Brothers surrendered temporarily by withdrawing their refund suit, but they still claim corporate tax exemption, and their suit was reinstated late in 1959. Under present federal policy, such exemption is granted to churchly manufacturers of liquor who are priests. (This exempts the Jesuits, who are priests, but not the Christian Brothers, who are technically not "sacerdotal.")

The Catholic hierarchy was so openly opposed to prohibition even after the passage of the Eighteenth Amendment that Father Conway's famous *Question Box,* a Catholic best seller for many years, which was published at the height of the prohibition era under the imprimatur of Cardinal Hayes, said: "The Prohibition law is a law not binding in conscience, because the drink evil has never assumed such enormous proportions in the United States as to render imperative so radical an interference with the liberty of all citizens."

Probably no pressure group in the history of American politics has ever had Congress so completely in the hollow of its hand as the Anti-Saloon League in the 1920s. Those days are past, and today the anti-liquor interests can no longer produce enough pressure in Washington to threaten the careers of city Congressmen. In some rural districts, however, there is still much anti-liquor sentiment, and rural Congressmen are likely to be quite respectful in their treatment of dry leaders. Several hundred towns and villages in the country—and the entire state of Mississippi—are still nominally dry.[41] It is primarily Protestant sentiment that keeps them dry.

It is also primarily Protestant sentiment—or at least the sentiment of Protestant clergymen—that has produced eight drives in the last twelve years in Congress for an interstate ban on liquor advertising. The National Council of Churches, the Methodist Board of Temperance, the Southern Baptist Convention and the W.C.T.U. have spearheaded the attack of more than fifty Protestant denominations. In 1958, in the last great drive, the liquor interests, the American Legion and many great national magazines (which garner enormous revenues from such advertising) appeared at hearings on the other side.[42]

The Catholic Church was officially silent on the issue, but its largest chain of diocesan newspapers—which carries liquor advertising in its own columns—published a comment that expressed the Catholic philosophy quite accurately: "Advertising liquor in itself is not evil. If it is morally right to sell a certain product, it is morally right to advertise it. Liquor is not an evil in itself; the morality of drinking is entirely in its use or abuse." [43]

Apparently Congress will not be moved by church pleas on the liquor advertising issue. At the end of the 1958 Senate hearings, all reform proposals were buried in committee without a public vote.

The same type of Catholic-Protestant split on moral policy appears in the field of gambling, although the issue rarely reaches a national level. All churches agree that all citizens must obey the national lottery law, which bars gambling promotion by mail. It was passed in Cleveland's second administration under the pressure of a powerful Protestant lobby, and it has been considered impregnable ever since. But at the present time, licensed gambling for charitable purposes, operating under local law, is spreading rapidly throughout the country with Catholic support and Protestant opposition. In Catholic moral manuals, gambling is not an evil per se; in most Protestant codes, it is. "History proves," said the Federal Council of Churches in 1939, "that all forms of gambling have a demoralizing influence upon character, and that in the end most of the losses are visited upon the poor." [44]

Bingo, recently legalized by constitutional amendment in New York State, has become an important means of financial support for Catholic parochial schools in many states. Congress, like many city governments, would prefer to look the other way when the problem is posed as a challenge to its own authority. Bingo is illegal in the District of Columbia, and the District is exclusively under the control of Congress, yet several of Washington's largest Catholic churches announce regular games with the full knowledge of the police.[45] (Congressmen who wished to participate in October 1959 would have found weekly games in operation at St. Mary's Church, 727 5th Street, N.W.; at St. Martin's social hall, 1912 North Capital Street; and at St. Aloysius Church, 19 I Street, N.W.) The only federal department that insists that such gambling enterprises should obey the law is the Post Office Department. It will not permit even a Catholic church to announce through the mails that a "game" is open to the public, regardless of whether the word "bingo" is used.

In matters of Congressional economic programs, Catholicism and Protestantism are closer together today than they have been at any time in decades. The moral weight of the churches is on the progressive side in the struggle for social amelioration. It is difficult to realize that less than forty years ago leaders of the (Protestant) Inter-Church World Movement were called "Bolshevists" and "Reds" for favoring the right of collective bargaining and the abolition of the twelve-hour day in the steel mills. It is also difficult to realize that the leaders of the Catholic hierarchy were largely responsible for the defeat of the proposed child labor amendment in 1924, on the ground that it would interfere with parents' control of their children.

Today the influence of all major church groups is in favor of child labor legislation, the right to organize, the right to strike, a living minimum wage for industrial workers and such remedial measures as slum clearance. The record of Catholic Congressmen in such matters is perhaps even more progressive than that of Protestant Congressmen, partly because nearly all the Catholic Congressmen represent heavily industrialized city areas where the labor vote is unusually strong. The pronouncements of Catholic prelates against the proposed right-to-work laws—really anti-union-shop laws—in six states in 1958 played an important part in defeating those laws. In Ohio, the key state in this fight, both the Catholic bishops and the (Protestant) Ohio Council of Churches openly opposed the right-to-work proposals. They are "clearly anti-union," said Charles P. Taft, Vice President of the National Council.

American Jews have naturally played a lesser role in affecting Congressional policy in the area of social welfare because of their relatively small numbers in the population and in Congress. However, it is an important role, far more important than a 3 per cent proportion in the general population would indicate. In general, the Jewish position has been left of center on nearly all matters of economic and racial policy and vigorously favorable to desegregation, civil liberties and the rights of labor.

Only one strictly Jewish welfare issue has reached the floor of Congress in recent years—the exemption of Jewish butchers and meat packers from the requirements of the new national law for the humane slaughter of animals. Traditional Jewish dietary law enjoins Jews from eating any meat not slaughtered according to Jewish formulas, and a substantial proportion of American Jews, though probably not the majority, still adhere to this law. Senator Humphrey, who started his campaign for humane slaughter in 1955, leaned over backwards in dealing with Jewish customs when he came to write a statute, and thought he had met all possible Jewish demands. He specifically exempted all Jewish practices—in fact, *all* religious practices—from the regulations.

He was surprised, therefore, when even this total exemption from regulation did not satisfy the Orthodox rabbis who represent the right wing of American Judaism. The rabbis expressed apprehension that the mere assertion of government authority over the methods used in handling and slaughtering animals might ultimately lead to government policies that would encroach upon their rabbinical control of Jewish butchering. Their fears seemed very far-fetched to the valiant army of American women who had fought against the cruelty of the stockyards for a generation; and they seemed especially extreme when a Jewish Senator like Richard Neuberger of Oregon, who had long been a leader in the fight for more humane treatment of animals, endorsed the new bill.

The humane slaughter bill was finally passed in 1958 in spite of Orthodox objections, with complete exemption for "shechita," the Jewish technique for slaughtering.[46] Although it is a welcome step toward more humane methods in the meat industry, it is not a very happy precedent in the field of church-state law. Should society ever apply health and welfare measures at two levels, public and sectarian?

Sectarian Dollars

I have described the problem of American relations with the Vatican as the most delicate religious problem Congress must face today. It is explosive partly because Congress has the power to face it squarely and reach a decision.

One other religious issue is far more important and equally explosive—the issue of public money for sectarian schools. But Congress lacks the power to adopt an over-all solution to this problem. Traditionally the support of education has always been a matter for state and local governments, and the Supreme Court has outlawed all general and direct appropriations of public money, state or federal, for the central activities of ordinary sectarian schools.

Congress, therefore, can only nibble at the edges of this problem. It can appropriate—or decide *not* to appropriate—federal money only for those benefits that have not yet been outlawed by the Court, such as school lunches, medical care, bus transportation and non-religious textbooks. It can appropriate money—or decide not to—for schools in special situations, such as those involving military reservations.

Congress has no serious problem in respect to school lunch money and medical care. These have been accepted as constitutional, and virtually all religious organizations concede that they are desirable for children as children. A tax dollar may follow a child into a sectarian school if the service rendered is for health and nutrition, not for education proper.

The rub comes when religious groups try to label substantial parts of their school costs as "welfare" and secure federal funds for such costs. Bus transportation, for example, has been brought within the scope of the child benefit theory. (However, no federal money has yet been spent on buses for ordinary sectarian schools.) Another possibility entered the Congressional picture in 1958 and 1959, when the administration proposed a plan under which sectarian as well as non-sectarian colleges could receive 25 per cent of the cost of new equipment and building bonds from federal education grants.[47] This type of aid is still only a proposal, and neither its constitutionality nor its acceptability in Congress has yet been determined.

On the question of using federal money for sectarian school buses, Congress is not divided on either party or denominational lines. Northern city Democrats tend to favor such grants, particularly if they are Catholic, but many Protestants and Jews, both Republican and Democratic, may be found on both sides of the fence. Neither major political party has brought the question of bus transportation within the official policy on "the separation of church and state" which both political parties have endorsed. Both parties are happy that no Congressional vote has been forced on the issue in recent years, since the cleavage on the underlying policy is denominational and deep.

Practically all approved and official Catholic propaganda in the country favors government financial aid to sectarian elementary schools and high schools.[48] Practically all approved and official Protestant and Jewish propaganda is opposed. "There is no doubt," says Dr. John C. Bennett of Union Theological Seminary, "that Protestants in America are almost unanimously opposed to any direct aid to parochial schools." [49] Leo Pfeffer has stated the prevailing Jewish position: "While the Jews do not feel as strongly on the question as the Protestants, their position is much the same and is held with much the same unanimity. They agree that public subsidies to religious schools would violate the constitutional principle of the separation of church and state to which they are strongly committed." [50]

Occasionally an individual Protestant or Jew speaks out for some particular item of aid to sectarian schools, and occasionally an individual Catholic publicly doubts the wisdom of making Catholic requests for government money at this time. These departures from the norm nearly always earn headlines and give the false impression that the faiths are divided in their attitudes. They are divided, of course, but the division is reasonably consistent along denominational lines. It is Protestant and Jew versus Catholic. The Catholic schools ask public money; the Protestant and Jewish schools do not.

When a Jewish professor, Will Herberg, announced his support of the principle of the Catholic financial demands in the Jesuit magazine *America* in 1957, not a Jewish organization in the country supported him.[51] When Reinhold Niebuhr conceded the bus case to Catholic schools in 1947, he received some Protestant commendation only because he did not favor complete support of parochial schools. When Cardinal Cushing declared in 1955 that he did not favor any Catholic requests for parochial building costs at the present time, he added: "I don't speak for the hierarchy of the United States." [52]

Even the so-called liberal intellectual journals of American Catholicism, *America* and *Commonweal,* fall in line with Catholic theory on this issue. They always support the principle of public aid to sectarian education, even when they question the strategy of pressing the demand at any particular moment. The National Council of Churches and all the great Jewish organizations have lined up on the other side of the argument.

This puts a considerable strain on Congressmen who wish to be all things to all faiths. They are very eloquent about the contributions of sectarian schools to American culture, especially during election campaigns when they are invited to speak to Catholic audiences. Usually they avoid all definite commitments on behalf of federal aid to sectarian schools, since they know that such a commitment might lose at least one Protestant or Jewish vote for each Catholic vote they acquire. For more than ten years, since 1949, they have avoided any direct vote on the issue, even in a Congressional committee. Catholic leaders, like John W. McCormack, have aided in the strategy of avoidance, presumably because they know that a Catholic drive even for federal bus money would fail at the present time. They also know that discussion of this controversial issue in Congress might jeopardize the position of any Catholic candidate for the Presidency.

The great Congressional battle on this issue took place from 1939 to 1949, and it created so much bitterness that no one inside Congress wants to raise the question again. Before 1939 the Catholic Church had been one of the chief enemies of all federal grants for education. Then the hierarchy gradually changed direction, and it finally decided to support federal aid in principle on condition that any specific measure should include auxiliary services for Catholic schools. The condition has never been met, and the failure of agreement has created the longest and most acrimonious church-state controversy in the history of Congress.

The climax of the battle came in June and July 1949, with Cardinal Spellman's bitter public attacks on Mrs. Roosevelt and Representative Graham Barden of North Carolina for a "record of anti-Catholicism." The "record of anti-Catholicism" consisted of opposing federal grants for auxiliary services for Catholic schools.

The Barden bill, appropriating federal money to public schools exclusively, became the focus of a great negative pressure campaign on Congress by Catholic individuals and agencies. The mail that flooded Congress created a ten-year continuing panic about controversial religious issues. The tone of many communications on the issue was exceedingly partisan, and most Congressmen reached the conclusion that there was more punishment than glory to be derived from taking sides on such a question. A Catholic Congressman from Michigan, John Lesinski, who was serving as chairman of the House Committee on Labor and Education, refused to call a meeting of his committee for four months after the Spellman-Roosevelt incident, in order to avoid action on the Barden bill, although the bill had been voted out of a subcommittee by a vote of 10 to 3.[53] The bill finally died without coming to a record vote on the floor.

The panic created in Congress was indicated by the fact that not a single Congressman ventured to reprint in the *Congressional Record* during the appropriate session the exchange of correspondence between Mrs. Roosevelt and Cardinal Spellman, although the correspondence was highly pertinent to the proceedings of Congress and almost everybody in America was talking about the exchange.

The amount of federal money involved in this whole ten-year controversy over auxiliary funds for parochial schools was quite trifling. Probably all the parochial school buses in the country involve a total annual expenditure of less than $35,000,000. At one time the Catholic Church was willing to accept a grant of $5,000,000 proposed by Senator Brien McMahon, but this was defeated in the Senate.[54] Later the Church seemed willing to take almost any token settlement in order to establish a principle and a precedent.

The legislative alternatives in this controversy, proposed over a period of several years, boiled down to three major proposals. The first was that some federal money should be given directly to sectarian schools for auxiliary services in all states regardless of whether the states permitted state money to be spent for such purposes. (That would have by-passed state law.) The second was that such federal appropriations should be given to states, and the states should then decide whether any portion should go to sectarian schools. (That would have given very little money to Catholic schools.) The third was that contained in the Barden bill, that all federal appropriations should go exclusively to public schools.

The Catholic Church and, for a time, the American Federation of Labor favored the first proposal. The second compromise proposal, advanced by Senators Taft and Thomas, received mixed support from a number of Congressmen as a better-than-nothing compromise. The third, all-public, proposal was supported by Mrs. Roosevelt, Graham Barden, the National Education Association and, eventually, nearly all the leading Protestant and Jewish organizations. The head-on collision between Catholic and non-Catholic forces resulted in a defeat for the Barden bill and all other federal aid bills.

It was evident at the Congressional hearings, stretching over a period of several years, that the real issue was not the few million dollars involved in bus transportation. The real issue was the separation of church and state. Protestant and Jewish spokesmen were far more frightened by the arguments used by the Catholic witnesses than by the costs involved. They visualized a pattern of fragmented sectarian school systems in the European manner if the Catholic claims were honored. They regarded the bus money proposal as merely an introduction to a larger scheme. "Protestants generally," said the official Protestant spokesman in the controversy, "believe that our American democracy would be impaired by an increasing fragmentation of education, and State support for sectarian schools would promote cultural segregation."

Nothing did so much to frighten non-Catholics as the testimony, repeated at several hearings, of a slender young priest from the National Catholic Welfare Conference—Father William Mc-Manus, later to become superintendent of Chicago's Catholic schools. McManus did nothing more than state the standard Catholic position on education, assigning to the government a minor supporting role and to the Church and parents a major role, but his educational theory sounded to non-Catholics like a message from the Dark Ages. Incidentally, another slender young Catholic listened without public protest to Father McManus and his medieval theories. This was Representative John F. Kennedy of Massachusetts, who promptly introduced a bill of his own to give a percentage of grants to his Church's schools for auxiliary services. But there is no reason to believe that he agreed with all of Father McManus' views.

Father McManus, making the most complete and official statement of Catholic claims ever presented to Congress, spoke in his first appearance of "the dangerous assumption on the part of so many people that education is a government service." Then he said:

In a democracy the functions of the government in education are restricted to:
1. Financing schools which meet standards set in terms of citizenship.
2. Enforcing compulsory education laws.
3. Engaging in direct educational activities in such fields as military science and government service.

Proposing a plan to by-pass state laws that bar the use of federal money by sectarian schools, Father McManus suggested that "the norms of distributive justice" demanded the granting of money to non-public schools. He concluded with this novel interpretation of the separation of church and state in education:

In the field of education separation of church and state bars Government from inquiring into the religious or non-religious character of any school receiving its aid. Government may only ask: "Is this school an institution to which parents may send their children in compliance with the compulsory education laws of the State?" If the answer is in the affirmative, the school is entitled to public support.[55]

Two years later, Father McManus repeated his reasoning and added: "I submit that the restriction of all federal aid to public school pupils alone is unjust, arbitrary and dangerous."

It is not surprising that when Cardinal Spellman joined the fray, attacking Mrs. Roosevelt for "discrimination unworthy of an American mother" and denouncing Representative Barden and his associates as "disciples of discrimination" who vented their "venom upon children," the non-Catholic world did not accept his claim that his Church was asking only for incidental services. The official testimony of Father McManus before two Congressional committees belied the claim.

Since then, the issue of sectarian educational dollars has rarely been mentioned on the floor of Congress. Catholic leaders inside Congress do not want to bring it up again unless there is a reasonable chance of winning an appropriation for parochial school buses. In May 1959, a House subcommittee on the District of Columbia voted unanimously, after protests from Protestant witnesses, against a public subsidy for half-price fares for students in private schools.

Catholic leaders outside of Congress continue to demand public dollars for their schools in no uncertain terms, and the National Council of Churches continues to oppose the demand. In January 1958 the presidents of twenty-eight Jesuit colleges and universities expressed the demand in a public statement calling for an "across-the-board" share in any federal aid.[56] The Jesuits would like to make Catholic approval of any federal aid program conditional upon the receipt of some auxiliary aid for Catholic schools, but it is doubtful if they can carry many Congressmen along with them. In May 1959 they issued a pronouncement directly opposing the chief federal aid measure of the 86th Congress, the Murray-Metcalf bill, on the ground that it was "intended to set a pattern for full, permanent and exclusive Federal support for public schools" and that "the necessity for outright grants of Federal money to overcome the classroom shortage is far from obvious." [57] The pronouncement was probably a bargaining stratagem designed to warn opponents of financial aid to parochial schools that the Catholic Church will oppose all federal aid unless it receives some share in the proceeds.

In May 1959, simultaneously with the pronouncement of the Jesuits, the National Catholic Welfare Conference itself made one of its rare public legislative appeals to Congress. In a letter signed by Archbishop Albert Meyer, episcopal chairman of the Department of Education of the N.C.W.C., and addressed to Senator James E. Murray of Montana, the Church opposed general and permanent federal grants to public schools and declared that "private and public education are partners on the American education scene and their welfare should be advanced simultaneously in any proposals for temporary Federal assistance." Congress, said the N.C.W.C., "cannot in justice be indifferent to parents of . . . non-public school children who bear heavy financial burdens." [58] For the time being the bishops were content to ask for themselves only low-interest government loans for their parochial schools, similar to the legal loans now given by the government for some sectarian college building projects, but their arguments were obviously directed toward the final goal of complete support for their schools.

While the Catholic bishops make these relatively polite and limited demands for federal funds in the public press, the Catholic diocesan newspapers stir up the emotions of their people with far more direct language. Once a year the chief diocesan newspaper in the United States, the *Register* of Denver, which has thirty-four diocesan editions, blasts all those who would obstruct the demands of the Church for public funds for its schools. Its 1959 blast, written by Catholicism's most influential American editor, Monsignor Matthew Smith, said:

The argument that the State should not give any aid to parish schools because the State should not support religion, under the American system, is mere balderdash. It is senseless jargon, nonsense, trash. . . . Catholics have never asked that the State support instruction in Christian doctrine by tax funds. What they ask is that, as in England, a certain amount of tax money be allocated to their schools for the general educative work these institutions do.

The foes of parish education want to kill the religious school system—a stand that is most certainly anti-constitutional.[59]

Two facts should be noted in connection with this editorial. No church or political group in the United States is undertaking to "kill the religious school system," which is fully protected under Supreme Court rulings. Also, England's Catholic schools now receive over 95 per cent of their total costs from the public treasury.

When the first general bill for federal aid to schools since 1892, the National Defense Education Act, was passed by Congress in 1958, no provision was included in its $887,000,000 appropriation for bus funds for sectarian schools. Catholic Congressmen did not demand sectarian dollars for auxiliary services as a condition of their support. In fact, most Catholic Congressmen now support federal aid unconditionally. The new scholarship act did include some minor testing and counseling service for sectarian schools at public expense, but the ghosts of the 1949 battle were not revived. Private non-sectarian colleges, under the 1958 act, may receive direct grants for equipment; sectarian colleges must be satisfied with loans and scholarship help. Sectarian colleges receive some indirect help in government loans, but not direct grants unless some direct service is rendered to the government.

The future drive for public dollars for sectarian schools is likely to take an entirely new tack with proposals for state and federal grants to parents for tuition in private schools. The scheme was presented to Congress quietly in 1957 at the request of a Massachusetts Catholic Congressman who inserted in the *Congressional Record* Cardinal McIntyre's 1956 address at the University of Dallas outlining the arguments for a new financial technique.[60] Under the plan, "aid would go to all children directly as it did to our returned heroes" under the G.I. educational bills. "The McCollum decision," said the Cardinal, "would be nullified as irrelevant."

Thus far no Congressman has dared to raise his voice on the floor for the Catholic hierarchy's new proposal for by-passing the Constitution. Most Congressmen, in fact, devoutly pray that the Supreme Court will save them from the embarrassment of a record vote on such a demand.

Meanwhile, a great many public dollars are being used in sectarian welfare work without bitter Congressional debate. Although some of the expenditures are of doubtful constitutionality, Congress is disposed to be uncritically generous and allow the Supreme Court to build the breakwaters after the expenditures have been voted. Millions of dollars' worth of government surpluses are being distributed abroad by church agencies—Catholic, Protestant and Jewish. No substantial opposition has developed in Congress to this very extensive church-state cooperation, although the law undoubtedly aids churches in their work of proselyting.

The largest direct grants of public dollars to sectarian institutions by Congress in recent years have gone to hospitals through the Hill-Burton Act.[61] About 70 per cent of the sectarian portion of these grants—$168,000,000 out of $237,000,000—has gone to Roman Catholic institutions. Protestant institutions have been outstripped in welfare competition for a number of reasons. Protestantism is fragmented; it does not pursue a policy of denominational separatism in welfare work; and it has no reserve supply of nursing nuns to serve at nominal wages. Also, Protestantism is divided over the basic principle involved in accepting government grants for sectarian hospitals. Methodists accept hospital grants with considerable alacrity. Baptists, particularly Southern Baptists, believe it is inconsistent to advocate the separation of church and state and simultaneously to accept outright government grants for welfare work. At the request of the Southern Baptist Convention, the Hill-Burton Act was revised in 1958 to permit a church to accept a loan instead of a grant for a sectarian hospital. A few— very few—Baptist hospitals under private boards continue to accept grants.

No such scruple of conscience deters the Catholic hospitals. They are booming with the help of federal aid. Although they are much more denominational in their trappings, their personnel and their medical codes than are Protestant and Jewish hospitals, their right to receive public grants has not been successfully challenged in the courts, and Congress is not disposed to alter its present policy of generous aid.

Chapter V

God, Man and the Presidency

I come now to the White House, and there is more awe than reverence in me as I approach the graceful, towering pillars of the north portico. Americans do not apply to their Chief Executive that special combination of reticence and adulation which many European newspapers reserve for their monarchs. The ground on which the President walks—or plays golf—is not holy ground. If we exalt our Presidents, we also bully and chastise them. We surround them with almost as much pitiless criticism as adulation. Few Presidents ever emerge from the White House with as good a reputation as they had when they entered it.

In this white mansion, which is also a great mechanized publicity factory, lives one of the world's most powerful individuals. He has more than 500 direct White House employees. He is the executive head of history's wealthiest society, the chief employer among the nation's employers, the chief promoter of American glory. He appoints the entire cabinet, the entire diplomatic corps and the entire federal judiciary. Directly or by delegation of authority, he also appoints thousands of others who control the daily operations of the government machine. He has limited veto power over every act of Congress. He initiates many of the nation's most important laws. He is the titular head of his political party. He is commander in chief of the armed forces, and although he cannot declare war by himself, he can easily maneuver the nation into a position where Congress has no other honorable alternative.

The growth of this position in our society can be measured

partly by the growth in the President's appointive power between the administrations of Washington and Truman. Sidney Hyman has summarized the contrast in his book, *The American President.* Washington supervised 9 agencies. Truman was responsible for 9 major departments, 104 bureaus, 12 sections, 108 services, 51 branches, 460 offices, 631 divisions, 19 administrations, 6 agencies, 16 areas, 40 boards, 6 commands, 20 commissions, 19 corporations, 5 groups, 10 headquarters, 3 authorities and 263 other miscellaneous bits of government machinery. These combined agencies employed 1 out of every 62 civilians in the nation, in contrast with 1 out of every 2,000 in Washington's day. Truman made 25,000 appointments in a single year.

In 1958 the *Saturday Evening Post,* making a general editorial comment on the election of that year and a particular comment on the election of Nelson Rockefeller as Governor of New York, reminded its readers that they were not called upon in 1960 to send Mr. America to the White House. This would be no beauty contest, the editors argued, but a struggle over political principles. Personality should be subordinate.

The warning was reasonable but quite futile. In a television age, every aspect of a President's personality is considered relevant to his alleged fitness. Millions of American voters are persuaded to vote one way or another by a Presidential candidate's smile, his family relationships, his speaking voice—*and* his religion.

Of course, Article VI of the Constitution declares that "no religious test shall ever be required as a qualification to any office or public trust under the United States." In interpreting this article, the emphasis should be placed upon the word "required." The provision makes any statutory barrier on the basis of religion unconstitutional; it does not cover the mind or the heart of the average voter. Each American voter at the polls retains his right under our system of secret ballot to use his own standards in judging any candidate. When the voting curtain is closed, he may vote for or against a necktie, a bald head or a twinkle in the eye, and no constitution or law can protect a candidate against such trivialities of judgment. It is part of the very nature of our democracy that political appraisal should be personal, and if many voters carry the mentality of a Superman comic strip into the voting booth in making their personal appraisal, we can only accept the result as inevitable.

The President of the United States has been transformed by the national processes of public information into a kind of Mr. Super America; and his religion, diet, recreational habits and family skeletons are no more private than those of a Hollywood star. Under the circumstances, it is idle to talk about a President's religion as being irrelevant. Everything about Mr. Super America is relevant.

The constitutional rule is that every native-born citizen of thirty-five is eligible to be President regardless of race, religion or sex. Every honest critic knows that this rule represents a very small portion of the reality. There are a score of unwritten taboos against certain classes, individuals and racial minorities.[1] While we say that a woman, a Negro, a Jew, a Catholic, a Jehovah's Witness, a Mormon or an avowed atheist can be President of the United States, we know in practice that only two of these—the Jew and the Catholic—stand any chance at the polls. And even their claims to equal rights are very much in doubt.

It is inconceivable that, in the present state of American opinion, a Jehovah's Witness, an atheist, a Mormon, a Negro or a woman could attain to the nation's highest office. It is also inconceivable that a President of the A.F.L.-C.I.O., a president of the National Association of Manufacturers or a Southern Baptist member of a White Citizens Council could be elected president. And it is very doubtful that any citizen of a small and unimportant one-party state could ever reach the White House directly.

To be elected to the Presidency, a candidate must have not only strategic location and non-controversial economic alignments but also some conformity in matters of religious faith. He must not be a religious extremist. Since this is a predominantly Protestant country, he must not be too far from the rather tolerant and mild Protestant norm. His religious manners must not be offensive, and he must not be transparently insincere. He must not be an atheist; and if he is an agnostic, he must be careful to state his doubts inoffensively. His church membership is usually accepted not as a proof of superior dedication to religious goals but as evidence of moral normality. He must be a "regular guy," a responsible citizen. Membership in some church or synagogue is one indication that he is acceptable.

After he reaches the White House, the candidate's code of religious conduct must be just as carefully managed as it was before and during the campaign. A President must be strictly neutral among Protestants, Catholics and Jews. That is one of the unwritten rules of our pluralistic society, and all Presidents in recent years have followed it quite strictly. Atheists and non-believers are not included in the White House book of religious etiquette, but they are usually treated with some courtesy if they are not too aggressive.

One of the White House rules is that secretaries, assistants and administrators should be chosen from among all three leading religious groupings so that no one grouping can feel neglected. Another unwritten rule is that, so far as possible, there must be strict equality in dealing with Protestant, Catholic and Jewish organizations whenever denominational public appearances are called for. This is managed by appropriate liaison men on the White House staff.

In this area, no religious sect can have any serious complaint about discrimination during the terms of Roosevelt, Truman and Eisenhower. During my years of work in Washington on church-state matters, I have never known of a deliberate act of sectarian favoritism by the White House. Although Eisenhower's chief liaison man with religious agencies has been a Congregational minister, his Protestantism seems not to have influenced his policies.

Primarily a White House contact man with community agencies, he has treated all groups alike whether they are sectarian or not.

In one great mutual security conference in 1958, when the cooperation of religious organizations in foreign aid was a major topic of discussion, the White House inadvertently put only one religious speaker on the program, Bishop Fulton J. Sheen. One quiet telephone call to the White House, pointing out that Protestants would feel inadequately represented by the chief proselyting agent of the Catholic Church in the United States, brought a quick "readjustment" of the program. A Protestant, a Jew and Bishop Sheen all spoke. Bishop Sheen, perhaps spurred on by the unexpected competition, made a speech which was obviously considered by the audience the best of the three.

This impartiality in the White House does not mean that all the executive departments and services of the government abstain from favoritism in dealing with the various sects, nor does it mean that these departments always administer the law without favoritism to religious taxpayers as against non-religious taxpayers. Sectarian favoritism sometimes appears in the armed forces; the three armed forces academies, for example, still require their cadets to attend a church or synagogue. The Internal Revenue Service has gone very softly in applying loosely worded laws on the taxation of churches to Baptists, Catholics and Mormons, but particularly to churches which have religious orders. The responsibility is partly that of Congress, but it will probably continue until the President himself inaugurates a new tax policy. At the present time, Catholic organizations and individuals are the chief beneficiaries of loosely administered laws.

Technically this tax favoritism is not granted officially to the Catholic Church but to churches which have sacerdotal (priestly) religious orders. Since sacerdotal religious orders are almost exclusively Catholic, the government's policy of allowing even subordinate commercial corporations under the control of such orders to engage in competition for profit and still evade the corporate profits tax amounts to preferential treatment of a single denomination.[2]

A Jesuit chaplain in the armed services is not obliged to pay an income tax on his salary because of a transparently partisan interpretation of an old tax decision; a Presbyterian chaplain, even with a wife and five children, must pay income taxes in the same way as any other citizen. The exemption applies even to Catholic nuns who are *public* school teachers. Their salaries, turned over to their religious orders, are treated as exempt contributions to their orders, although it is clearly unconstitutional for any government unit to make such contributions. Several Protestant organizations have suggested amendments to the Internal Revenue Code establishing a denominationally impartial and functional test for tax-exempt revenues of churches. The House Ways and Means Committee now has the whole problem under advisement.

The Protestant Monopoly

For 171 years there has been a Protestant or near-Protestant monopoly in the Presidency. No Catholic or Jew has ever been President or Vice President; with one exception, no Catholic or Jew has ever been the candidate of a major political party for these posts.[3] Several Presidents have been non-Protestant in the sense that they have refused to join churches, but they can fairly be classified as belonging in the Protestant orbit. They have not been Catholic or Jewish, and most of them have attended Protestant churches while in office.

Washington, Madison and Monroe were Episcopalians; the Adamses were Unitarians, and so was Jefferson informally. Abraham Lincoln and Rutherford B. Hayes never joined a church. Lincoln was so unorthodox that most of the Protestant ministers of Springfield, Illinois, opposed him as too unorthodox to be President.[4] (Jefferson also was severely attacked as an "infidel" when he ran for President. He was very cautious about stating his religious views until his political career was ended.) Grant attended a Methodist church without joining. Altogether we have had in the White House nine Episcopalians, six Presbyterians, four Unitarians, four Methodists, and two Baptists, with scattered representatives of other Protestant denominations.[5]

The significance of this Protestant White House history can easily be exaggerated. It is not in itself clear proof of anti-Catholic or anti-Semitic prejudice. When a great majority of the people of a country belong to one religious grouping, it is almost inevitable that their chief executive should be drawn from that grouping. Until the Civil War, about 90 per cent of the American people were either Protestants or near-Protestants in their personal allegiance or family connections. Catholics comprised less than 1 per cent of the population when the nation was formed, and their proportion did not rise above 10 per cent until the great secondary waves of Irish and Italian immigration had transformed the eastern cities.[6] There were only about 200,000 Jews in the United States at the end of the Civil War, and Jews probably have never comprised more than one-thirtieth of the American population. Today almost four out of five Americans are non-Catholic and non-Jewish.

It is not surprising that a President should come from such a substantial religious group in the population as the Protestant bloc, even when that bloc is far from being cohesive. Indeed, it would be surprising if he did not. The tendency toward group identification is present in all societies, and all politicians take account of it. Professor Franklin Giddings used to call it rather elegantly "consciousness of kind." The political bosses and the politically minded prelates call it "voting for our own people."

Many nations in the world even today require their monarchs to profess the religion of the traditional majority. The kings of Norway and Denmark must be Evangelical Lutherans; the king of Greece must be Greek Orthodox; the monarch of Britain must be "in communion with the Church of England." The Catholic diocesan press of the United States, which constantly protests the Protestant Presidential monopoly, is delighted to condone the laws of Catholic countries like Spain, Argentina and Paraguay which exclude all Protestants and Jews from the highest state offices.

The American Protestant monopoly has not spread downward to include the cabinet and the working leadership of the great political parties. In these posts the members of religious minority groups have been quite well represented. Up to 1959, fifteen Catholics had served in the cabinet, and the direction of political campaigns had become almost a Catholic specialty. In the Democratic National Committee, every chairman from James A. Farley to Paul M. Butler has been a Catholic. Only two Jewish leaders have served in the cabinet, but many others have held very powerful administrative posts just below the cabinet level.

This is not to say that America is free from religious prejudice, but prejudice rarely comes in a single package. It is mixed with geography and genuine tolerance and ethnic jealousy and the self-love of like-minded majorities. Every student of American history knows that there has been a great deal of anti-Catholic prejudice in our national background and that prejudice has had some effect upon the nomination and election of candidates of all faiths. Anti-Semitism has been less evident, partly because there are so few Jews in the nation. The Catholic-Protestant relationship has always caused the most anguish and ill feeling because of the historic antagonism between the two branches of Christendom and the fact that Catholic power has enormously increased in this originally Protestant country.

Usually it is safe to assume that when anybody in America talks about "the religious issue" in a Presidential campaign he means the Catholic-Protestant issue. Specifically he means: Can a Catholic be nominated and elected President or Vice President of the United States; and if so, under what circumstances? It would be idle to pretend that this is not *the* religious issue in American politics.

Perhaps another religious issue will arise in America some day when the question is asked: Can a Jew be nominated and elected President or Vice President of the United States; and if so, under what circumstances? Thus far, no Jewish candidate has come within striking distance of a Presidential nomination. Some anti-Semitism still exists in the United States and it might become an overt factor if a Jewish candidate appeared. Occasionally it has been a factor in Presidential campaigns in the past. In the 1868 campaign, there was a slight flurry because Grant, while serving as a general in Tennessee, issued an order giving all Jews in the region twenty-four hours to leave the area. A campaign pamphlet appeared under the title "General Grant and the Jews," implying that the general was anti-Semitic.[7] Lincoln reversed the Tennessee order when he heard about it; and Grant, very apologetic, explained that he had merely tried to get certain peddlers out of the disturbed area and that most of the peddlers happened to be Jews. When Grant became President, his policies were in no way anti-Semitic.

Bias in Campaigns

Mormonism and Quaker pacifism could easily become "religious issues" if a Mormon or a Quaker pacifist ever came forward as a candidate. Thus far, no Mormon candidate has appeared, and all Quaker candidates on major national tickets have been decidedly non-pacifist. "Atheism" could easily become a decisive factor if any candidate appeared who was as unorthodox as Lincoln or Jefferson.

Anti-Catholicism has been a factor in many Presidential campaigns, but it has almost never been a pure and undiluted factor.

The great waves of Irish-Catholic immigration before and after the Civil War and the rise of the new Irish political bosses created almost automatically a Catholic-versus-Protestant situation in which the Catholics were usually Democrats and their non-Catholic opponents were Republicans. The Republican Party was not always averse to employing both anti-Catholicism and native economic jealousy to fight the Democratic enemy, and the Democratic Party was sometimes ready to reply in kind.

Anti-Catholicism in the Republican Party proved to be a boomerang in the 1856 campaign: the report was spread that the Republican candidate, John C. Frémont, was a Catholic, and many Know-Nothing voters turned against him. Actually he was an Episcopalian who had been married by a Dutch priest in a runaway marriage, after several Protestant clergymen had refused to perform the ceremony. In the Hayes-Tilden campaign of 1876, the Republican Party went so far that it issued a documentary denunciation of "the Romish Church" and charged it with the "endeavor to overthrow the Republican Party, and with it the free school system which it sustains." [8]

It is possible that James G. Blaine lost the Presidency to Grover Cleveland in 1884 because of last-minute Catholic reprisals. He was defeated by the electoral vote of New York State alone, and a transfer of 600 votes within that state would have sent him to the White House. He seemed to be fairly sure of election until the closing weeks of the campaign, largely because Cleveland had alienated Tammany and its Catholic following in his home state. Cleveland, said the well-organized whispering campaign, was a "Presbyterian bigot," and anyway he had an illegitimate child. True, his mother had some Irish blood, but Blaine's mother was a Catholic!

Then, one morning at the Fifth Avenue Hotel, only a few days before the election, when the weary Blaine appeared briefly before a meeting of Republican Protestant clergymen, one of them made an introductory address in which he scored the Democratic Party

as the party of "Rum, Romanism and Rebellion." The phrase ran
through the Tammany wards like an electric shock. It was pounced
upon by the Democratic press and distributed on handbills in front
of all New York Catholic churches. The "clerical Presbyterian
sandwich," as it was called, turned out to be full of political arsenic.
Enough wavering Catholic voters came back to the fold to send
Cleveland to the White House for his first term.[9]

Taft was caught in a similar but milder exchange of religious
animosities in his successful campaign of 1908, an exchange in
which both Unitarianism and Catholicism played a part. Orthodox
Protestant groups questioned his fitness not only because of his
theological liberalism but also because, it was charged, he had been
too generous to the Vatican while serving as Civil Governor of the
Philippines. It was his misfortune that while acting for President
Theodore Roosevelt and Congress he had helped to give the Pope
a payment of $7,200,000 for extensive tracts of land which had
formerly belonged to those Spanish friars evicted during the Span-
ish-American War. Since the Spanish friars had acquired 400,000
acres of the best agricultural land in the Philippines, and their
reputation as landlords was not of the best, they had earned the
hatred of millions of the Philippine people. They had also earned
the hostility of American Protestants. After they were ousted, Taft
had the unpleasant task of arranging for their compensation. Instead of settling the bill in the Philippines, he went to Rome and
took with him as assistant the Catholic Bishop of South Dakota.
That was bad enough, but when the settlement was made, Taft
accepted from Leo XIII a golden goose quill. His critics had the
opportunity to say that he had been the goose and that the Pope
had gotten the gold.

Taft might well have been defeated if he had not had behind
him the overwhelming prestige of Theodore Roosevelt, who at that
time was riding the crest of a wave of national popularity. Even so,
Taft's biographer, Henry Pringle, expressed the opinion that Bryan
would at last have gone to the White House in 1908 if the Demo-

crats had added to their religious arsenal an authenticated statement of Taft's very liberal theological views. They did not locate the priceless ammunition until after the election. "I am a Unitarian," said Taft in writing a letter to his brother. "I believe in God. I do not believe in the Divinity of Christ, and there are many other of the postulates of the orthodox creed to which I cannot subscribe." [10] That statement in 1908 would have profoundly shocked the bucolic electorate, and even today a parallel statement might cost a candidate the Presidency.

Faint echoes of orthodox anxiety about Unitarianism and Catholic anxiety about a divorced President appeared again in the two campaigns of 1952 and 1956 when Adlai Stevenson was nominated by the Democrats. But most observers believed that neither of these factors cost him the electoral vote of a single state. Stevenson was doubly protected because he had never specifically repudiated in public the major items of the Christian creed. When he calmly joined the Presbyterian Church in 1955 and simultaneously retained his Unitarian membership, the unusual combination seemed to delight as well as to satisfy the public. Several Unitarian and Presbyterian ministers expressed complete satisfaction. No one asked him what part of the Apostles' Creed he believed when he recited it in the Presbyterian Church, or what interpretation he put upon the divinity of Christ when he continued to be a Unitarian.

The elder Roosevelt was caught in a Catholic-versus-Protestant dilemma after he had retired from the White House. Privately he was not friendly to Catholicism, but he was such a superb politician that he never allowed himself to be maneuvered publicly into any anti-Catholic posture. His public pronouncements on religion were jewels of tri-partisan tolerance.

Just before he retired from the White House in 1909, he confided to his aide, Archie Butt, that "the Catholic Church is in no way suited to this country and can never have any great permanent growth except through immigration, for its thought is Latin and entirely at variance with the dominant thought of our country and institutions." [11] But he coupled this personal view with a code that was completely without prejudice or discrimination. "Any discrimination for or against a man because of his creed or nativity strikes me as infamy," he declared.

He had the temerity to apply this gospel against the Pope when Pius X had what Roosevelt himself described as "an elegant row" over a canceled invitation to visit the Vatican. On his way back from Africa through Rome in 1910, Roosevelt had expected to visit the Pope, and preliminary plans had been made for the visit. But Vice President Charles W. Fairbanks, a Methodist, had been in Rome ahead of his chief and had annoyed the good Pius X, one of history's most reactionary theologians, by visiting the Rome headquarters of the Methodist Church. After that, Pius refused to see him, since the Pope could not endure even an inference that other religions should be treated on a basis of equality with Catholicism in the Imperial City.

Pius let Roosevelt know that, in keeping with the precedent he had established in the Fairbanks incident, T.R. would be welcome at the Vatican only if his religious visitation was exclusive. Roosevelt calmly declined such a condition, describing it to his friend Henry Cabot Lodge as "a proposition that a Tammany Boodle Alderman would have been ashamed to make." The American people cheered him for his decision. This was a matter of national pride, they felt. It was, to use Roosevelt's own words, an assertion of "my freedom of conduct." [12]

American belief in freedom of Presidential conduct is even stronger today than it was fifty years ago. No Pope in these days would be tactless enough to challenge the right of the President or Vice President of the United States to assert his interest in Protestantism, even in Rome. In the United States, however, politicians never know how far they can go in the direction of freedom of conduct in selecting a Presidential or Vice Presidential candidate whose personal past may have been "offensive" to the Catholic hierarchy. An ex-Catholic is commonly considered less "available" than a Catholic. Technically, under Catholic rules, any baptized Catholic who deliberately leaves his Church as an adult and joins a Protestant church is an apostate, automatically excommunicated and consciously shunned as a moral leper.[13] Also, under Catholic rules, the Catholic who breaks the narrow mixed marriage rules of his Church is a sinner and in danger of public condemnation. If he marries a Protestant or a Jew, he is supposed to marry inside his Church if his marriage is to be considered valid, and all his children must be reared as Catholics. In selecting Presidential candidates, these Catholic taboos always cause some anxiety in the smoke-filled party caucus rooms.

The "apostate" taboo undoubtedly worked against James F. Byrnes of South Carolina in the Democratic conventions of 1940 and 1944. He had been baptized a Catholic but had transferred his allegiance to the Episcopal Church after his marriage. When this "irregular" religious history was revealed, Byrnes was stricken from the eligible list for Vice President on the Democratic ticket at the behest of boss Ed Flynn of New York, a Catholic.[14]

Oddly enough, the United States had already had one technically apostate Catholic Vice President without being generally aware of it. Charles Curtis of Kansas, who served under Hoover, was baptized a Catholic in his infancy. His Catholic mother had died soon afterwards, and he had been reared a Methodist by a Methodist grandmother. He was not held responsible for this checkered past, since his apostasy had not been of his own choosing.[15]

The political taboos against "bad" Catholics are now fading away so rapidly that any repetition of the Byrnes incident seems quite unthinkable. Frank Lausche of Ohio has been elected Governor of Ohio five times and Senator once, although he is a Catholic who was married outside his Church and has failed to rectify that "sin." Governor Meyner of New Jersey left the Catholic Church as a young man and became a Protestant, but the shift in religious loyalties has not seemed to affect his vote-getting power, even in a state which is 42 per cent Catholic. Probably the Catholic Church would not be able to carry many voters along with it if its hierarchy publicly attempted to impose a ban on such a man as Meyner for making a free choice in faith during his adult life.

Protestants, of course, have no official political problems in a candidate's apostasy or mixed marriage. Protestant feelings may be involved, but there are no Protestant taboos. All Protestant churches recognize the marriages of all citizens as valid whether performed by a clergyman of any faith or by a public official, and no penalties are prescribed for change of church allegiance. This does not mean that a candidate's departure from Protestant norms would go unnoticed. It simply means that the penalty, if any, would be personal and informal.

The relatively relaxed and informal character of Protestant practices in marriage was well illustrated by the story of Herbert Hoover's marriage. It created a two-day sensation in the newspapers during the pre-convention campaign of 1928 and was then forgotten. Hoover's young schoolteacher wife, an Episcopalian, had elected to be married by a Catholic priest who had taught religion after school hours to some of the pupils in her California private school. Quaker Hoover genially fell in with the suggestion that the priest should marry them. A special dispensation had to be secured from the Catholic bishop, since bride and groom were unwilling to abandon their Protestantism. They were finally married by the priest, not as a priest but as a civil magistrate.[16] American Protestants were amused by the story, not annoyed. Anyway, said the public, they were married. If Hoover lost a few fundamentalist votes because of the circumstances of his marriage, he was probably compensated by a few Catholic votes.

The Smith Campaign

It was unfortunate that, in the first great attempt to break through the Protestant monopoly in the White House, a Catholic Democratic candidate was chosen who labored under two great handicaps that had nothing to do with his religion. In 1928 millions of non-Catholics who would otherwise have welcomed the opportunity to vote for a Catholic refused to support Al Smith. He was able and conscientious, they admitted, but he was a wet at a time when a considerable proportion of the people still believed in the "noble experiment," and he had come up to state power through Tammany Hall. Moreover, he was a politician from a great city who pronounced radio "raddio" and talked with a New York accent. A Protestant wet with such a background might have gone down to defeat by almost as wide a margin.

Some observers, with the usual unrebuttable hindsight, believe that Senator Thomas J. Walsh of Montana, a Catholic defender of prohibition who had no Tammany taint, might have won the 1928 battle for the Presidency in spite of his Catholicism. Probably they are wrong, but there is no way to disprove the speculation. Smith had already accumulated so much popular favor before the 1928 Democratic convention at Houston that his rejection would have split the Democratic Party wide open.

If religion played an important part in the defeat of Al Smith —and no one can deny this—it was partly because he inherited some of the ancient bitterness that had been created in the 1920s by the revival of the Ku Klux Klan. That hooded order, originally an anti-Negro terror organization of the Reconstruction period, was re-created in 1915 and had taken on Catholicism as one of its auxiliary villains. Its anti-Catholic bias was partly sustained by a small and fanatical Missouri newspaper, *The Menace,* which began publication in 1911 and climbed to an alleged circulation of 250,-

000. The Klan itself reached a peak of power and membership about 1925, claiming nearly nine million followers before it rapidly declined. It was strong not only in the South but also in many parts of the Middle West, particularly in Indiana, and in such Pacific states as Oregon.[17]

I have always felt that the Klan's role in the politics of the 1920s was somewhat exaggerated in the Eastern press because its hooded figures and fearsome ceremonials made good pictorial copy. A burning cross and a sheeted Kleagle are easy to write about, and such illustrated stories tend to boost newspaper circulation. (I played a modest role in fighting the Klan in many Southern communities in those days, and at the time of the election I was serving on the editorial staff of a New York magazine that supported Smith, so I have some basis for my opinion.)

The Klan's peak moment of political power in this century came not with Smith's second defeat in 1928 but with his first defeat in 1924 at the Madison Square Garden convention of the Democratic Party. There, after 103 noisy ballots, the Democrats finally nominated John W. Davis for President against Coolidge. The fight for the nomination in that convention between William Gibbs McAdoo and Al Smith was essentially a Protestant-Catholic fight, and McAdoo condoned if he did not sanction some of the Klan propaganda. The Hooded Order was powerful enough to block Smith without being able to capture the convention for McAdoo, its own choice. John W. Davis, a pathetic compromise, was chosen after the convention had rejected by a three-vote margin a resolution specifically denouncing the Klan.

By the time Al Smith was nominated in 1928, the religious climate of America had improved. Although there was still enough fanatical literature in circulation to give the Klan an appearance of strength, it had lost much of its power. On the floor of the Senate, in 1927 and 1928, Senator Tom Heflin of the gaudy vests ranted against the Knights of Columbus and "the bold and brazen agents of Rome's political machine." But he exercised little influence and it is doubtful that he controlled the deciding votes on any major issue. He was severely criticized by three leading papers of his own state—the Montgomery *Advertiser,* the *Public Register* and the *Birmingham Age-Herald.*

The new challenge to Smith and his Catholicism in the 1928 campaign came not from Heflin and his kind but from Northern intellectuals. On the lower level, the old anti-Catholic bigotry continued in such journals as the *New Menace* and the *Fellowship Forum,* a Klan organ published in Washington. On the upper level the intellectuals began to ask whether there was not a real conflict between the principles of the Catholic Church and the Constitution.

The Unitarians led off in January 1927 through Dr. Albert C. Dieffenbach, editor of their national journal, *The Christian Register.* He was an extreme liberal in matters of dogma, and no one could charge him with Klan sympathy. Dieffenbach declared in an editorial that "it is futile for any person under heaven to attempt to prevent the immediate and protracted discussion of the most difficult and delicate problem that has ever confronted the American people . . . the subject is religion, and the two opposite ways of taking your religion, especially the two opposite ways of taking your religion into the state. . . . Let superficial and fatuous talk about religion not have anything to do with politics be gone from this time forth. . . ." Then he quoted a paragraph from a letter in the *New York Times* by a Michigan clergyman which seemed to express the major anxieties of non-Catholics as well as they could be expressed:

In short, we may as well face the issue. Before the class of intelligent and fair-minded Protestants I have in mind can be mentally at peace on these issues, they will want to know whether an American Catholic Presidential candidate endorses the claim of the Papacy to temporal power, its toleration, not its acceptance, of American principles, its attitude toward American public schools, and its rejection of the claims of millions of American Christians to the right of self-government in religion, as well as in politics.

The last clause seemed to be a challenge to an internal policy of the Catholic Church, and some Protestants doubted the wisdom of it. But it brought a fundamental question out into the open. Protestants feared Catholic policy partly because it was made by an undemocratic process and partly because some papal directives applied to areas which they considered political. Dieffenbach's challenge got a mixed reception in the religious press, but he announced that a majority of Protestant clergymen he had polled supported his criticisms.

Smith did not answer Dieffenbach directly, but four months later, when the *Atlantic Monthly* published an open letter addressed to him by the scholarly Episcopalian lawyer Charles C. Marshall, Smith and his advisers decided that the time had come for a reply.[18] Fortunately for him, the Marshall letter was rather general, and Marshall was given no opportunity for a rebuttal. Marshall argued that the two-powers theory of Catholicism on church and state was in conflict with the American theory and that Catholic principles on education and marriage were not in accord with American principles:

The Roman Catholic Church, of course, makes no claim, and never has made any claim, to jurisdiction over matters that *in her opinion* are solely secular and civil. She makes the claim only when the matter in question is not, *in her opinion,* solely secular or civil. . . . The education of youth, the institution of marriage, the international relations of the State, and its domestic peace . . . are, in certain exigencies, wrested from the jurisdiction of the State. . . . Do you, sir, regard such claims as tolerable in a republic that calls itself free?

Marshall was particularly caustic about Catholic marriage doctrine, charging that, under Catholic theory, "jurisdiction touching marriage is wrested from the State and appropriated to the

Roman Catholic Church, its exercise reposing ultimately in the Pope. . . . The Church . . . claims, at its discretion, the right to annul and destroy the bond of the civil contract."

The whole country waited for Smith's reply; and when it came, the editor of the *Atlantic Monthly* loaded the scales for Smith quite shamelessly by asking in an introductory note: "Is the principle of religious tolerance, universal and complete, which every schoolboy has repeated for 150 years, mere platitudinous vaporing? . . . Is the United States of America based on a delusion?" But even with these handicaps, it is not certain that Marshall came off second best in the total exchange. Smith's answer won the immediate victory partly because American editors made no attempt to evaluate Marshall's substantive case. They accepted Smith's reply as a personal reply, and as such it was successful and sincere.

"Taking your letter as a whole," Smith wrote, "and reducing it to commonplace English, you imply that there is a conflict between religious loyalty to the Catholic faith and patriotic loyalty to the United States. Everything that has actually happened to me during my long career leads me to know that no such thing as that is true. . . . I have never known any conflict between my official duties and my religious belief."

Although he did not discuss the general marriage policy of his Church, Smith ended with an eloquent two paragraphs, stating his credo on Americanism and Catholicism, which covered the whole field:

I summarize my creed as an American Catholic. I believe in the worship of God according to the faith and practice of the Roman Catholic Church. I recognize no power in the institutions of my Church to interfere with the operations of the Constitution of the United States or the enforcement of the law of the land. I believe in absolute freedom of conscience for all men and in equality of all churches, all sects, and all beliefs before the law as a matter of right and not as a matter of favor. I believe in the absolute separation of Church and State and in the strict enforcement of the provisions of the

Constitution that Congress shall make no law respecting any establishment of religion or prohibiting the free exercise thereof. I believe that no tribunal of any church has any power to make any decree of any force in the law of the land, other than to establish the status of its own communicants within its own church. I believe in the support of the public school as one of the corner stones of American liberty. I believe in the right of every parent to choose whether his child shall be educated in the public school or in a religious school supported by those of his own faith. I believe in the principle of noninterference by this country in the internal affairs of other nations and that we should stand steadfastly against any such interference by whomsoever it may be urged. And I believe in the common brotherhood of man under the common fatherhood of God.

In this spirit I join with fellow Americans of all creeds in a fervent prayer that never again in this land will any public servant be challenged because of the faith in which he has tried to walk humbly with his God.[19]

Most of the public probably accepted the picture of Smith which emerged from the Smith-Marshall exchange as quite genuine, even if they suspected that he had not written the actual words himself. He was a downright and honest American Catholic who was perfectly loyal to American institutions. He was not an expert in regard to his own religion or Vatican policies. A story, probably apocryphal, gained wide credence that when Smith was asked how he could reconcile some papal encyclicals with the American policy on the separation of church and state, he replied: "What in hell is an en-kick-lical?" In his autobiography, Smith gave full credit for assistance in the preparation of his statement to Father Francis J. Duffy, famous war chaplain, and to Judge Joseph M. Proskauer.

Strangely, neither side in the Smith-Marshall exchange came down to earth enough to discuss specifically the question whether Catholic officials should favor public appropriations for parochial schools. The issue was not then a live issue in Washington or in many states, and most Americans were unaware that the demand for such public support was an integral part of world Vatican policy. Smith's general declaration for public schools and his pro-public-school record were accepted as counter-balancing one minor item in his record, an incident in the New York State Constitutional Convention of 1915. In that Convention Smith had introduced a resolution calling upon the state to take out of its constitution the phrases that prohibited appropriations for denominational schools. When this incident was mentioned in the pre-campaign months, Smith's biographers explained that the resolution was only a legislative maneuver used for trading purposes to prevent something that would have been worse from his Church's point of view.[20] The maneuver was successful, and Smith was never called upon to press his resolution or to explain it to a curious public in 1928.

The voters who had made up their minds in advance not to accept any explanation from Smith which "white-washed" his Church soon had plenty of additional anti-papal ammunition when a French Catholic magazine branded Smith's statement as quite heretical because it "deliberately contradicts that of the Syllabus of Pius IX." [21] In 1930 the Vatican chose to assert some of its most reactionary teachings on birth control and creedally segregated education.

The Smith-Marshall exchange did not stop the whispering campaign or quiet the rumors. Preachers, priests and rabbis jumped in on both sides. The Pope, Tammany and the liquor traffic were entangled in a campaign medley which included Al's cigar, his love of cocktails and even the social inadequacies of his wife. From the subterranean depths of some print shop came thousands of copies of that fraudulent old-time masterpiece, *The Awful Disclosures of Maria Monk or The Hidden Secrets of a Nun's Life in a Convent Exposed*. In New York a fundamentalist divine named John Roach Stratton proclaimed that Al Smith was a tool of vice and sin.

Smith finally felt compelled to strike back in one campaign speech. He chose Oklahoma City late in September as the site for his counter-attack on "the religious issue." Denouncing the "wicked motive of religious intolerance," he declared: "The world knows no greater mockery than the use of the blazing cross, the cross upon which Christ died, as a symbol to instill into the hearts of men a hatred of their brethren, while Christ preached and died for the love and brotherhood of man." It was too late then to stop the campaign bitterness, and when Smith secured only eighty-seven votes in the electoral college, many critics described his overwhelming defeat as essentially a defeat of minority rights by religious bigotry.

The 1928 election returns can be read in many ways, and few analysts agree in their assessment of the factors. Smith in defeat polled over 6,500,000 votes more than Davis' vote in 1924. William F. Ogburn of the University of Chicago estimated that prohibition sentiment was three times as decisive an influence in the result as the religious issue. Two professors at New York University summed up the disgust of most intellectuals over the tone of the campaign:

A party campaign is not a rational process. It is an emotional spree, an orgy of self-seeking, venality and tomfoolery. . . . One must conclude that fears, prejudices, likes and dislikes, susceptibility to the quality of dignity, habit, pride in party, sympathy for the underdog, rebelliousness arising from inferiority complexes and thwarted ambitions—all these, and many other factors in motivation decide the result. The chances are good that the few voters who apply their critical intelligence to the task of discerning the public interest swing not a single district.[22]

Two-Way Bigotry

In 1949, discussing one phase of Catholic education, I spoke very critically of "the type of personal bigotry which disgraced the country during the Al Smith campaign." I referred, of course, to anti-Catholic bigotry. Like many liberal journalists of the Al Smith era, I had followed the exposures of Protestant and "dry" bigotry in the old *New York World,* and I had read such scholarly works as Professor Ray Billington's *The Protestant Crusade, 1800-1860* and such Catholic works as Michael Williams' *The Shadow of the Pope*.

In perspective, I believe that these analyses of our anti-Catholic past were substantially true but that the picture they drew of the Catholic-Protestant struggle in American history was decidedly one-sided. The worst pronouncements of the lunatic fringe of Protestantism have often been accepted as typical. Recent books about Al Smith and his times, written by such able historians as Oscar Handlin of Harvard and Edmund A. Moore of the University of Connecticut, have been impeccable in their scholarship but astonishingly inadequate in discussing the underlying reasons for anti-Catholicism. They have also, it seems to me, neglected the pro-Catholic bigotry which helped to keep anti-Catholic bigotry alive.

Much of the popular literature about anti-Catholicism in the past begs the whole question of whether there is a real conflict between Catholic policy and American political institutions. The evasion is accomplished by avoiding any analysis of Catholic policy. And too often the critics assume without argument that any person opposed to the ecclesiastical or political interests of a minority group is per se a bigot.

One can scan the serious historical works about the Al Smith period without finding a single mention of the two basic policies of the Church that probably did more to create anti-Catholicism than all the speeches of the Heflins and the Bishop Cannons. The first of these policies, embodied in Canon 1374 and promulgated in 1918, obliges every American parent to boycott the public school unless he receives a special episcopal dispensation. The second policy, embodied in the *Ne temere* decree on marriage and applied to the United States in 1908, makes any American Catholic marriage to a non-Catholic absolutely invalid unless all children of the marriage are reared as Catholics.[23] These two rules, imposed upon American Catholics by fiat, have made Catholicism a kind of society within our society, existing in a state of separateness that permanently bars complete community cooperation.

The *Atlantic Monthly* did publish, early in 1928, a series of articles summarizing the views of an anonymous American priest about the clerically promoted policy of separatism in American life. The articles, incidentally, were greeted in the Catholic press by a storm of vituperation and in the daily press by dead silence. "We are a people self-ostracized," said the priest. "We must have our own schools, our own charities, our own graveyards. We are the modern Pharisees who will not sit with publicans. Bitterly we complain of the prejudice that has arisen against us. We may thank our own aloofness for it. The spirit of segregation is diametrically opposed to the spirit of Christ. . . ." [24]

Earlier this same priest was quoted as saying that, within the cultural system of his Church, the priest "must stand before his people in the guise of a medieval pedagogue. To be true to his trust he must be a reactionary. . . . Rome demands absolute intellectual submission of him." In pained surprise, after the priest's series was completed in the *Atlantic,* the editor remarked:

Here is a topic of intense interest which has elicited a correspondence almost unparalleled in our experience, but not one newspaper in the United States (barring church publications) has mentioned it. The topic is absolutely and consciously tabu. A similar debate upon Protestant issues would be a favorite, almost a universal, subject of discussion. Is it well for the Republic, is it well for the Roman Catholic Church, that her affairs, and her affairs only, are outside the pale of public debate?

The policy that the *Atlantic* editor described as a "tabu" was in force during the Al Smith era, and it has been in force in most literature about religious controversy ever since. A South Dakota scholar, Professor Charles L. Sewry, has examined the American literature of anti-anti-Catholicism quite carefully and has found it consistently oversimplified. He believes that many historians of anti-Catholicism have been guilty of "attitudinizing." [25] They consider it "inconsistent with the liberal, urbane and sophisticated demeanor they wish to present before the world to appear to take seriously the highly agitated and frequently vulgarly expressed outbursts of contending religious parties." They also consider it "more chivalric to champion the presumed underdogs in such conflicts." Only a few historians have recognized that in the vulgar conflicts over "no Popery" and "anti-Catholic bigotry" a great cultural struggle is in progress in which individual freedom and American self-government are involved.

Almost all writers about the Al Smith period have also ignored the Catholic bigotry in the diocesan press in 1927 and 1928. It was less vulgar in style than the Klan-inspired bigotry, but it was not far superior in balance and broad-mindedness. It certainly must have had a part in creating anti-Catholic feeling.

One can take, for example, the *Catholic News* of New York, which can fairly be described as Al Smith's home newspaper. It spoke for his archdiocese and carried the endorsement of Cardinal Hayes on its masthead. During 1927 and 1928 its columns contained many extreme and antagonistic comments on Protestantism and many highly emotional accounts of anti-Catholicism in America's past.

During a large part of the campaign, the *Catholic News* and thirty-five other diocesan papers ran a provocative serial about American anti-Catholic literature and Catholic patriotism written by the noted historian Dr. Peter Guilday, who declared that "the political philosophy back of American freedom came to the Founders of the Republic straight from the heart of the Catholic Church." [26] He also declared that Catholics had come to realize that "Protestantism as a religion and as a policy carried in its very heart the seeds of the dissolution of the Republic." [27] In one article, published just three months before Smith's nomination, Guilday said: "Democracy was all but annihilated by the so-called Reformation. Protestantism meant, for all practical purposes, the destruction of the right to life, property and personal freedom; it meant the abolition of freedom of conscience, of speech, of the press. Its most appalling consequence was the decay of education and the outlawing of charity."

Under the heading "Must Catholics Never Resent Insult?" the editors warmly supported the old Catholic boycott of the *Washington Post,* which had been instituted when that paper published one letter in its letter columns mildly criticizing a Catholic welfare institution in the capital.[28] The *Catholic News* warned newspapers to be "fully aware that, if they appeal for Catholic patronage, their columns must be closed to insults or slanders against the Church and its institutions." Commenting on the *Atlantic Monthly* articles by the anonymous priest, it accused the magazine of "stooping to the depths of the old-time *Menace* and Maria Monk" and of printing articles such as "we look for from an Imperial Wizard." [29] It was equally gentle in describing the Unitarian Dr. Dieffenbach as a man who has "exposed completely the countenance of bigotry in all its ugliness and vindictiveness." [30]

One of the sad lessons of the Al Smith campaign is that even the most dignified discussion of Catholic policy and Presidential fitness is likely to receive the same treatment in the Catholic press as the fulminations of the Ku Klux Klan.

The word "bigotry" is entitled to more judicious handling than it received in the Al Smith campaign. According to Webster's, a bigot is "one obstinately or intolerantly devoted to his own church, party, belief or opinion." The early meaning of the word was that of a religious hypocrite; in current usage, it has been transformed into an epithet to be hurled at any person who is hostile to a minority group. But in practice, hostility to a bigoted minority group may be the very opposite of bigotry. At times, such hostility may even be a social necessity for those who believe in freedom. Witness the organized opposition to Tennessee's anti-evolution fanatics!

Toward the end of the Al Smith campaign, the most important Protestant journal in the country, the *Christian Century* of Chicago, tried to rescue the church-political discussion from semantic confusion. Said the editor: "We have yet to hear of any Protestant, even the most 'bigoted,' who proposes to vote against Governor Smith because of his mode of worship or the religious doctrines which he professes." Then the editor asked and answered his own questions as follows:

> Just what kind of a motive is it that actuates a Protestant to vote against a Roman Catholic for the presidency? Why does he not wish to see a Roman Catholic in the White House?
>
> It is not because he would restrict religious freedom.
>
> It is not because he is a religious bigot.
>
> It is not because he does not believe in the Roman Catholic religion or does not like its way of worship.
>
> It is not because he disregards the constitution.
>
> It is not because he fears that Al Smith as President will "take orders" from the Pope. Such a fear is surely groundless if for no other reason than the fact that the Pope is no foe.
>
> The anti-Catholic voter is no more a bigot than the anti-Wall St. voter, or the anti-bolshevist voter, or the anti-pacifist voter, or the anti-militarist voter, or the anti-Volstead voter. He is opposed to the occupancy of the White House by a Roman Catholic because he sees, or thinks he sees, a real issue between Catholicism and American institutions.[31]

The *Christian Century* probably overestimated the capacity of the average Protestant voter to divest himself of personal prejudice and vote according to pure rational principle. But on one thing the editor was entitled to unanimous agreement. He declared that the question involved is "one that every voter should answer for himself in the light of the study of the facts, and he cannot do this unless the facts can be talked about openly and freely, without innuendo, without bullying, and without any cant about 'bigotry.' "

Can a Catholic Win?

Since Senator John F. Kennedy of Massachusetts almost won the Democratic Vice Presidential nomination in 1956, no question has been more popular among political columnists than the question: Can a Catholic be elected to the Presidency in 1960? In groping for an answer to that question, countless commentators have exhumed and re-examined the ghost of the Al Smith campaign. Most commentators, in order to stave off Catholic wrath, have repeated over and over again the assurance that they themselves are free of all bigotry but that, since somebody else may raise "the religious issue," it should be considered, etc. etc. Then, without discussing any fundamental policies of Catholicism, they usually proceed to speculate on those superficial and practical aspects of the situation that are concerned solely with the possibilities of victory or defeat. Usually the prophecy centers on whether there will be more or less opposition to a Catholic candidate in 1960 than there was in 1928. Since the 1928 sampling is far from pure, the comparison is bound to be slightly unscientific.

It seems clear that the comparative prophets are correct in saying that a Catholic candidate's chances in 1960 are greater than Al Smith's chances were in 1928. Smith was a wet and a product of Tammany Hall. He was also a cigar-chewing politician from a big city who lacked social finish and had never gone to college. Those handicaps do not affect any of the potential Catholic candidates of 1960. Prohibition has disappeared as a national issue; Tammany has no candidate on the political horizon; and all available Catholic candidates are suave, learned and gracious. Kennedy, as a Harvard graduate and an author, has a special appeal to intellectuals that Al Smith never had.

It is also clear that since 1928 there has been a great increase in tolerance for Catholic candidates at the state level. To what extent this new tolerance is a consciously promoted result of propaganda is not clear. Such organizations as the National Conference of Christians and Jews have ceaselessly promoted the belief that Americans should feel guilty for the "bigotry" demonstrated in the 1928 election and that they should purge their souls by banishing any thought of discrimination in the future. There is enough substance in this description of the past by the N.C.C.J. to win the sympathy of many liberals, although it should be noted that the organization never criticizes any religious organization for bigotry or separatism promoted by its own clergy.

The election of so many Catholic Governors and Senators in 1958 clearly proves that there is a new tolerance toward Catholic candidates as individuals. Several states elected their first Catholic Governors or Senators in 1958 despite the small proportion of Catholic voters in their population. Pennsylvania, with a Catholic population of only 30 per cent, elected a first Catholic Governor. Maine, with 27 per cent, elected a first Catholic Senator.[32] Montana, with a Catholic population of only 22 per cent, has two Catholic Senators. It is clear that a majority of Protestant voters in the Democratic Party do not discriminate against Catholic candidates on grounds of religion, at least at the state level.

The fact that the Catholic increase in officialdom is almost wholly a Democratic as against a Republican achievement should not detract from its Presidential significance. The Democratic Party is now a stronger national force than the Republican Party, as the recent elections have proved. It occupies a much more strategic position in relation to the Presidency than it occupied in 1928. The fact should also be noted that the front-running Catholic candidate, Senator John F. Kennedy, underscored his eligibility by capturing his home state in 1958 by an unprecedented majority of 870,000 votes.

Regardless of the name of any potential Catholic President or Vice President, the prophets always assume that he will be a Democrat. This assumption is strengthened by the fact that most of the big city machines are Democratic, that many of these machines are dominated by Catholic political leaders and that these Catholic leaders have actually "done it once," in 1928. It is assumed that they will force the nomination of a Catholic before the Republican Party succumbs to similar pressure, and that if the Republican Party follows suit its choice of a Catholic will be in the nature of a rejoinder. There seems to be no good reason for disputing this rather obvious political soothsaying.

The power of urban Catholic leaders is strengthened by another statistical fact. Nine key cities in nine pivotal states could quite possibly swing those states one way or another and thus elect a President. Before Alaska and Hawaii entered the picture, statistical analysis indicated that 222 of the 266 electoral votes necessary to elect a President came from those nine key states—New York, Illinois, Massachusetts, Michigan, Wisconsin, Pennsylvania, Ohio, Missouri and California.[33] The 1959 *National Catholic Almanac* indicates that the population of these states is nearly 29 per cent Catholic as against the national proportion of about 20 per cent. Probably the percentage is not so important as the Catholic concentration in the key cities. According to the *Catholic Almanac,* that concentration has risen sharply since 1928.

What these figures are worth as a basis for political forecasting depends on several imponderables. Is it safe to assume that Catholics will vote almost solidly for a Catholic candidate? Will their solidarity be sufficiently apparent to arouse the competing solidarity of Protestants; and if so, what will be the effect of *that* bloc sentiment? Will an overwhelmingly Protestant South switch to the Republican ticket, as several Southern states did in 1928, rather than support a Catholic? Does the rise of a considerable Catholic population in the North to new economic status in the middle class mean that more Catholic voters will desert to the Republican Party? (If both major parties nominate Catholics for Vice President, that maneuver would doubtless cancel out religious factors.)

Taking the easiest question first, it is not safe to assume that almost all Catholic voters would vote for a Catholic candidate. Probably the majority would if he were a Democrat, but perhaps these same voters would support a Democratic ticket in any case if the Democratic candidates revealed no substantial anti-Catholic bias. While the Irish wards in Boston gave Al Smith an all-time high tribute in 1928, Truman in 1948 actually exceeded Smith's vote in many heavily Catholic districts.[34] A Baptist Democrat seemed to suffer no handicaps in those wards. It is obvious that in some ways "a Catholic vote" is more Democratic than Catholic.

Of course, all party alignments would be abandoned by most Catholic voters if a head-on collision between Catholic and Protestant policy were involved in an election. But there is no indication that such a collision is imminent. On the contrary, it seems safe to predict that the last thing a Catholic candidate could desire would be a Catholic platform. In order to avoid any unpleasant collision any Catholic candidate is likely to eschew any suggestion of subservience to papal policy.

The Catholic voters who have moved up the economic ladder from the Irish and Italian pick-and-shovel brigades of the nineteenth century are expected to show some sympathy for the Republican Party regardless of the religion of its candidates. Many studies of the class structure of American religious groups have indicated a great change in recent years. As early as 1946, one study estimated that at least one-third of American Catholics were members of the upper and middle classes.[35] While Catholics as a whole are still more proletarian than Protestants as a whole, Catholic voters are moving away from the views and status of an underprivileged immigrant minority. The Irish Catholic ghettos of many Eastern cities have almost disappeared. Most political analysts of the 1952 and 1956 elections believe that many prosperous Catholics crossed over party lines to vote for Eisenhower in 1952 and 1956.

An outburst of religious feeling during a Presidential campaign might upset all the mathematical predictions and throw almost all Catholic votes into the Democratic camp. But religious feeling can serve as a double-edged sword. The same partisan excitement that produced solidarity among Catholic voters might also produce a new solidarity among Protestant voters, and the two aroused partisanships might cancel each other out. Potentially, an aroused Protestant electorate is far more powerful than an aroused Catholic electorate, and Protestant partisanship could be aroused almost as easily in the Middle West as in the South. Such Middle Western states as Indiana, Kentucky and Kansas have strong anti-Catholic traditions. Among them they have only one Catholic member in Congress, a lonely Representative from Louisville.

Every serious study of voting behavior in recent years has indicated that there are probably several million people in the United States who would still refuse to vote for a Catholic Presidential candidate under any circumstances. Samuel Lubell, whose political studies in depth have won respect in scholarly circles, estimated in 1958 that the presence of a Catholic Presidential candidate on the Democratic ticket would probably cause a shift in the votes of one in every six or seven voters—about 14 to 16 per cent. But he reasoned that for every five votes lost among non-Catholics, three votes would be acquired by Republican Catholic transfers to the Democratic Party.[36]

Gallup poll studies indicate a considerably larger influence on the result by voters who cherish an anti-Catholic bias. Gallup's American Institute of Public Opinion polls in 1958 and 1959 used the same questions that had been used in several previous polls: "If your party nominated a generally well-qualified person for President, and he happened to be a Catholic, would you vote for him?" It should be noted that this question is "loaded" for an affirmative answer. It forces the person interviewed to take a specifically anti-Catholic position, and many voters who cherish prejudices are reluctant to disclose such attitudes. Using this question as a measure of anti-Catholic feeling, the Gallup poll found that 68 per cent of the persons interviewed said *Yes* in 1958 and 1959; 73 per cent in 1956; 60 per cent in 1955; and 62 per cent in 1940.[37]

Many newspapers carried a headline over the 1958 results in this poll: "Prejudice in Politics Declining." The conclusion seems hardly justified. If the figures are stated negatively, they indicate that a prodigious amount of unqualified anti-Catholicism is still present in the American electorate. From one-fourth to one-third of our voters belong to a boycott bloc. They would refuse to vote for a Catholic Presidential candidate under any circumstances. That is what the *No* vote means in these Gallup polls.

Almost any person with an open mind concerning the fitness of a Catholic candidate would unhesitatingly vote *Yes* on such a carefully slanted question—as I would—and leave the final judgment to the campaign. Those who would vote *No* can fairly be described as the last-ditch diehard opponents of Catholicism, who would desert their party rather than follow a Catholic standard-bearer. It is a disturbing fact that this group is so large.

In this anti-Catholic bloc there are probably some independent and well-educated voters who base their extreme opposition to Catholicism on sound knowledge of Catholic reaction in other countries, and who therefore do not trust any Catholic leader to remain independent of Vatican control. But it is more than likely that most of the voters in this bloc belong to the narrow-minded and under-educated segment in our society associated with Protestant fundamentalism. About one-third of all Southern voters, apparently, favor a boycott of Catholic candidates. Professor Stouffer's 1955 studies indicated that the most narrow-minded people in America were Protestants from the old South.[38] Ironically, the second most narrow-minded people in America appeared to be those Catholics against whom the prejudice of the Southern fundamentalists is directed.

Many voters are, of course, more reluctant to vote for a Catholic Presidential candidate than for a Catholic Governor or Senator. They accept the President as the national symbol, and presumably they do not like the thought of a Catholic national symbol even when they respect the Catholic individual. It is difficult to measure this difference in attitude toward state and national candidates.

Many non-Catholics are evidently afraid of Catholicism as an international political force operating from a church-state capital in

Rome. They feel that they can take care of Catholicism in America at the local level but that a Catholic President might commit the nation to too much pro-Vatican policy abroad. And personal opposition to the Pope as an absolute ruler over a church state still persists. This feeling is undoubtedly strengthened by reports in American newspapers concerning Catholic political parties in Europe. "I wouldn't want the Pope running the country for us" was the sentiment discovered among a substantial number of voters by the Gallup poll of 1959.

The feeling about a Vice Presidential candidate is very much weaker, although no one could prove this statistically. American voters are notoriously careless about the qualifications of their Vice President in spite of the fact that eight Vice Presidents have succeeded to the Presidency by reason of death at the White House. The party conventions continue to choose the second man on the Presidential tickets in the final mad hours of political bargaining when the perorations about disinterested devotion to the nation have been forgotten. The ticket must be "balanced," whatever that means. The Presidential candidate's personal choice of a running mate is nominally paramount; but beyond that personal courtesy, the tactical considerations as seen by the party machine leaders seem to be more important than fitness.

The Vice Presidency is often a mere regional pawn in a party chess game, and it could easily become an ethnic and religious pawn designed to capture the "offended" Catholic vote by appeasement. Ergo, most political critics in Washington believe that the first Catholic to reach the White House is much more likely to get there via default and the Vice Presidency than by any direct route. It is significant that a *Congressional Quarterly* poll of Democratic Congressmen in 1959 showed twice as many members in favor of Senator Kennedy for Vice President as for President.[39]

One of the important imponderables in the situation is the number of votes that would be lost to any political party which seemed to reject a leading Catholic candidate at the last moment for reasons of religious prejudice. Two acute critics of Washington affairs, James Reston of the *New York Times,* and Richard Rovere of the *New Yorker,* have suggested that the rejection of a candidate like Kennedy after many months of front-running and ballyhoo might so anger so many Catholic voters that the Democratic Party would pay a heavy price for the rejection.

The Jesuit magazine *America* has underscored this potential resentment of Catholic voters: "If the Senator from Massachusetts fails to get either the Presidential or the Vice Presidential nomination from the Democrats, the Republicans will still need a Catholic —in this event to attract the votes of resentful Catholic Democrats." [40] As bait for the "resentment vote," *America* mentioned the Catholic convert Claire Booth Luce and Secretary of Labor James P. Mitchell.

But for every "resentment" vote lost to the party rejecting a Catholic candidate, there may be at least one gained—the "anti-prestige" vote cast by the voter who believes that any Catholic President, no matter how loyal to American concepts, would be used by the Vatican to increase its own power and prestige in the world. The line of argument espoused by such a voter might run something like this: Catholicism as a world force is reactionary and opposed to the American concept of church-state separation. It is growing rapidly. No matter how sincerely a Catholic President asserts his independence, the Vatican will unfairly exploit his religious status as evidence of Catholic control of the United States.

Another imponderable factor in the situation is the number of votes that might be cast for the *first* Catholic Presidential candidate in this era by liberals who have no particular sympathy for Catholicism or great admiration for any particular Catholic candidate. These liberals might reason that they wish to "rid the national soul of guilt" for past discrimination by breaking the Protestant monopoly, regardless of the quality of the candidate. The psychology of this potential group of voters might be akin to that of those Harvard seniors who, some years ago, elected the first Negro marshal of a Harvard graduating class. The Negro victor in this election was a worthy leader of his class, but his personal qualities were secondary. His victory was a victory over racial intolerance. He was the symbol of something much larger than himself. Similarly, the first successful Catholic Presidential candidate may be regarded by some liberals as a symbol of the battle against religious prejudice.

Professor Lawrence Fuchs of Brandeis University, in a perceptive article in the Jesuit magazine *America* in 1958, summed up the balance of probabilities quite neatly; "The arithmetic of an election which threw Kennedy against a Republican candidate comes down to a calculation of the number and location of votes which would be lost to the Democrats because of anti-Catholic prejudice and the number and location of votes won because of Catholic pride." [41] Probably several hundred thousand Catholic voters would cross any party line to vote for a Catholic candidate. In the May 1959 Gallup poll, a special question was asked of Catholic voters only which was designed to measure the number of these potential transferees: "If a party other than the one you normally vote for nominated a man for President in 1960, who happened to be a Catholic, do you think you might vote for him, or not?" About 52 per cent of the Catholic voters said *Yes,* 37 per cent *No* and 11 per cent *Don't know*.

While any prophecy in this highly controversial area can be nothing more than a guess, let me record my own impression that a Catholic *can* be elected to the Presidency but that the hurdle of hostility is still too great to make the choice attractive to the leaders of either political party. Since politicians like to take the easy way out from any dilemma, they are much more likely to install a Catholic in second place than in first place.

Clichés That Bar Discussion

Assuming, then, that a Catholic *can* be elected President—*should* he be elected?

Obviously, the answer must depend on the individual candidate's total qualifications. His Catholicism is relevant only as it affects his total qualifications, but anything in a candidate's religion which might affect his conduct as President is pertinent. If his record and utterances indicate that he personally stands for certain policies of his Church that are objectionable to the voter, he cannot avoid responsibility for those policies simply because they are associated with his religion. If his record and utterances indicate no allegiance to those policies, some presumption has been created that he has independence of judgment.

All these things seem dreadfully obvious, but they need to be said because too often they are treated as silent assumptions which one side in the dialogue accepts without expression and the other side rejects without discussion.

There is another silent assumption which should be recorded: that any Catholic candidate would be instantly rejected by the voters if he stood without qualification for the development in the United States of the whole Catholic program in political, social and economic life. It is assumed—I think rightly—that a Catholic candidate, in order to be successful at all, will not run on a Catholic platform. In Europe, on the other hand, it is assumed that a Catholic candidate who seeks the endorsement of his Church leaders *will* accept without serious question all six of those major Vatican social policies which, as I mentioned in Chapter I, threaten our present democratic society.

These policies are not merely incidental opinions of individual prelates but basic teachings of the Church, promulgated in papal encyclicals or Canon Law and made applicable to all Catholics in

the United States and elsewhere. They are all discussed and codi-
fied either in the encyclicals or in the standard, American-approved
text, *Canon Law, Text and Commentary* by Father T. Lincoln
Bouscaren and Father Adam C. Ellis. This text is serially arranged
so that the following Canon Law references can be found as easily
as the words in a dictionary:

1. *Complete abolition of divorce:* Canon 1118.
2. *Complete prohibition of contraceptives:* Encyclical *Christian Marriage* by Pope Pius XI. (The most complete documentation is in
   Alvah W. Sulloway's *Birth Control and Catholic Doctrine,* Beacon
   Press, 1959.)
3. *The obligation of the state to support Catholic schools with public
   funds:* ("The system of taxation which burdens Catholic citizens
   with the support of so-called 'public' schools which Catholics may
   not in conscience attend, is an evident violation of fundamental
   justice.") [42]
4. *Church censorship:* Canon 1399, which forbids all Catholics to read
   without episcopal permission any book or periodical directly criticizing Catholic teaching.
5. *Discrimination against Protestants, Jews and unbelievers in mixed
   marriage:* Canons 1060 ff., and Canons 1070-71.
6. *Creedal segregation of Catholic children in a separate school system,
   with theological penalties for parents who refuse their bishops'
   orders to boycott public schools:* Canon 1374.

Before we can discuss these six social policies and their relation to a Catholic candidate, we must open the pathway to a rational discussion, now cluttered with certain obstructive clichés
which are mind-blocks to clear thinking. Often these clichés seem
reasonable on the surface, but they will not stand examination.

*Cliché One: Religion has absolutely nothing to do with a
man's qualifications for the Presidency.*

That depends, of course, on what one means by "religion."
Usually this cliché is wielded as a club by someone who attaches a

very narrow meaning to the word and who infers that the questioner is a bigot for denying some good Catholic his right to be President.

No fair-minded voter questions any Catholic's right to adhere to the devotional aspects of his faith without penalty. But the complex moral and political code that passes for religion in the Catholic Church includes a great many policies and principles that non-Catholics consider governmental. Most non-Catholics believe that if these policies and principles are to be withdrawn from discussion because they bear a religious label, the withdrawal will constitute a fundamental denial of free speech. They insist, therefore, that a candidate's religion is relevant to his qualifications for the Presidency to the extent that his faith involves such political policies.

Cliché Two: The questioning of a Catholic candidate about the policies of his Church is discrimination against a minority group.

This is the favorite cliché of many liberals because it gives a kind of moral dignity to evasion. Unhappily, it seems to have made an impression upon some Jewish liberals; Judaism has also been a minority religion in American history, and minorities tend to be sympathetic with each other. A moment's reflection will show that the cliché begs the whole question.

Deliberate ethnic or religious discrimination against a minority group, either because it is a minority group or because it is unlike the majority group in some way, is always to be condemned. But opposition to a minority group is not necessarily based on either prejudice or discrimination, and the fact of minority status should not confer immunity from criticism. If a minority stands for policies that are reactionary or stupid or undemocratic, those policies should be attacked just as vigorously as if they were the accepted program of the majority.

Cliché Three: Opposition to Catholicism is prejudice.

Some of it is and some of it isn't. The anti-Catholic spectrum ranges all the way from the Ku Klux Klan to humanists and leaders of the Unitarian Church. It is fraudulent to represent the whole phenomenon in terms of its most fanatical specimens. Sometimes an individual is vigorously anti-Catholic precisely because he is opposed to prejudice and because he considers the Catholic Church the most deplorable form of congealed religious prejudice in modern society.

Peter Viereck's famous quip: "Catholic baiting is the anti-Semitism of the liberals" may be taken as a horrible example of a sub-variety of this cliché. It is not only untrue; it is the direct opposite of the truth. Catholic baiting is the anti-Semitism of the stupid and the reactionary. The discerning liberal who opposes some Catholic policies for sound reasons is usually opposed to anti-Semitism for much the same reason: he wants a free culture where neither church nor state can penalize men for religious non-conformity.

Cliché Four: Membership in a church should never be held against a candidate.

Why not? Membership in any social organization creates some presumption of agreement with the principles of that organization. If a church teaches certain principles and policies that are contrary to American constitutional policies, a candidate's membership in that church is highly relevant to his fitness for the Presidency.

A member of the Daughters of the American Revolution is presumed by virtue of her D.A.R. membership to be an economic and cultural reactionary. The assumption is rebuttable in any individual case. The analogy between the D.A.R. and the Catholic

Church is reasonably sound; both emphasize the worship of the past and both claim a special status in modern society by virtue of tradition.

Cliché Five: It is discriminatory to single out Catholic candidates for questioning without subjecting Protestant and other candidates to the same inquiry.

Whether this criticism is sound depends upon the nature of the questions asked. General questions on the separation of church and state are appropriate for all candidates of all faiths and should be addressed to all alike. But if the policies under consideration are exclusively Catholic, it would be absurd to question Protestant candidates about them. This is the case in respect to the Catholic social policies on divorce, birth control, the support of sectarian schools out of the public treasury, Church censorship, mixed marriage and the boycott of public schools. No large Protestant group in America supports any one of these policies.

Moreover, no large Protestant group in America makes its church-state program so officially and punitively binding upon its members by including the program in its codes of conduct and belief. And all Protestant groups functioning in America determine their policies in the United States through a reasonably democratic process, in sharp contrast to the Catholic method of determining social policies through a self-perpetuating hierarchy in Rome.

Cliché Six: A Catholic is loyal to the Pope rather than to the United States, and is therefore automatically disqualified for service as President.

This will probably be the second most popular cliché of any campaign involving a Catholic candidate, and it is just as much an oversimplification as Cliché One.

It is true that if a Catholic candidate faithfully obeyed *every one* of the directives of the Popes in respect to governmental institutions he would be disqualified for responsible service in a pluralistic democracy. Several past Popes have issued formal statements placing loyalty to their Church above loyalty to civil governments. Even today, in some of its most extreme claims of exclusive authority, the Church demands loyalties that are quite inconsistent with American sovereignty—in domestic relations law, eugenic sterilization and diplomatic preference, for example. (Some of these claims are documented in this volume; others are documented in *American Freedom and Catholic Power,* Beacon Press, 1958.)

But most men are born into their religion in the same way that they are born into their nationality, and there must be a reasonable limit to the accountability of a Catholic candidate for the reactionary concepts of his Church's hierarchy. The concept of superior loyalty to the Pope is now hedged with so many verbal and actual conditions, and the record of American Catholics in serving the nation in war and peace is so notable, that I believe this whole issue should be expunged from any Presidential campaign. There are plenty of other issues, far more specific, which clamor for discussion.

The Inescapable Issues

How much should a Catholic candidate be held accountable for the social policies of his Church? Of course, the purely devotional and theological policies of his Church are irrelevant; nothing that is concerned wholly with philosophy or worship should be brought into a Presidential campaign. But what of those six social policies which overlap and to some extent contradict American legal traditions?

There are important technical differences among these six policies. Divorce, mixed marriage and censorship might be considered irrelevant for discussion in a Presidential campaign, partly because they are matters within the primary power of the states. On the other hand, public appropriations for parochial schools and the boycott of public schools under the threat of ecclesiastical penalties are undoubtedly relevant. These issues obviously have some national significance, legislative or moral. Birth control falls in an in-between category because it is both local and international in significance.

But this very distinction between relevant and irrelevant issues in Catholic social policy is itself irrelevant to the actual opposition of many voters to a Catholic candidate. The distinction between national and state fields of jurisdiction may please the political scientists, but when a voter questions the independence and liberality of a Catholic candidate, his questioning will not stop at state lines. He will want to know about the total character and outlook of any man he votes for. He is bound to question anything in the candidate's viewpoint which seems to contradict or deny freedom of thought or the practice of tolerance in an open society.

If—to take the most "irrelevant" issue—a Catholic candidate actually accepts and acknowledges the right of his bishops to prevent Catholic legislators from voting for a more liberal divorce law (as has happened in Albany for the last thirty years), that acceptance and acknowledgment of a supra-legal moral authority must be considered relevant to his Presidential fitness. Even if he should be excused from all responsibility for discussing divorce specifically in the campaign, his liberal critics, to be honest, would have to declare their opinion that a man who followed the Albany pattern of obedience is unfit for the White House.

Liberals would instantly vote against any candidate of any party or faith who actually proposed the abolition of the right of divorce in the United States, or who actually announced that he would follow ecclesiastical directives on such an issue. Is it not reasonable, then, for them to take into account the fact that a Catholic candidate belongs to an organization which destroys the right of divorce everywhere in the world where it has the power to do so—in Italy, Spain, Portugal, Ireland, Quebec and Brazil, for example—and which forbids its legislators to liberalize divorce laws in such states as New York, just as it forbids them to liberalize birth control statutes in Massachusetts and Connecticut?

In such circumstances, it would seem that a Catholic candidate cannot escape from the consequences of his own Church's reactionary policies. These negations of human freedom are too important to be ignored. He must—at least, if he wishes to secure the vote of honest liberals—shoulder the burden of proof that he does not accept such clerical limitations on his democratic conscience.

Similar reasoning may fairly be applied to the Church's policy on marriages between Catholics and non-Catholics. Marriage is within the jurisdiction of the states; it could not, within the foreseeable future, be a direct issue in a Presidential campaign. But non-Catholics are bound to ask whether a Catholic candidate actually believes in the obligatory discrimination against non-Catholics which the priests now impose on all mixed marriage ceremonies, requiring these Protestants, Jews and non-believers to agree to raise all their future children as Catholics if they wish to have their marriages considered valid. A Catholic candidate who complains of religious discrimination will be particularly vulnerable to such questions, since the Catholic mixed marriage rule is probably the most patent form of religious discrimination now being practiced on any large scale in the United States.

Some Catholic critics may protest that such questions as divorce and marriage cannot logically be injected into a Presidential campaign when no national divorce and marriage proposals are before the voters. Their logic is technically sound but quite unrealistic. Voters who are suspicious of certain anti-democratic and reactionary features of Catholic policy will not make such fine distinctions. Everything that the word "Catholic" actually implies in politics will be considered relevant in a campaign, especially if it involves a potential conflict between Catholic policy and prevailing American policy.

This oversimplified attitude of the skeptical voter may be somewhat unfair to a Catholic candidate, but it is not without some justification. The Church is—and claims to be—a monolithic and centralized organization which promotes the same fundamental policies everywhere in the world through its prelates, political parties, parishes, trade unions, missions and social organizations. It cannot suddenly disclaim responsibility for those policies when one of its sons becomes an American candidate for President. Nor can the candidate disclaim his responsibility entirely, especially if he remains conspicuously Catholic.

The voters will want to know: What does it mean to be a Catholic? Must every Catholic conform with the world policies of his Church? The Catholic candidate may be victimized by the assumption that he agrees with some policies of his Church which he secretly loathes, but this is part of the burden he must bear for his tacit consent. If he were a Methodist and Methodists had a Pope who championed such policies, he would be compelled to face a similar challenge. Indeed, this analogy can quite fairly be applied to all candidates of all churches which have social or political programs in conflict with the institutions of American democracy.

A candidate from any church which challenges the Constitution by any formal statement purporting to bind the conscience of its members should be held responsible for such statements, whether the ecclesiastical defiance is concerned with racial segregation in education or with financial claims for creedally segregated education. If Quaker meetings attempted to bind all their members to obligatory pacifism, a Quaker candidate could scarcely expect to escape public questioning about his contradictory obligations to his church and his government. In practice, such questions are not raised against Quakers because they have complete freedom of individual conscience in their informal and creedless church. Their denominational principles are considered only advisory, and the leading Quakers who have served in national office have been quite conventional in their views on military matters.

If a Quaker candidate for the Presidency actually included all-out pacifism in his personal profession of religious faith, most voters would undoubtedly regard him as ineligible for the Presidency. If they were asked to square this attitude with the constitutional rule against a religious test for public office, they would probably reply that it was not a strictly religious test they were applying but a test of a candidate's fitness to serve as head of the nation's defense forces. Voters are bound to apply this type of reasoning to any candidate of any faith if they are convinced that there is anything in his faith that conflicts with American policy.

Catholic policies and attitudes in the areas of education and international relations are clearly relevant to a Catholic candidate's suitability for the Presidency. In a sense, the conflicts arising in both these areas involve the separation of church and state. In both instances the intrusion of church power into the province of democratic power lies at the heart of the problem. In both instances the Vatican has drawn a line between church and state which gives the Church more power and the state less power than these institutions have in the American form of government.

America is firmly committed to the gospel of public responsibility for education on a non-creedal basis. The Roman Catholic Church is publicly committed to the policy of creedal operation of a private school system under denominational control. It has formally condemned the theory that education is the primary responsibility of government, and it has formally forbidden its people to send their children to schools of "mixed" religion unless they receive a special dispensation from their bishops. In addition, it has formally condemned the Supreme Court's interpretation of the constitutional principle of separation as it applies to tax appropriations to religious schools.[43]

No Catholic candidate for the Presidency can avoid this fundamental clash in policy since Vatican policy and American policy in this area are mutually exclusive. The Catholic school policy is especially relevant at the present moment because federal monetary aid for public schools has actually begun and Catholic leaders have demanded amendments of the present federal laws to give their schools financial equality with public schools.

The conflicts in the area of international relations are more amorphous and more difficult to chart. The Roman Catholic Church is not only a church but also a state with its own foreign office and diplomatic corps. Yet its foreign policy as a state has not caused as much concern as might have been expected because that policy has been anti-Communist, and anti-Communism is now the chief ingredient in all American foreign policy. There might be some anxiety, however, in regard to the influence exerted upon a Catholic President by the Vatican in his dealings with Catholic dictators. Would his Catholicism influence his judgment in regard to such Catholic dictators as Franco and Salazar? Would he seek to give his Church increased prestige by sending an American ambassador to the Vatican? Would he, through his appointments of American representatives in the United Nations, strengthen the anti-birth-control bloc in that organization?

This last question is of vital importance now because every significant move in United Nations committees in recent years in behalf of population control through contraception has been blocked by the opposition of Catholic countries.[44] Population control can no longer be considered a purely local, national or personal matter. In the years to come, it will be one of the greatest of the moral challenges that confront an American President.

There are also several general reasons why the six reactionary and separatist policies listed above are bound to enter into any Presidential campaign involving a Catholic candidate. They are not simply matters of personal and spiritual devotion. They affect many American public institutions directly. In a sense, they are six aggressive claims filed by an authoritarian power against a tolerant, democratic state. They are dictated policies, imposed as a

"moral duty" on American Catholics with no pretense of democratic process, and this arbitrary imposition naturally raises a pivotal question: can a candidate who has accepted dictation on such
issues as an individual Catholic demonstrate sufficient independence as the nation's Chief Executive?

The problem of the separation of church and state is as much
a problem of jurisdiction as of wall-building: The location of the
wall is as important as the wall itself. As Justice Frankfurter
pointed out in his assenting opinion in the McCollum case,
". . . agreement in the abstract that the First Amendment was
designed to erect a 'wall of separation between Church and State'
does not preclude a clash of views as to what the wall separates."
The hierarchy of the Catholic Church would place the wall essentially where it stands in Europe, bringing education, marriage, divorce, birth control and certain kinds of censorship within the
primary authority of the Church. In the American tradition, all
of these areas belong primarily within the domain of the state, and
decisions on policy are to be made by popular choice, not by ecclesiastical dictation.

A Catholic candidate cannot have it both ways. If he accepts
his Church's six policies literally, he cannot accept the prevailing
American concept of the separation of church and state. If he believes in freedom of choice as the foundation of all democracy, he
must somehow square that conviction with the system of dictation
under which these policies are imposed on Catholics by fiat. If
he is faced with searching questions about these six policies, and
if he answers them candidly, he will be compelled either to reject
the basic principles of American democracy or to assert an independence which his Church's hierarchy will interpret as contrary
to Catholic teaching.

A Candidate Versus His Church

Once it has been determined that the conflict between certain Catholic policies and certain American governmental policies should be brought into the open in a Presidential campaign, it becomes essential to do this with a minimum of distortion and hate-mongering. No realist can be optimistic about all elimination of fanaticism on either side in such a controversy. The most that can be expected is a calm and candid exchange between leading Catholic candidates and their potential critics concerning the major anxieties of non-Catholics. The political conventions and the party platforms will doubtless attempt to smooth away all anxieties with euphonious phrases, and the campaign speeches are likely to follow the same strategy. The best possibility of realistic discussion seems to lie in written questions directed to Catholic candidates.

When strategic maneuvering for the 1960 Presidential campaign got underway in 1957, many Catholic leaders and some non-Catholic editors took the position that it would be discriminatory to single out Catholic candidates and ask them special questions about the relation of their particular Church to American policies and institutions. Sometimes stronger language was used: such questions were "insulting" or "unconstitutional." The Jesuit magazine *America* said that the questions were "in the long tradition of anti-Catholic bigotry."

Senator John F. Kennedy at first took this attitude toward a series of questions addressed to all Catholic candidates by P.O.A.U. (Protestants and Other Americans United for Separation of Church and State). This organization, headed by leading Protestants, announced that it was opposed to the formation of any Catholic or anti-Catholic political party, that it deplored any blanket boycott of Catholic candidates and that it "recalled with regret those chapters in our history when religious prejudice ran amok in the Know-Nothing movement and the Ku Klux Klan." But it declared also that "the religion of a candidate for president or vice president of the United States should not be used as a shield to conceal his own opinions on matters of church-state policy," and it suggested three questions to be asked of every Catholic candidate as "a wise and necessary precaution designed to protect our American traditions":

1. The Canon Law of your church (Canon 1374) directs all American Catholic parents to boycott our public schools unless they receive special permission from their bishops. Do you personally approve or disapprove of this boycott rule?

2. The bishops of your church, in an official statement in November 1948, have denounced the Supreme Court's interpretation of the religion clause of the First Amendment and have urged that the Constitution actually permits the distribution of public money on an equitable basis to sectarian schools and other sectarian institutions. At present the Catholic press and ranking prelates are promoting a plan—see *United States News and World Report,* October 25, 1957—for securing grants of federal money to parents to cover the costs of parochial school tuition by laws which would parallel the G.I. education bills. What is your personal attitude toward your bishop's interpretation of the Constitution, and toward the new plan for financing parochial schools?

3. Many nations recognize your church as both a church and a state, and send official ambassadors to the Holy See. If you became president, what would be your policy concerning the appointment of an American ambassador or a personal representative to the Vatican? [45]

Senator John F. Kennedy, as the leading Catholic aspirant, was immediately deluged with correspondence calling upon him to give specific replies to these questions. At first he took the attitude that the questions were "somewhat insulting" and reminded his correspondents that Article VI of the Constitution forbids any religious test for public office. He soon realized, however, that such replies would not satisfy serious critics. He was confronted with the same challenge that faced Al Smith, but this time it had become much more serious because his Church had made its narrow doctrine on education and birth control more specific than it had been in 1928. Also, twenty years after the Al Smith campaign, in 1948, the

American hierarchy had come out openly against the Supreme Court on the question of public appropriations for parochial schools, and this bolder position required a more specific answer than Al Smith's generalized statement.

Kennedy was intelligent enough to see that he would lose more by silence than by frankness. He gave to *Look* magazine, for publication on March 3, 1959, a statement that was quite remarkable for its candor and breadth, and much more direct than Al Smith's 1927 credo. Kennedy said:

Whatever one's religion in his private life may be, for the office-holder, nothing takes precedence over his oath to uphold the Constitution and all its parts—including the First Amendment and the strict separation of Church and State. Without reference to the Presidency, I believe as a Senator that the separation of Church and State is fundamental to our American concept and heritage and should remain so.

I am flatly opposed to appointment of an ambassador to the Vatican. Whatever advantages it might have in Rome—and I'm not convinced of these—they would be more than offset by the divisive effect at home.

The First Amendment to the Constitution is an infinitely wise one. There can be no question of Federal funds being used for support of parochial or private schools. It's unconstitutional under the First Amendment as interpreted by the Supreme Court. I'm opposed to the Federal Government's extending support to sustain any Church or its schools. As for such fringe matters as buses, lunches, and other services, the issue is primarily social and economic and not religious. Each case must be judged on its merits within the law as interpreted by the courts.

On the whole, the non-Catholic public was pleased by this statement, especially by Kennedy's frank rejection of his Church's claim that public appropriations for sectarian schools were constitutional. A few critics undoubtedly disagreed with his suggestion that bus appropriations to sectarian schools could be considered social and economic rather than religious. But they conceded that he was within his rights in treating some fringe benefits in this way since the Supreme Court had declared that transportation payments did not violate the federal Constitution.

Many non-Catholics were somewhat startled to see that Kennedy received almost no support in the American Catholic press. He was specifically chastised by several leading Catholic journals, and not a single Catholic editor praised him unconditionally. *America* blustered: "It is humiliating for Catholics that even a man with the brilliant war record of Senator Kennedy thought himself obliged to answer questions that everyone knows are the remnants of the bad old days of Know-Nothingism." Then the Jesuit editors disclosed the basis of their annoyance by rebuking Kennedy on the money question:

He is against Federal aid to Catholic schools except for "fringe" benefits. . . . The issue is not a "religious" one, nor a "socio-economic" one, but rather an elementary question of equal treatment under the law. In the years to come, Catholics are confident that a fair-minded public, and the Supreme Court itself, will finally recognize that the theoretical right of a sizable population of U.S. citizens to maintain their own schools is not a right at all when coupled with a denial of the necessary means.[46]

The *Catholic World* of April 1959 carried a picture of Senator Kennedy on its cover, with a signed article by the magazine's editor, Father John B. Sheerin—"Senator Kennedy Vetoes Aid to Catholic Education." Kennedy "will find few Catholics in agreement with his views," declared Father Sheerin; and he argued: "To refuse to grant a Catholic parent his proper share of tax funds seems to strike down a precious right guaranteed by the First Amendment."

The *Commonweal,* edited by liberal Catholic laymen, followed a milder line, rebuking the Massachusetts Senator for giving away the case for federal aid for Catholic schools by his words "It's unconstitutional." The editors averred that such an attitude was "presumptuous and/or unsophisticated" in view of "the long and shift-

ing history of opinion on this Constitutional question." [47] They
argued that there is no "Catholic position" on these matters. They
carefully refrained from telling their readers that the American
Catholic bishops had published a clear "Catholic position" in all
the newspapers of November 21, 1948, interpreting the Constitution as permitting public grants to sectarian schools.

The Jesuits were, quite naturally, the most angry critics of
Senator Kennedy. They had carefully promoted a campaign for
federal aid for Catholic schools as constitutional, and now they saw
their work of years undone by one candid statement from a *Catholic* Presidential aspirant! Said Father Virgil Blum, S.J., author of
the McIntyre plan to pay federal money to Catholic parents: "It
seems somewhat strange to see a Boston Catholic in the 'strict
separation' camp usually occupied almost exclusively by the POAU
and its adherents." [48] *America* reminded its readers that Kennedy's
gesture was especially ungracious in "one who himself never went
to a Catholic school." Said the *Catholic Review* of Baltimore:
". . . he appears to have gone overboard, in an effort to placate the
bigots. . . ."

Perhaps the most significant comment on Kennedy's statement appeared in the Catholic magazine *Ave Maria*. Acknowledg-
ing that the Senator was technically correct in describing the
payment of federal funds to Catholic schools as unconstitutional
under present Supreme Court decisions, the editors said:

We believe that a legitimate question can be asked of any candidate—Do *you* believe that the Supreme Court's decision was a wise
and fair one? Does it do justice to those American citizens, who, for
reasons of conscience, choose to send their children to religious
schools? Or are they being unfairly penalized for exercising freedom
of religion?

Here in *Ave Maria*'s editorial was a statement in exact reverse
of the grounds of apprehension voiced by the predominantly Protestant P.O.A.U. This Protestant organization had argued that a
Catholic should not go to the White House until he had reassured

the citizens about his personal support of the Supreme Court's denial of public money to sectarian schools. It wanted a man in the White House who really believed in the Supreme Court's point of view on this question. *Ave Maria* wanted the reverse, a man in the White House who believed that the Supreme Court had not done justice to Catholics by such a ruling.

One Catholic writer, John Cogley of *Commonweal,* came to the defense of Senator Kennedy on the constitutional issue. Quoting the Supreme Court's ringing words in the Everson case against the use of public money for sectarian institutions, Cogley said:

I do not think Senator Kennedy was far off base when he described this doctrine as "strict" separation. Certainly when the decision was handed down, in 1947, it was roundly condemned as being altogether too narrow by many Catholic spokesmen. But the point is this: a President does not swear to uphold the Constitution as Catholic leaders, or any other leaders, think it should be interpreted but as the Supreme Court interprets it. He does this not because Supreme Court justices are infallible but because observance of their authority, especially by the President, is necessary to stable government.[49]

Kennedy emerged from the encounter with increased stature. He had spoken courageously on the Supreme Court's side against the interest of his Church's hierarchy, and he had convinced some of his critics that, on the money question, he believed in the Court's interpretation of the separation of church and state. This was the kind of independence that apprehensive non-Catholics had been hoping to see in a Catholic candidate. The *Washington Post* praised the Senator in an editorial headed "Senator Kennedy's Candor." [50]

The most important question which Senator Kennedy ignored in his first reply to his non-Catholic critics was that of his attitude toward his Church's boycott of public schools. The Kennedy family had been exempted from any obligation under Canon 1374 to send its children to Catholic schools, although Cardinal O'Connell had issued a public statement threatening excommunication for parents who disobeyed this rule at the very moment when young John, then twelve years old, was attending a non-Catholic school.[51] (Kennedy never went to a regular parochial school, but he did attend a private Catholic preparatory school for one year.) There is no evidence that Kennedy believes in the coercive principle of Canon 1374. Indeed, his education, which has been almost wholly non-Catholic in character, creates the presumption that he rejects the coercive features of that Canon.

Should the Catholic boycott rule be considered irrelevant in any campaign involving a Catholic candidate? A liberal Jewish scholar believes it should:

Although I oppose orthodoxy, including the orthodoxies of the Catholic Church, I do not believe that all the rules embodied in Canon Law have operative significance in American politics. The citation of Canon 1374 which forbids every Catholic to attend a non-Catholic school without special permission from his bishop is really irrelevant to the [Presidential] issue. If a Catholic presidential candidate gave any evidence that he felt this particular Canon to be of high significance and one which could govern his attitudes toward legislation affecting the public schools, then I would be in serious doubt as to his qualifications to govern in a democracy.[52]

There is much to be said for this reasonable phrasing of the issue, and it applies with some appropriateness to all the Catholic candidates now on the Presidential horizon. Apparently they are genuine friends of the public school who have never openly favored the enforcement of their Church's narrow boycott. Catholics can also point to the fact that the boycott is not universally enforced in the United States: it is a rule of perfection, usually enforced very strictly in Catholic countries but often relaxed in non-Catholic countries.

Nevertheless, so long as this restrictive rule is in the Catholic code, it is difficult to see how it can be kept out of a campaign, and probably any Catholic candidate will be obliged to face it. Non-

Catholic critics are likely to argue that, if this rule is a mere formality, it will be an easy matter for any candidate to say so and repudiate its application to the United States. For non-Catholics the rule seems to constitute the keystone of Catholic separatism in education. They do not understand how Catholic spokesmen can talk about "freedom of education" and at the same time endorse theological penalties for parents who send their children to public schools in opposition to their bishops. They want an American President who will commit himself against any kind of coercion, theological or physical, designed to maintain sectarian segregation in education.

This attitude of non-Catholics toward clerical coercion in education is undoubtedly shared privately by millions of Catholic laymen. Until the coercive rule was officially applied to the United States in the 1880s, there was widespread and open opposition to it by both laymen and bishops. At the time of its application, Professor Robert D. Cross reports in his *The Emergence of Liberal Catholicism in America,* "the liberals begged the Third Plenary Council not to coerce priests and laymen into building and attending parochial schools. Bishop Fitzgerald of Little Rock thought that parents should only be advised and urged." [53] Probably every prominent Catholic leader in American political life today would agree with Bishop Fitzgerald that parents should only be "advised and urged," not coerced by theological penalties.

They know that most Americans consider coercion in such matters the essence of intolerance.

Will the American Catholic hierarchy permit its political spokesmen to take this broad-minded and tolerant attitude without rebuke? The Catholic bishops have not given an official reply, but apparently the answer will be in the negative. When Kennedy's answer to his critics was being discussed in 1959, the question of the official Catholic boycott of public schools received very candid treatment in an editorial in *America* by its associate editor, Father

Neil McCluskey. Father McCluskey frankly defended Canon 1374 as an "integral part" of the Catholic faith binding on all Catholics, and added: "To insist that a Catholic Presidential candidate renounce the authority of Canon Law is, reductively, to deny him his freedom to be a Catholic." Then Father McCluskey proceeded to defend the Catholic boycott of public schools as "natural law": "The natural law obliges parents to protect the spiritual and moral well being of their off-spring. Consequently, parents may not allow their children to frequent any place (schools included) where their faith and morals would be exposed to grave danger." [54]

Father McCluskey's statement, published as an editorial in the country's leading Catholic journal, constitutes an answer to the liberal Jewish scholar who believes that the boycott "is really irrelevant." It cannot be considered irrelevant unless the Catholic Church releases Catholic candidates from an obligation to observe or promote the boycott. As long as this rule is presumed by the Church itself to have "operative significance in American politics," the burden of proof will rest upon any Catholic candidate to show that he does not personally approve of its application to American citizens.

The "operative significance" of the Catholic rule against contraception will be equally embarrassing to a Catholic candidate. In the face of overwhelming protests from scientists and social reformers, the Vatican has refused to yield an inch to the advocates of contraception, either for its own people or for the non-Catholics of India, China and Massachusetts. The issue will be particularly difficult for Senator Kennedy, since he comes from one of the two states in which clerical power has outlawed contraceptives for both Catholics and non-Catholics, and since he remained silent during the last great legislative struggle in his state on this issue. His position was rendered even more precarious when the American Catholic bishops made birth control a major political issue by announcing on November 26, 1959 that "Catholics" will not "support any public assistance, either at home or abroad, to promote artificial birth control."

The Responsibility of the Voter

Can we expect *any* calm and rational discussion of such issues in a Presidential campaign? Although the history of past campaigns is not reassuring, any liberal believer in democracy must feel that open discussion is better than either scandal-mongering or the evasions of hypocrisy. The issues are too important to be ignored. We can only hope that there is enough sanity and fair-mindedness in the American electorate for it to discuss the basic issues with more light than heat. Both leading political parties have declared themselves in favor of "fair election practices," whatever that means. A Fair Campaign Practices Committee has been organized under the chairmanship of the distinguished liberal Charles P. Taft.[55] Its "Code of Fair Campaign Practices" includes the pledge: "I shall condemn any appeal to prejudice based on race, creed, or national origin."

The committee does not presume to suppress or condemn any reasonable questions addressed to Catholic candidates, or candidates of any other faith, concerning the policies of their church. It will undoubtedly have its hands full attempting to eliminate the grosser forms of scandal-mongering embodied in such outrages as the famous fake oath of the Knights of Columbus which purports to bind all members of the organization to "hang, burn, waste, boil, slay, strangle, and bury alive" their heretical, Protestant and Masonic enemies.[56] From the literary sewers of Florida and Georgia there will undoubtedly pour forth hundreds of thousands of copies of the fraudulent old work *The Awful Disclosures of Maria Monk* —this book is still being circulated through the United States mails from obscure post office box numbers in the South, accompanied by vague Protestant labels.

The counter-propaganda in the Catholic press will undoubtedly classify virtually all severe criticism of Catholic policy as "bigotry." Several leading Catholic journals have already used such words as "hate-mongers" and "bigots" to describe all critics who put questions on church-state policy to Catholic Presidential candidates. The cry of "No Popery" is certain to be revived by anti-Catholics, especially if some Catholic candidate is indiscreet enough —as Al Smith was—to be caught by a camera in the act of kneeling before a cardinal or bishop.

The Fair Campaign Practices Committee would make a real contribution to political sanity if it could persuade all factions to drop such words as "bigot" and "No Popery" from the campaign lexicons. But no committee can hope to suppress—nor should it attempt to suppress—the feelings and concepts which lie behind such words. It is part of the democratic process that citizens should have an opportunity to express their apprehensions and anxieties in their own language, so long as they do not descend to specific slander.

Before the beleaguered voter finally pulls the curtain behind himself in the voting booth, he will have the responsibility of studying each candidate's pronouncements and record to determine how much truth and how much falsehood there is in each claim and counterclaim. The ultimate question he will have to decide in his own conscience is whether the Catholic candidate whose merits he is considering has demonstrated in good faith enough independence from his Church's hierarchy. One ingredient in that required demonstration of independence will be a direct or indirect assurance that the candidate's election will not promote the six basic and reactionary social policies considered in this chapter.

Such a question is not personal in any invidious sense; it is institutional. It is directed not to a candidate's personal faith but to the consistency of his belief in the American policy of the separation of church and state. That policy is in mortal danger from the pressures of a powerful, authoritarian Church, and any member of that Church who aspires to be the nation's chief executive must shoulder some of the responsibility for his Church's social platform.

Although my personal conviction is that several of the Catholic aspirants are quite worthy as individuals of being President of the United States, their individual qualities can scarcely be appraised in isolation. To some extent they are bound to be scrutinized and assessed as representatives of a Church which is also a state with a world-wide political and social program. Millions of voters, fairly or unfairly, will place upon them the burden of proof for demonstrating that their worthiness is more than personal and that it rises above all sectarian commitments.

Chapter VI

Pluralism and the Good Society

It seems clear that God is not absent from Washington and that organized religion plays a considerable role in American politics. Washington is not an island, either religiously or politically. As a representative capital, it reflects the attitudes and ferments that permeate the entire nation. Presidents, Supreme Court justices, members of Congress and administrators are bound to take religion into account as one of the significant forces in American life. As representatives of a religious people, they would consider themselves untrue to their public trust if they did not give religion due recognition.

Quantitatively the interactions between government and religion at the national level have been increasing in recent years. The federal government has become more and more involved in religious ceremonies. Federal expenditures have been authorized for sectarian hospitals; and local tax appropriations have been declared constitutional, under some circumstances, for sectarian bus transportation and other "welfare" expenses. Clergymen have gained official exemption from military service in two world wars. The government has granted religious conscientious objectors a special status.

Such old and established favors as tax exemption and government chaplaincies have been confirmed and extended. Released-time religious instruction has received permissive federal sanction in connection with public schools. "In God We Trust" has become the national motto. Conspicuous loyalty to some form of theism has become almost obligatory for entrance to the White House.

These facts seem to refute the notion, frequently suggested in religious journals, that our culture is being secularized by a Godless government. Perhaps the nation is becoming less devout in spite of increasing church membership; but, if so, Washington is not responsible. On the contrary, Washington, in spite of the official separation of church and state, is a pro-religious capital. It could scarcely be otherwise in a nation with such a pro-religious hinterland.

If De Tocqueville should come back from some heavenly outpost to the America of the twentieth century, he would undoubtedly record the same reaction to the American scene that he did in 1832. Religion is unofficially one of the nation's foremost political institutions, and the spirit of freedom and the spirit of religion seem intimately united under the aegis of a friendly government.

The federal government's greatest achievement in the area of religion has been the almost universal acceptance and enforcement of religious freedom. Often this achievement has been attained over the protests and obstruction of local officials insensitive to the meaning of the First Amendment. Chiefly through the power and wisdom of the Supreme Court, federal authority has penetrated to the most remote and religiously monolithic communities and has guaranteed even to the most unpopular fanatics the right to speak for or against any article of faith. Where such federal authority has failed to prevent religious discrimination and guarantee religious equality, the failure has more often been local than national.

On the whole, Congress and the executive have supported the Supreme Court in its championship of religious liberty and religious equality. In spite of Congressional shortcomings, no major law has come out of Washington in this century abridging religious freedom in any way or granting to any single faith any discriminatory advantage. No impediments have been erected by Congress to the free flow of religious influence into political institutions. We can safely assert that the maintenance of religious liberty in the

United States is not at the present time a serious problem. It will become a serious problem only if some single church gains enough political and religious power to threaten our beneficent pluralism.

It is quite a different matter with the partial establishment of religion and the resultant violations of the principle of the separation of church and state. This is still a very critical issue, and it is becoming more critical with the growth of church power. The pressure on the government by churches for sectarian privilege is far stronger than any pressure on the churches by government for conformity. It can be truly said that the state is in need of protection from the church, not the church from the state.

No church is in deliberate opposition to the state, but the pressure of organized religion is automatically a pressure inspired with self-interest. Politicians are not prepared to resist it. For them, church support is a constant political temptation; they are offered sweet rewards without unpleasant responsibility. Since almost no one is against God, it is profitable to appear to be on God's side—which often means, in practice, on the side of some religious group that is asking for special favors. For powerful religious organizations, the temptation is even more compelling. The public treasury is there: why not partake of it? The public school is there: why not adapt it to promote religion? The majority of the people are professing Christians: why not use state machinery to maintain the Christian brand of Godliness?

The encroachments upon the neutral state during the last fifty years have not been massive or sensational. Each encroachment has been in the nature of a tiny erosion of the wall of separation between church and state, relatively insignificant in itself but meaningful as an indication of a trend. A "Pray for Peace" cancellation stamp on American mail is followed by an "under God" phrase in the pledge of allegiance to the flag and the adoption of "In God We Trust" as the national motto. No one wishes to protest against such sentimental gestures, but each gesture is used as a precedent for a more substantial favor. Hundreds of Protestant communities in the South are defying the Supreme Court's ruling that religion must not be taught in public classrooms, and several scores of Catholic communities in the Middle West are defying the same Court's ruling against the use of public money for sectarian schools by ironing their nun-directed "captive schools" into the public treasury.[1] Even a Senate committee directed by an outstanding liberal does not dare to expose these violations of the First Amendment for fear of the counter-charge of bigotry or hostility to religion.

The chief danger in the situation is not conscious, creeping secularism or conscious, creeping clericalism, but unconscious, creeping sentimentalism. The underpinning of America's policy of church-state separation is being eroded by goodhearted people with exalted moral motives who are willing to make step-by-step concessions in order to maintain religious peace and good will. Too often, the good will between established faiths is considered more important than the national policy of state neutrality which has made it possible for all sects to live together with comparative good will.

The public school is the institution most seriously threatened by the encroachments of sectarianism, both Catholic and Protestant. (There is no substantial Jewish threat to public school neutrality at the moment.) Its above-the-battle status in respect to religion irks the clerically minded of all sects. Its neutrality is condemned on two counts by our largest church, the Roman Catholic Church.

The first Catholic count against the public school is that elementary education must be suffused with religion in order to be good education, and the public schools neglect religion. The second count is that the public school should not monopolize public financial aid; rather, such aid should be awarded in equal measure to sectarian schools. These two counts in the Catholic indictment are made more serious by the hierarchy's open rejection of the line of demarcation that the Supreme Court has drawn between church and state in the public school.

The Protestant attitude toward public schools is in sharp

contrast. The major denominations of American Protestantism made possible the rise of the American public school in the nineteenth century by agreeing to send Protestant children to religiously neutral schools and by abandoning denominational plans for separate, sectarian systems. Sometimes nineteenth-century Protestantism intruded itself into public classrooms in a way that discredited its own claims to unselfishness; but on the whole, the Protestant churches remained true to the concept of public school independence.

Protestantism still stands firmly for the neutral school and against any use of public money for competing sectarian systems. But throughout the years there have been many signs that some groups within Protestantism wish to use the public schools for promoting Christian faith. Movements have begun in many cities for classes in "moral and spiritual values," and both Jewish and humanist parents have been disturbed by certain sectarian accompaniments of such programs. Many of the 68,000,000 people in America who do not belong to any church have watched with increasing dismay while the supposedly neutral public schools have yielded to both Catholic and Protestant pressure, and some parent-taxpayers have felt compelled to challenge these sectarian encroachments in the courts.

Here is a very delicate problem in social adjustment, and there is no single, dogmatic solution. Almost all citizens believe in the moral values inherent in the great religions. The differences arise when one party attempts to give these moral values a theological content. When anyone declares that "God" belongs in the public school, the citizen of a pluralistic society naturally inquires: Whose God? If it is not *his* God, he protests that he is not receiving equal protection under the First and Fourteenth Amendments, and he may be perfectly correct in this claim.

On the whole, the American Protestant churches recognize the delicacy of the situation in a nation which is predominantly Protestant in orientation, and they are using their power with great circumspection in most communities. The latest unofficial study report, "Christians and Public Schools," issued by the Committee on Religion and Public Education of the National Council, firmly opposes any grant of tax funds to sectarian schools, and just as firmly declares against "religion expressed in sectarian, theological, doctrinal, dogmatic, or ecclesiastical terms" in public classrooms.[2] When sectarian, theological, doctrinal, dogmatic and ecclesiastical religion are all excluded from public classrooms, there is not much left but the moral dedication to ideals, which even humanists can also accept.

But Protestantism is not quite willing to reduce its claim to this purely moral level. While asking for obedience to the Supreme Court in its definition of the boundary line between church and state, the authors of "Christians and Public Schools" favor the inclusion of material *about* religion in the public school. Few persons will question this concept if properly administered. They then suggest not only high school credit for outside Bible classes but the possibility that "where sensitively and skillfully done, and when [done] by common consent, the class or school can include a prayer, a Scripture reading or similar and appropriate religious observance."

Can such religious manifestations be "sensitively and skillfully done" in one part of the country without undermining the whole concept of the neutral public school throughout the whole country? The difficult answer, I believe, must be made by the American people through conscientious support of the national policy laid down by the Supreme Court. In the nature of our democracy, only the Constitution as interpreted by the Court can adequately guarantee the continuing neutrality of the public school, and the Constitution itself cannot protect our public institutions unless the people believe in it and insist that its principles be applied without fear or favor.

Many citizens' first reaction to the suggestion that the federal government should protect the public school from clerical encroachments is that such a task is not Washington's business. It belongs by law and custom to local and state governments. The local control of education is one of the most basic principles of our democracy.

Technically the rejoinder is correct, and, fortunately, the great majority of American state and local governments are enforcing the American policy of church-state separation conscientiously and successfully without federal help. But federal intervention to maintain constitutional rights is often most necessary in the very situations in which local governments are most powerful. Power makes partisanship more dangerous. If strong local governments happen to be partisan, racially or religiously, a racial or religious minority may be quite helpless. That has been one lesson of the American experience in trying to maintain equal protection for Negroes in segregated public school districts in the South. The same lesson can be derived from the three great Supreme Court cases which comprise America's charter of church-state separation—the Everson, New Jersey, bus case; the McCollum case on religious instruction; and the Zorach case on released time.

In each of these three famous cases involving religious encroachment on the neutrality of the public school, Washington, through the Supreme Court, was obliged to step into a local community and draw the line between church and state in public education in a way that would guarantee equal protection to the believer and the unbeliever. Without federal intervention, many citizens would have lost their constitutional rights. The Court forbade religious instructions in public classrooms and all expenditure of public funds for the central activities of sectarian schools. It permitted, under careful restrictions, public expenditures for sectarian buses and released-time religious classes away from public school buildings. The American people accepted this federal intervention in spite of our long tradition of the local control of public schools, since the intervention seemed necessary to protect religious freedom and prevent religious favoritism.

Several writers in this field have recently suggested that government policy on religion and the public schools could well be left in part to local determination, with full freedom to permit practices that are now rated unconstitutional.[3] The consequences of such an exercise of local autonomy might be quite chaotic in certain regions. Catholic-dominated regions might install a virtually Catholic "public" school system—that feat has been accomplished in quite a number of Midwestern communities—and some Protestant-dominated regions would no doubt follow suit in imitation. Local schools would become forensic and political arenas for sectarian competition. The resulting educational fragmentation and conflict might be a cultural disaster of the first magnitude. The public school system as we know it might cease to be a primary cultural force in many parts of the country.

Such alarmist words are not purely speculative. The nightmare of a fragmented educational system divided along denominational lines is a reality in many of the leading nations of the West. When Lord Bryce, in 1884, expressed his pleasure in finding in America a nation without an established church, and when he contrasted our relative peace with the bloody record of those European nations where church and state have engaged in continuous warfare, he was describing a permanent difference between the old world and the new. And perhaps the most important factor in maintaining that difference has been the religious neutrality of our common schools. This neutrality has made possible the spread of tolerance to other institutions in our society. Children who learn to live together in their formative years without religious distinctions are prepared as adults to build a more cooperative world. They do not think of themselves as living in a sectarian society within our larger democratic society. Their pluralistic public school becomes for them a training ground for a good society.

Europe and Canada have endured much agony because, unlike the United States, they have not had the non-sectarian principle built into their systems of publicly supported education.

England, which for many years has granted sectarian schools approximately 95 per cent of their total costs out of the public treasury, has recently, after a bitter struggle, increased the proportion a little through larger building grants. In spite of their great community service, the English sectarian schools have divided the people along creedal lines and have long delayed the development of an adequate public school system. In some Canadian provinces the experience has been just as unfortunate. With school systems in four provinces supported out of public revenue and divided into public schools and "separate" schools—the Protestant schools are "separate" in Quebec, and the Catholic schools are "separate" in Ontario—a deep cultural division in the population has been accentuated.

France and Belgium have been torn for fifty years by the struggle between public and sectarian educational systems, both supported out of public revenue. Most significant of all, the Netherlands, a predominantly non-Catholic country, has been split three ways by its policy of "separate but equal" treatment for sectarian and public schools. Today four out of five Dutch children attend Catholic and Protestant schools, while most of the public schools are left to the anti-clerical socialists. The cultural cleavage begun in the schools has spread through the whole life of the nation, with Catholic and Protestant political parties and Catholic and Protestant labor unions[4] continuing the divisive tendencies among adults. A Catholic worker who joins a non-Catholic labor union is excommunicated. According to a Rotterdam dispatch to Religious News Service, "A Catholic Chess Association has been formed here among correspondence chess players. To insure the Catholic character of the Association, the players are under obligation to say prayers for each other."

The neutral public school will not, of course, guarantee a tolerant society, nor does a sectarian system necessarily produce intolerance. England is probably more religiously tolerant than the United States in spite of its divided school systems, but that is partly because the population is relatively homogeneous. The United States, with a great diversity of religious and ethnic groups, is in far greater need of neutralism in public education and government than are most European countries. Our ethnic divisions need to be softened and neutralized in the amalgam of a cultural institution which includes all creeds—as well as all races.

The mere development of "good relations" among adults of Catholic, Protestant and Jewish faith is not enough to produce a genuinely cooperative society without the underlying experience of growing up together which the public school alone makes possible. Unfortunately, this elementary lesson is not taught in our public schools themselves. They refuse to blow their own trumpets.

While anti-public-school doubts are drummed into the heads of parochial school students through such phrases as "Godless education," there is no corresponding emphasis in public schools on the triumph and significance of democratic education offered free of charge without discrimination to children of all creeds. Most American children go through the public schools with no appreciation of the American policy of church-state separation as it applies to education. One of the first necessities in defending the American tradition would seem to be the insertion into the public school curriculum of a clear and simplified version of the Supreme Court's position on this subject.

It sounds trite to say that the only answer to the sectarian pressure against the American policy of church-state separation is the eternal vigilance of citizens who believe in the Constitution. But it *is* the only answer. Even a Supreme Court cannot defend the Constitution without massive popular support.

We have chosen freedom in pluralism, and it has been maintained in our society with remarkable success. But its maintenance is not automatic. We are surrounded by nations that have chosen religious favoritism as a way of life, and a large bloc of citizens within our republic can easily be led to champion a partial union of church and state in the name of piety and exclusive truth. To counteract such influences there must be a great body of affirmative belief in the neutral state as the only good society for free men. That affirmative belief must make itself felt in Washington by organized expression. It scarcely seems necessary to say that citizens who hold this belief should not speak primarily as Protestants, Catholics or Jews but simply as Americans committed to a national ideal.

In striving to secure the ingredients of this good, pluralistic society, there are certain purposes and aims upon which most citizens of all faiths can agree:

We want complete religious freedom to preach, teach, proselyte or deny, together with the right to operate sectarian school systems or to denounce them as divisive.

We want continuing legal equality among all sects, with no legal preference of any sort.

We want the public school to remain a neutral institution open to the children of all creeds and of no creed, without discrimination or sectarian promotion.

We want no new types of public appropriations for sectarian purposes; the present drift in that direction has already gone beyond the proper functional limits of a neutral state.

We want no religious or anti-religious political parties.

We want no citizen to be excluded from public office or elected to public office merely because of his religious faith.

Having suggested these aspirations as a kind of citizens' code for the maintenance of the separation of church and state, I can think of no more inspiring plea for their attainment than the words of Justice Frankfurter in the McCollum case:

Separation means separation, not something less. Jefferson's metaphor in describing the relation between Church and State speaks of a "wall of separation," not of a fine line easily overstepped. The public school is at once the symbol of our democracy and the most pervasive means for promoting our common destiny.

In no activity of the State is it more vital to keep out divisive forces than in its schools, to avoid confusing, not to say fusing, what the Constitution sought to keep strictly apart. "The great American principle of eternal separation"—Elihu Root's phrase bears repetition—is one of the vital reliances of our Constitutional system for assuring unities among our people stronger than our diversities. It is the Court's duty to enforce this principle in its full integrity.

We renew our conviction that "we have staked the very existence of our country on the faith that complete separation between the state and religion is best for the state and best for religion."

Notes

The source material for a study of this kind consists largely of countless personal conversations and countless newspaper stories, and it would clutter up the record too much to identify such sources in all cases. I have been careful to identify sources when some important factual or theoretical issue is discussed; and in the chapter on "God, Man and the Supreme Court" I have appended many legal citations so that legal students may follow up the appropriate cases. In order to save space, I have occasionally bunched a number of references under one note. In general, where current documentation seemed advisable I have relied heavily upon the *Congressional Record*, the Religious News Service, the *New York Times*, and the *Washington Post*.

In the field of books, two works have been of immense value, Canon Stokes' three-volume *Church and State in the United States* and Leo Pfeffer's *Church, State and Freedom*. Several other books have been almost equally helpful, and I shall include them now in this list of abbreviated titles used in the Notes.

Annals—*Annals of the American Academy of Political and Social Science.*
CR—*Congressional Record.*
Canon Law—T. Lincoln Bouscaren and Adam C. Ellis, *Canon Law, Text and Commentary*, Bruce Publishing Company, 1946.
Catholic Almanac—*National Catholic Almanac, 1959*, Doubleday.
Ebersole—Luke Ebersole, *Church Lobbying in the Nation's Capital*, Macmillan, 1951.
Konvitz—Milton R. Konvitz, *Fundamental Liberties of a Free People*, Cornell University Press, 1957.
NYT—*New York Times.*
Pfeffer—Leo Pfeffer, *Church, State and Freedom*, Beacon, 1953.
RNS—Religious News Service.
Stokes—Anson Phelps Stokes, *Church and State in the United States*, Harper, 1950.
WP—*Washington Post and Times Herald.*
Yearbook—Benson Y. Landis, editor, *Yearbook of American Churches for 1959*, National Council of Churches, 1958.

Chapter I

Personal Prologue: The Church-State Battle Front

1. *The Jewish Yearbook* of 1959 estimated the Jewish population of the United States at 5,260,000; that of Israel at 1,789,000; and of New

223

York City, 2,018,000. *The Catholic Almanac, 1959* estimated the Catholic population of Brazil at 57,660,000; Italy, 48,058,500; France, 36,-935,000; and the United States, 35,868,900. The Brazil figures indicate baptisms, but many Catholic authorities have estimated that only about 10 per cent of the Brazilian people practice Catholicism; and similar estimates have been made that about 20 per cent of the people of France practice Catholicism. In view of the well-known Catholic defections in Italy, and the above estimates, it is probable that the United States today has the largest number of practicing Catholics, Protestants and Jews among all the nations. For financial statements about American Catholic contributions, see Bernard Wall, *The Vatican Story,* Harper, 1957, p. 127.

Chapter II

"One Nation Under God"

1. CR, August 20, 1958, p. A746.
2. Stokes, III, p. 596.
3. *Zorach v. Clauson,* 343 U.S. 306 (1952).
4. The estimate is that of the American Association of Fund-Raising Counsel, as published in the *Register,* national Catholic weekly of Denver, February 2, 1958.
5. See analysis of "Characteristics of American Organized Religion" by Winfred E. Garrison in a special issue of the *Annals,* March 1948, on "Organized Religion in the United States"; also Stokes, I, p. 229.
6. Bureau of the Census, *Population Report,* February 2, 1958.
7. For all formal membership figures I have used the *Yearbook,* which secures its estimates from each denomination, and the *National Catholic Directory.* For comparative purposes I have assumed a Catholic population in the United States of 36,000,000 in a national population of 175,000,000. Both figures are shifting constantly, and all church figures are nothing but rough approximations, in view of the absence of a religious census.
8. WP, January 3, 1959.
9. *Catholic Almanac,* p. 411.
10. *Time,* October 15, 1956, based on National Council of Churches figures.
11. Statement by Protestant Council, NYT, April 26, 1959.
12. See, for example, Lawrence H. Fuchs, *The Political Behavior of American Jews,* Free Press (Glencoe, Ill.), 1956.
13. Samuel A. Stouffer, *Communism, Conformity and Civil Liberties,* Doubleday, 1955, p. 32.
14. CR, April 2, 1948. Representative John W. McCormack has coined the phrase "atheistic capitalism" to describe those phases of the business system which he does not like.
15. *America,* April 2, 1955.
16. CR, April 2, 1958.

17. See Stokes, III, pp. 129 ff., for a good discussion of Congressional chaplaincies.
18. See CR, July 23, 1956, p. 12686. A history of the new motto was in NYT, July 7, 1956.
19. *Lewis v. Allen*, 159 N.Y.S. 2d 807; see also *Catholic Lawyer*, Autumn 1957.
20. Report of the International Cooperation Administration, Advisory Committee on Voluntary Foreign Aid, November 10, 1958. See also *National Council Outlook*, June 1958.
21. *Christian Century*, June 18, 1958.
22. *Hughes v. Priest*, District of Columbia Court of Appeals, dismissed May 1956.
23. In a delightful article by Dr. Miller, "Piety Along the Potomac," *Reporter*, August 17, 1954. See also Leo Pfeffer's article on "Blasphemy on the Potomac," *Christian* (now *Unitarian*) *Register*, March 1955.
24. Alexander Miller, *The Renewal of Man*, Doubleday, 1955, p. 168.
25. Norman Cousins has much interesting material on Jefferson in his *In God We Trust*, Harper, 1958.
26. Stokes, I, p. 501.
27. See WP, March 3, 1959, District Commissioners' census report.
28. Louis J. Putz, editor, *The Catholic Church U.S.A.*, Fides (Chicago), 1956, p. 174.
29. WP, January 1, 1959.
30. The N.A.E. includes about forty of the smaller Protestant denominations, the largest of which is the Assemblies of God, with headquarters in Springfield, Missouri. The N.A.E. headquarters are in Wheaton, Illinois. The organization has an efficient office in Washington, but its affiliates are not strong in this area.
31. *National Council Outlook*, September 1956.
32. See "Taste and the Censor in Television" by Charles Winick, Fund for the Republic pamphlet.
33. Brooklyn *Tablet*, March 1, 1958.

Chapter III

God, Man and the Supreme Court

1. Fred Rodell, *Woe Unto You Lawyers*, Reynal and Hitchcock, 1939, pp. 72 and 35.
2. The oath, administered under Title 28 of the U.S. Code, is not strong enough to suit Senator Thurmond of South Carolina, who has suggested a stronger one. To compel a justice to acknowledge God would violate the phrase in Article VI of the Constitution which forbids any religious test as a qualification for office.
3. Catholic justices and their periods of service have been: Roger B. Taney (1836-1864); Edward D. White (1894-1921); Joseph McKenna (1898-1925); Pierce Butler (1922-1939); Frank Murphy (1940-1949); William

J. Brennan, Jr. (1956-   ). Jewish justices have been: Louis D. Brandeis (1916-1939); Benjamin N. Cardozo (1932-1938); Felix Frankfurter (1939-   ). A breezy and informative discussion of the Court is *Marble Palace* by John P. Frank, Knopf, 1958. The writings of Anthony Lewis in the *New York Times* are always informative, especially NYT, October 26, 1958.

4. In 1959 Representative John W. McCormack, chief Catholic spokesman on Capitol Hill, solicited the attendance of non-Catholic as well as Catholic officials at this Mass on his official House stationery. The publicity in the Catholic press has given the occasion the appearance of a state function. Eisenhower was the first President to attend a Red Mass while in office. Governor Rockefeller attended a similar Mass in Albany in February 1959.

5. The two key decisions were 295 U.S. 495 and 301 U.S. 1. The shift in view is discussed by Robert Carr in *The Supreme Court and Judicial Review*, Farrar and Rinehart, 1942.

6. In his *The Nature of the Judicial Process*, Yale, 1922, p. 65.

7. In *West Virginia v. Barnette*, 319 U.S. 624.

8. *Roth v. United States*, 354 U.S. 476 (1957); and *Kingsley Books Inc. v. Brown*, 354 U.S. 436 (1957). A scholarly analysis of Brennan's record is "Mr. Justice Brennan and His Legal Philosophy" by Francis P. McQuade and Alexander T. Kardos in *Notre Dame Lawyer*, May 1958.

9. *Buck v. Bell*, 274 U.S. 200. The Catholic rule on eugenic sterilization is expressed by Monsignor Francis J. Connell, former dean of the School of Sacred Theology at the Catholic University, in his *Morals in Politics and Professions*, Newman (Westminster, Md.), 1946, p. 33: ". . . in those states which now prescribe or permit eugenic sterilization for certain types of defectives and criminals, no circumstances can justify a judge in giving a decision that the law should be put in operation."

10. *Bradfield v. Roberts*, 175 U.S. 291 (1899).

11. *Cochran v. Louisiana State Board of Education*, 281 U.S. 370 (1930).

12. *McCollum v. Board of Education*, 33 U.S. 203. A recent book lauding the record of Justice Reed is *Justice Reed and the First Amendment* by F. William O'Brien, S.J., Georgetown University Press, 1958. It has an unusually good bibliography in this field. Vashti McCollum has told her own story in *One Woman's Fight*, Beacon, 1952.

13. *Zorach v. Clauson*, 342 U.S. 306 (1952).

14. See Philip Williams, *Politics in Post-War France*, Longmans, Green, 1958.

15. Vol. II, p. 695.

16. See Stokes, II, pp. 722 ff., for discussion of proposed amendment, and the 1958 work *The Presidential Election of 1880* by Herbert J. Clancy, S.J., Loyola (Chicago), 1958, for a discussion of Garfield. Garfield fought against an appropriation of $25,000 to a Catholic hospital in Washington, stating that "the divorce between church and state should be absolute."

17. In *Cantwell v. Connecticut*, 310 U.S. 296 (1940). See Konvitz, Appendix, "Adoption of the Bill of Rights"; Pfeffer, Chapters 4 and 5;

and for a Catholic interpretation of constitutional history, the article "Law or Prepossessions?" by Father John Courtney Murray in *Law and Contemporary Problems* (Duke University), Winter 1949.

18. *Washington Ethical Culture Society v. District of Columbia,* 249 Fed. 2d 127. See also *Fellowship of Humanity v. County of Alameda,* 315 Pac. 2d 349 (Calif. App. 2d [1957]).

19. *Watson v. Jones,* 80 U.S. 679 (1872). The decision on *Lady Chatterley's Lover* was *Kingsley Pictures Corp. v. N.Y. Board of Regents,* 360 U.S. 684.

20. See the interesting discussion on church status by Professor Howe, Leo Pfeffer and others in Volume I of the *Conference Proceedings* of "The Institute of Church and State" of Villanova University, 1958.

21. *Kedroff v. St. Nicholas Cathedral,* 344 U.S. 94 (1952). See discussion in Konvitz, pp. 92 ff. The Pittsburgh case cited was *St. Peter's Roman Catholic Parish v. Urban,* 394 Pa. 194, 146 Atl. 2d 724 (1958); denied certiorari May 4, 1959, No. 749.

22. *Pierce v. Society of Sisters,* 268 U.S. 510 (1925).

23. *Cantwell v. Connecticut,* 310 U.S. 296. The limits of religious freedom for Witnesses are also discussed in several other important cases, notably *Prince v. Massachusetts,* 321 U.S. 158 (1944), and *Marsh v. State of Alabama,* 326 U.S. 501 (1946). The Fund for the Republic's pamphlet of 1958, "Religion and the Free Society," contains a popular legal discussion of this area, with citations. See also Wesley McCune's *The Nine Young Men,* Harper, 1947.

24. *Burstyn v. Wilson,* 343 U.S. 495 (1952).

25. *First Unitarian Church of Los Angeles v. County of Los Angeles,* 357 U.S. 545. The principles are more completely discussed in the companion case, *Speiser v. Randall,* 357 U.S. 513.

26. *Reynolds v. U.S.,* 98 U.S. 145 (1878). The other important Mormon polygamy case is *Davis v. Beason,* 133 U.S. 333 (1890). RNS of November 10, 1955, reported that a Utah fundamentalist Mormon mother, deprived of the custody of her children by a juvenile court, would appeal on the ground that she had a religious right to teach them the moral validity of polygamy.

27. See *Bunn v. North Carolina,* 336 U.S. 942 (1949).

28. *Kissinger v. U.S.,* 356 U.S. 958 (1958); facts in 250 Fed. 2d 940.

29. *Jacobson v. Massachusetts,* 197 U.S. 11 (1905); and a later case, *Dunham v. Board of Education,* 154 Ohio St. 469; certiorari denied, 341 U.S. 915.

30. *U.S. v. Ballard,* 322 U.S. 78 (1944), and *Ballard v. U.S.,* 329 U.S. 187 (1946).

31. *Boston Herald,* July 30, 1958.

32. *Labrenz v. Illinois,* 104 N.E. 2d 769 (1951), certiorari denied, 344 U.S. 824.

33. *Minersville School District v. Gobitis,* 310 U.S. 586 (1940).

34. *West Virginia v. Barnette,* 319 U.S. 624 (1943). Henry Steele Commager in his *Majority Rule and Minority Rights,* Oxford, 1943, a book dedicated to Justice Frankfurter, ably defends Frankfurter's view, emphasizing the point that "the place to meet, and to defeat, unwise

or unconstitutional legislation is in the legislature or in the arena of public opinion."

35. Two key cases are *Presiding Bishop v. City of Porterville,* 338 U.S. 939 (1949), 90 Cal. App. 2d 563; and *Wisconsin Lutheran High School v. Sinar,* 349 U.S. 913 (1955), 65 N.W. 2d 563. Two 1956 state zoning cases in New York were decided in favor of religious groups by the state's highest court, *Diocese of Rochester v. Planning Board,* 1 N.Y. 2d 508, 136 N.E. 2d 827; and *Matter of Community Synagogue v. Bates,* 1 N.Y. 2d 445. See 70 *Harvard Law Review* 1428 (1957) for summary; also *Notre Dame Lawyer,* May 1958. For background discussion of principles see Pfeffer, p. 563. In the latest zoning case the Supreme Court by denying certiorari indirectly supported a planning ordinance, in *Milwaukee Company of Jehovah's Witnesses v. Mullen,* 330 Pac. 2d 5 (1958); denied certiorari, May 4, 1959, No. 767.

36. *Boston Pilot,* June 27, 1959; the case was *Crown Kosher Super Market v. Gallagher,* May 1959, now on appeal. Pfeffer has a good discussion of Sunday laws; see also his *Creeds in Competition,* Harper, 1959, p. 111. For an older, documented treatment by Seventh Day Adventists, see *Separation of Church and State in the United States* by Alvin W. Johnson and Frank H. Yost, Minnesota, 1948. Stokes, III, pp. 153 ff. has a substantial historical treatment.

37. *Matter of Rupp,* 33 App. Div. 468.

38. In *The Wall of Separation Between Church and State,* Beacon, 1951, p. 174. This important book has not received the attention it deserves.

39. *Soon Hing v. Crowley,* 113 U.S. 703 (1885).

40. *People v. Friedman,* 302 N. Y. 75 (1950); and *Friedman v. New York,* 341 U.S. 907 (1951), in which the appeal was dismissed for want of a substantial federal question.

41. The Court's denial of certiorari to an Ohio plaintiff came on December 8, 1958, in the case of *Ohio v. Ullner,* 167 U.S. 521, 150 N.E. 2d 413, in which the American Civil Liberties Union filed an amicus brief.

42. Stokes, III, p. 421. Pfeffer's discussion, pp. 183 ff., is comprehensive. See also 49 *Columbia Law Review* 968 (1949) for source material. The 1885 case is at 116 U.S. 404.

43. *Lundberg v. Alameda County,* 286 Pac. 2d 1; appeal dismissed, 352 U.S. 921. In this case California's highest court said that not a single case could be found in American law which declared that tax exemption for churches violated the no-establishment principle.

44. RNS, December 1955, published the statement by the executive director of the National Council's Department of Benevolences that Protestant, Roman Catholic and Jewish institutions received more than $200,000,000 in bequests in the past ten years.

45. *Selective Draft Law Cases of 1918,* 245 U.S. 366.

46. See, for example, *United States v. Macintosh,* 283 U.S. 605 (1931).

47. *Everson v. Board of Education,* 330 U.S. 1; *McCollum v. Board of Education,* 333 U.S. 203; *Zorach v. Clauson,* 342 U.S. 306. A legal volume, partly in this field, is *Political and Civil Rights in the United States* by Thomas I. Emerson and David Haber, Dennis and Co. (Buffalo), 1958.

48. *The Catholic Almanac,* p. 469, lists these seventeen states as states in which "some non-public school students ride on public school buses": California, Colorado, Connecticut, Illinois, Indiana, Kansas, Kentucky, Louisiana, Maryland, Massachusetts, Michigan, New Hampshire, New Jersey, New Mexico, New York, Oregon, and Rhode Island. In many of these states parochial school children are picked up only if they live along established routes to public schools. Hawaii permits the practice in some counties.

49. Many states have language more strict than the federal Constitution prohibiting such services as bus transportation for sectarian schools, and they have rejected any attempt to make the Supreme Court's permissive decision in the Everson case a mandate to alter their own practices. The highest court of the state of Washington in *Visser v. Nooksack Valley School District,* 207 Pac. 2d 198 (1949), refusing to permit state funds to be used for sectarian buses, said of the Everson decision of the Supreme Court: "Although the decisions of the United States Supreme Court are entitled to the highest consideration as they bear on related questions before this court, we must, in the light of the clear provisions of our state constitution and our decisions thereunder, respectfully disagree with those portions of the Everson majority opinion which might be construed, in the abstract, as stating that transportation, furnished at public expense, to children attending religious schools, is not *in support* of such schools." The most valuable statutory summary of state laws in this area is *The State and Non Public Schools,* published by the Office of Education in 1958. See also Document Miscellaneous No. 27, 1956, of the Office of Education, "Pupil Transportation."

50. *Bradfield v. Roberts,* 175 U.S. 291 (1899).

51. *Cochran v. Louisiana State Board,* 281 U.S. 370.

52. *Catholic World,* April 1955.

53. As stated by the Catholic bishops of the United States in "The Christian in Action," a long official pronouncement reprinted in full in the *New York Times* of November 21, 1948. The bishops declared that "in the McCollum case the majority opinions pay scant attention to logic, history or the accepted norms of legal interpretation." (Text in *National Catholic Almanac,* 1949, pp. 86 ff.) The *Catholic Almanac* has carried in many annual editions a summary of the Catholic position which includes the following introductory paragraphs:

"In the United States the use of local, state and federal funds to support denominational schools is prohibited by law. State constitutions and laws explicitly forbid state tax aid to any school giving sectarian instruction. The U.S. Supreme Court has ruled that the First Amendment to the U.S. Constitution prohibits federal aid to sectarian schools.

"Catholic authorities maintain that these laws are unjust and discriminatory because they arbitrarily deny tax aid to schools which, like the public schools, prepare children for the responsibilities of citizenship. They see no reason why the inclusion of religious instruction in a school's curriculum should deprive it of tax support so long as the school complies fully with all the requirements of compulsory education laws."

54. Perhaps the most powerful legal attacks at the time were published in Duke University's *Law and Contemporary Problems,* Winter 1949, with Father John Courtney Murray and Professor Edward S. Corwin of Princeton taking the critical side and Professor Milton Konvitz the defense. On the whole, this publication was loaded against the Supreme Court's point of view.

55. *Christianity and Crisis,* July 5, 1948.

56. CR, March 16, 1948, p. A1683.

57. CR, April 2, 1948, p. 4076.

58. *Religious Education,* January-February 1956.

59. F. William O'Brien, S.J., *Justice Reed and the First Amendment,* Georgetown University Press, 1958, p. 178. Some overemphasis on the concessions in the Zorach case has crept into the literature issued by the Fund for the Republic, which has published several pamphlets in the area of religion and education. In its pamphlet "Religion and the Free Society," Maximilian Kempner declares that the words of Justice Douglas "might serve to support a future holding that non-preferential aid to religious education is valid." Although the publications of the Fund in this area are scholarly and moderate in tone, the controlling personnel of its project "Religious Institutions in a Democratic Society" are almost unanimously committed against the Supreme Court's decision in the McCollum case. For an analysis of the past records of Fund representatives, see my article in *The Churchman,* March 1958.

60. The two standard cases in the religious field are *Massachusetts v. Mellon,* 262 U.S. 447 (1923), and *Doremus v. Board of Education,* 342 U.S. 429 (1952). Pfeffer's discussion of the principles is at p. 168, Konvitz' analysis of the Doremus case at p. 69. For a differing point of view see Sutherland, 62 *Harvard Law Review* 1306 (1949).

61. *Elliott v. White,* 23 Fed. 2d 997 (1928).

62. *Harris v. City of New York,* 357 U.S. 907 (1958), and *William Gart v. Cole,* Case No. 771 (1959).

63. *Maryland v. Baltimore Radio Show,* 338 U.S. 912 (1950); see also *U.S. v. Carver,* 260 U.S. 482 (1923).

64. Konvitz, p. 71.

65. For background facts in this area see *Research Bulletin* of the National Education Association, 1956, "The State and Sectarian Education"; an American Jewish Committee pamphlet of February 1958 on the rulings of state attorney generals; and Pfeffer, Chapter 11.

66. *Carden v. Bland,* 288 S.W. 2d 718.

Chapter IV

God, Man and Congress

1. Technically this is not a public document but a report to Congress by the Library of Congress.

2. CR, June 10, 1958, p. 9541.
3. CR, April 1, 1957, p. 4321.
4. Regulation of Lobbying Act, Public Law 601, Title II, 79th Congress. A valuable discussion of the recent operations of this law is that of Dr. Belle Zeller in a special issue of the *Annals,* September 1958, on "Unofficial Government." It is significant that this issue contains scarcely any mention of religious lobbies. Ebersole has written the standard work on religious lobbies, reviewing the facts up to 1950.
5. WP, October 5, 1958.
6. The National Council's Washington legislative newsletter is called *Memo.* It contains useful summaries of bills without recommendations. The *Congressional Quarterly* prepared for a number of Protestant denominations and boards a somewhat more editorialized summary of measures and votes by members of Congress called "The Christian Looks at the 85th Congress."
7. CR, August 20, 1958, p. 17369.
8. RNS, May 19, 1954, and August 10, 1954. See also article in *The Unitarian Register,* December 1958, by Harold Rafton. The Christian Amendment Movement has headquarters at 804 Penn Ave., Pittsburgh 21.
9. See NYT, August 31 and September 7, 1958; and my article in *The Christian Herald,* February 1958.
10. Holy Office decree of July 3, 1949, published in NYT, July 14, 1949. Later decree, NYT, April 14, 1959.
11. *The Secret Diary of Harold L. Ickes,* Simon and Schuster, 1954, II, p. 390.
12. CR, March 17, 1953. See *Hearings,* House Committee on Un-American Activities, July 21, 1953, and article in *Christian Century,* August 5, 1953, by Harold Fey. For a more hostile treatment of Bishop Oxnam see *United States News and World Report,* August 7, 1953. Bishop Oxnam has written his own story eloquently in a book, *I Protest,* Harper, 1954.
13. The most comprehensive treatment of the Matthews incident is in *The Progressive,* April 1954.
14. The action was described in American newspapers of November 22, 1958; a partial disclaimer by the National Council of Churches was contained in NYT, December 4, 1958. Protestant counter-attacks were published in *Time,* January 5, 1959. The Catholic criticism was featured in *America,* December 20, 1958; McCormack's attitude in CR, January 12, 1959, p. A85; while Dr. Harris' statement was in CR the same day at p. A90.
15. CR, May 6, 1959, p. 6798.
16. RNS, April 1, 1955.
17. Reinhold Niebuhr skillfully sifted out the true from the false rumors about this situation in an article on "Communism and the Clergy" in the Christian Century of August 19, 1953.
18. CR, April 23, 1917, p. 952.
19. In 1959 the American Legion estimated that there were 62 veterans in

the Senate, of whom 61 were members of the Legion, and 260 veterans in the House, of whom 240 were Legion members.

20. See Robert M. Miller, *American Protestantism and Social Issues,* University of North Carolina Press, 1958; also James H. Nichols, *History of Christianity,* Ronald, 1956, p. 408; Ray H. Abrams, *Preachers Present Arms,* Round Table Press (New York), 1933; and especially the historical summary by Stokes, III, Chapter XVI.

21. In this same year a constitutional amendment was proposed in a Senate hearing, Joint Resolution 45, 72nd Congress, beginning: "War for any purpose shall be illegal."

22. The Methodists took the lead, and they were supported by a 2 to 1 vote against compulsory military training by the executive committee of the Federal Council of Churches, in November 1947.

23. *Hearings,* House of Representatives Committee on Armed Services, January 30, 1959, p. 176.

24. Stokes, III, p. 295. The history and present status of conscientious objectors can best be appreciated by reading *Handbook for Conscientious Objectors,* published by the Central Committee for Conscientious Objectors, 2006 Walnut St., Philadelphia, Pa.; the monthly *Washington Newsletter* of the Friends Committee on National Legislation, 104 C St., Washington 2; and Stokes' long treatment in Vol. III.

25. *Hearings,* House Committee on Armed Services, January 30, 1959.

26. Loftus E. Becker, legal adviser of the State Department, wrote in 1957: "The United States . . . recognizes the fact that the Vatican City is a sovereign state." See my "The Papal Election and American Law," *Christian Century,* November 19, 1958.

27. See Ray A. Billington, *The Protestant Crusade, 1800-1860,* Rinehart, 1952, Chapters 15 and 16; and Gustavus Myers, *History of Bigotry in the United States,* Random House, 1943.

28. Both Stokes and Pfeffer discuss background facts. Early history is told in Leo F. Stock's *Consular Relations Between the United States and the Papal States,* Catholic University Press, 1933. A good brief summary is James Robert Gray's "Behind the Vatican Mission," *Christian Century,* October 19, 1949. See also "Truman and the Vatican," *Christian Century,* April 8, 1950.

29. My story from Rome about the Taylor mission was in *The Nation,* July 29, 1950; my discussion of the Vatican ambassador mission with Arthur Schlesinger, Jr., in *The Atlantic Monthly,* January 1952. The Catholic position is stated in a 1952 pamphlet published by America Press, "Diplomatic Relations with the Vatican" by Robert A. Graham, S.J., and Robert C. Hartnett, S.J.

30. The National Council's statement was in NYT, November 1, 1951.

31. CR, April 4, 1952, p. 3545.

32. My detailed discussion of these policies is contained in two articles, "The Case of Archbishop O'Hara," *Christian Century,* May 6, 1953, and "The Papal Election and American Law," *Christian Century,* November 19, 1958. The legal prohibition is contained in 8 U.S. Code 1481, where appropriate citations may be found.

33. CR, June 5, 1956, p. 8622.

34. See series of articles in *Wisconsin Law Review* by John P. Frank in 1941 and his book *Marble Palace,* Knopf, 1958. Alfred Lief's *Brandeis, A Personal History,* Stackpole (Harrisburg), 1936, tells of the opposition to Brandeis as a "radical" by seven former presidents of the American Bar Association.

35. *Hearings,* Senate Committee on the Judiciary, February 26-27, 1957.

36. From a series of articles by John Wicklein on the Churches and Segregation, NYT, July 1959.

37. In 1946 when the Council adopted the recommendation of its Commission on the Church and Minority Groups.

38. Published in CR, July 13, 1956, p. 11592. See *Christianity and Crisis,* March 3, 1958, for summary, "The Southern Churches and the Race Question." The Catholic bishops' statement on "Discrimination and the Christian Conscience" was issued November 14, 1958, and is contained in *Catholic Almanac,* p. 105. The Catholic teaching on miscegenation is contained in *Moral Problems of Interracial Marriage* by Father Joseph F. Doherty, Catholic University Press, 1949. Many valuable documents summarizing Catholic social policies in the United States and Europe are in the gigantic symposium *Church and Society,* edited by Joseph N. Moody and published with the Imprimatur of Cardinal Spellman by Arts, Inc. (New York), 1953. See especially "American Catholicism and the Socio-Economic Evolution in U.S.A." by Francis Downing.

39. Arthur Schlesinger, *The Rise of the City,* Macmillan, 1933, p. 355. For early Catholic attitudes on the liquor traffic see also Robert D. Cross, *The Emergence of Liberal Catholicism in America,* Harvard, 1958, pp. 124 ff.

40. *Canon Law,* 118-120. The California suit described was filed under the trade name of the De La Salle Institute; it was Civil Action 7499, District Court for the Northern District of California, Northern Division, January 17, 1957, and amended. The suit for a refund was withdrawn after P.O.A.U. asked to intervene on the government's side, and then re-instated later.

41. The facts are summarized in NYT, December 7, 1958. Mississippi's farcical "prohibition" is described in NYT, May 11, 1959.

42. *Hearings,* Senate Committee on Interstate Commerce, April 22-30, 1958.

43. *Register,* May 11, 1958.

44. *Federal Council Bulletin,* January 1939. The Catholic attitude on gambling was summarized in an article on "Bingo, Morality and the Criminal Law" in the *Catholic Lawyer,* No. 1, 1955. The conclusion reached was that "the wisdom and prudence of operating bingo for humanitarian purposes should be left to the discretion of the administrators of religious, charitable and fraternal organizations and the criminal law should control but not prohibit bingo under such auspices." But Catholic Archbishop Rummel of New Orleans banned bingo in his diocesan churches in 1956, and there is some Catholic opposition to the game.

45. Such gambling is illegal under Title 22, Section 1504, of the District of Columbia Code.

46. The 1956 hearings were on May 9 and 10, 1956; the 1958 hearings were before the Senate Agriculture and Forestry Committee in April. For Orthodox Jewish opposition see NYT, April 24 and 30, 1958, and also NYT May 4, 1958. See CR, February 4, 1958; and for Jewish criticism of Orthodox Jewish attitudes, the *Jewish Newsletter*, June 2, 1958.

47. In the Frelinghuysen bill, H.R. 4267, 86th Congress, 1st session.

48. For example, *Canon Law*, p. 574; the statement already cited in the *Catholic Almanac* of 1949 by the Catholic bishops; Father John Courtney Murray's article on "Law or Prepossessions?" in *Law and Contemporary Problems*, Winter 1949; *Freedom of Choice in Education* by Father Virgil C. Blum, S.J., Macmillan, 1958, the essence of which was published in *United States News and World Report*, October 25, 1957; "Roadblocks to Federal Aid" by Father William E. McManus, *America*, October 29, 1949; "A National Educational Policy" (pamphlet) by Archbishop Karl J. Alter of Cincinnati, 1956; "Federal Aid to Education" (pamphlet) by Robert C. Hartnett, S.J., America Press. Pius XII established the official policy in characteristically oblique language on September 15, 1951, in his "address to Teaching Sisters" when he asked that legislators throughout the world should see that Catholic schools "be not placed in a worse condition than the state schools."

49. John C. Bennett, *Christians and the State,* Scribner, 1958, p. 246. The official National Council statement on this subject was made at Evanston, May 19, 1954, opposing all federal aid except to public schools.

50. Leo Pfeffer, *Creeds in Competition*, p. 89.

51. In *America*, November 16, 1957. See reply by Rabbi Nathan Perilman, *America*, January 11, 1958. See also Herberg's article in *Commentary*, November 1952, and replies thereto in issue of January 1953.

52. RNS, December 5, 1955.

53. CR, October 11, 1949, pp. 14280 ff. Conrad Moehlman in *Wall of Separation Between Church and State*, Beacon, 1951, summarizes the Barden bill, p. xv. The Roosevelt-Spellman correspondence is reprinted and discussed in my *Communism, Democracy and Catholic Power*, Beacon, 1951. Pfeffer's section on federal aid is invaluable—pp. 478 ff.

54. CR, April 1, 1948.

55. *Hearings* on Federal Aid, Senate subcommittee, April 25, 1947. His testimony in 1949 was before the House Committee on Education and Labor on June 3. Kennedy's bill was H.R. 5838, 81st Congress, 1st session, introduced August 1, 1949. It provided for $300,000,000 annually to be distributed among states, of which 10 per cent was to go for auxiliary services for schools. It arranged to by-pass state prohibitions in order to provide for these auxiliary services for private schools by direct grants when necessary. It was defeated in committee.

56. NYT, January 5, 1958.

57. *America*, May 9, 1959.

58. Brooklyn *Tablet* (N.C.W.C. dispatch), May 9, 1959.

59. *Register,* January 4, 1959.
60. CR, January 16, 1957.
61. Officially the Hospital Survey and Construction Act of the 79th Congress. More than half of the total appropriations under this act have gone to non-sectarian hospitals.

Chapter V

God, Man and the Presidency

1. Sidney Hyman has listed nine tests for Presidential hopefuls in the *New York Times Magazine,* January 4, 1959.
2. The abuses in regard to tax exemption on unrelated business income of religious organizations, ranging from radio stations to distilleries, come under Section 511 of the Internal Revenue Code, as interpreted in a regulation published in the *Federal Register,* January 21, 1956. The abuses in income tax exemption, even for nuns who are public school teachers, come under Section 170 of the Code, as misinterpreted by an irrelevant Tax Court decision of 1949, *L. F. Ratterman v. Commissioner of Internal Revenue,* 177 Fed. 2d 204. See my testimony at House hearings on internal revenue taxation, November 19, 1956, and January 27, 1958. The dangers of excessive tax exemption for churches were emphasized in an important article in *Christianity Today,* August 3, 1959, by Eugene Carson Blake, former president of the National Council of Churches. He advocated the repeal of all exemption from corporate profits taxes for all churches engaged in business acitivity not related to the purpose or activity of the church itself.
3. Charles O'Conor, a New York Catholic lawyer, was nominated by the "straight" Democratic National Convention at Louisville in 1872, but Grant and Horace Greeley were the two leading candidates, and O'Conor polled less than 30,000 votes nationally.
4. See *Lincoln and the Preachers* by Edgar DeWitt Jones, Harper, 1948, p. 180. Only three of Springfield's twenty-six ministers supported him. When he was described as an "infidel" in the Congressional campaign of 1846, he issued a handbill saying: "I have never denied the truth of the Scriptures, and I have never spoken with intentional disrespect of religion in general or of any denomination of Christians in particular." But he admitted that he belonged to no church, and he gave no affirmative assurances of belief. (Lincoln's *Collected Works,* II, p. 382.)
5. A complete list of Presidents by denominations is contained in Ernest B. Fincher's *The President of the United States,* Abelard-Schuman, 1955.
6. See *Annals,* March 1948, and Stokes.
7. See Lawrence H. Fuchs, *The Political Behavior of American Jews,* Free Press (Glencoe, Ill.), 1956, for this and much other valuable material.
8. See James M. King, *Facing the Twentieth Century,* p. 270. This very

partisan book, published in 1899 by the American Union League Society, is an interesting exhibit of a certain type of anti-Catholicism in the 1890's. The author was an active participant in the struggle.

9. King, who helped to arrange the affair, tells the inside story. Stokes, II, has another version.

10. *The Life and Times of William Howard Taft* by Henry Pringle, Farrar and Rinehart, 1939, I, p. 45.

11. *Letters of Archie Butt,* Doubleday, 1924, p. 298.

12. *Theodore Roosevelt* by Henry Pringle, Harcourt, Brace, 1956, p. 362.

13. See *Catholic Encyclopedia,* "Excommunication." The marriage rule and its American application are discussed under Canon 1094 in *Canon Law,* pp. 516 ff.

14. See *Catholic World,* January 1959, and James F. Byrnes, *All in One Lifetime,* Harper, 1958.

15. *Catholic News,* June 30, 1928.

16. *Ibid.,* February 18, 1928.

17. Among many accounts of the Klan, perhaps the best known is Gustavus Myers' *History of Bigotry in the United States,* Random House, 1943. See also Edmund A. Moore, *A Catholic Runs for President,* Ronald, 1956.

18. *Atlantic Monthly,* April 1927. Marshall's reasoning was developed into a book, *The Roman Catholic Church and the Modern State,* Dodd, Mead, 1931.

19. *Atlantic Monthly,* May 1927.

20. Norman Hapgood and Henry Moskowitz, *Up From the City Streets,* Harcourt, Brace, 1927, and Father Edward M. Connors, *Church-State Relationships in Education in the State of New York,* Catholic University, 1951.

21. Moehlman, *Wall of Separation Between Church and State,* Beacon, 1951, p. 50.

22. *The 1928 Campaign* by Roy V. Peel and Thomas C. Donnelly, New York University Bookstore, 1931, p. 112. Oscar Handlin's *Al Smith and His America,* Little, Brown, 1958, has many illuminating details of the campaign. Ogburn's analysis was summarized in NYT, January 19, 1930.

23. *Canon Law,* pp. 704 and 517.

24. *Atlantic Monthly,* February 1928.

25. *Christian Century,* May 14, 1956, and June 25, 1958.

26. *Catholic News,* June 30, 1928.

27. *Ibid.,* August 25, 1928.

28. *Ibid.,* April 21, 1928.

29. *Ibid.,* January 21, February 4 and March 31, 1928.

30. *Ibid.,* August 25, 1928.

31. October 11, 1928.

32. I have used the *Catholic Almanac* for all Catholic proportions.

33. See *United States News and World Report,* November 23, 1951.

34. Samuel Lubell, *The Future of American Politics,* Harper, 1952, p. 213. For analysis of class factors in voting see also *Annals,* March 1948, "Religion and the Class Structure" by Liston Pope. Senator Paul

Douglas expressed his views in an article in *Coronet,* March 1959, "A Catholic *Can* Become President." One of the best analyses is that of Lawrence H. Fuchs, "A Catholic as President?" in *America,* September 13, 1958. Three valuable articles, largely historical, by Helen Hill Miller, on "A Catholic for President?" were published by the *New Republic,* beginning November 18, 1957.

35. See *Information Service,* Federal Council of Churches, May 15, 1948. Will Herberg's *Protestant-Catholic-Jew* Doubleday, 1956, has valuable material and an excellent bibliography, but he glosses over the short-comings of Catholic policy. See also Herbert Schneider, *Religion in 20th Century America,* Harvard, 1952, and James Hastings Nichols, *Democracy and the Churches,* Westminster (Philadelphia), 1951.

36. United Feature Syndicate release, October 8, 1958.

37. WP, May 7, 1959, October 26, 1958, and June 24, 1956; also *Time,* May 18, 1959. The proportion favoring boycott of a Catholic candidate might be higher in a campaign, since the majority of Protestants voting in the 1959 Gallup poll did not know that Kennedy was a Catholic. In a Presidential campaign they could hardly escape such knowledge.

38. Samuel F. Stouffer, *Communism, Conformity and Civil Liberties,* Doubleday, 1955.

39. *Congressional Quarterly,* January 30, 1959.

40. *America,* April 4, 1959.

41. *Ibid.,* September 13, 1958.

42. Bouscaren and Ellis, *Canon Law,* p. 574. See also Chapter IV, Note 48, for statements by Pius XII and others; and Chapter III, Note 53, for official American Catholic pronouncements.

43. Discussed above, citing Canon 1374 and NYT, November 21, 1948.

44. This has been asserted repeatedly by Brock Chisholm, former director general of the World Health Organization. The Catholic pressure is especially strong against any contraceptive measures, even in Asia, since a former head of Italy's Catholic Action, Dr. Vittorino Veronese, has become head of UNESCO. See *Birth Control and Catholic Doctrine* by Alvah W. Sulloway, Beacon, 1959.

45. Issued as leaflet by P.O.A.U., 1633 Massachusetts Ave., N.W., Washington 16.

46. *America,* March 7 and 14, 1959.

47. *Commonweal,* March 6, 1959. This magazine reprinted many comments on the Kennedy statement from Catholic papers in its issue of March 20, 1959, including the *Ave Maria* statement used here, and ran a series of three columns on the subject by John Cogley, beginning in this issue.

48. Brooklyn *Tablet,* February 28, 1959. The *America* comment was in the issue of March 7, 1959.

49. *The Davenport Catholic Messenger,* April 9, 1959.

50. WP, March 22, 1959.

51. NYT, September 1, 1929. It is interesting to note that this extreme sample of Catholic narrowness was not published in the *New York World,* although the *World* had specialized in exposing religious bigotry for several years.

52. From a personal letter to me.
53. P. 139.
54. *America,* March 21, 1959.
55. Founded in 1954, with offices at 8 East 66th St., New York 21.
56. This fake oath has been exposed as fraudulent on many occasions. Published in the *Congressional Record,* February 15, 1913, p. 3216, it was offered not as true but as an election fraud by Eugene C. Bonniwell of the 7th Congressional District of Pennsylvania, defeated Democratic candidate. He argued that it had been circulated with the knowledge of his victorious Republican opponent, Thomas S. Butler. Butler promptly repudiated the oath as "spurious" and claimed no knowledge of its circulation.

Chapter VI

Pluralism and the Good Society

1. Tennessee may be taken as an example of Protestant violations. It has been estimated that seventy-five Tennessee high schools give credit for Bible classes. Indiana and Texas afford good illustrations of schools captured by Catholic religious orders while the nuns stay on the public payrolls. Jasper, Indiana, has a public and a captive school, both supported out of public revenue, only four blocks apart. The Catholic "public" school is carried in the *Catholic Directory* as a parochial school and in the state directory as a public school. An almost identical situation in Bremond, Texas, has finally produced a lawsuit, appealing to the McCollum decision, *McIntyre v. Hoblinski,* No. 113,261; 126th Judicial District, Travis County, Texas, 1959. Important earlier state cases exposing the sectarian struggles over public schools are *Harfst v. Hoegan,* 349 Mo. 808 (1942); *Zellers v. Huff,* 55 N.M. 501 (1951); *Wooley v. Spalding,* 293 S.W. 2d 563, Kentucky, 1956, and still being fought; and *Rawlings v. Butler,* 290 S.W. 2d 801, Kentucky, 1956. A Catholic summary of recent cases in this church-state field is in *Notre Dame Lawyer,* May 1958.
2. "Christians and Public Schools," Working Paper issued November 8, 1958, not to be cited as an official position of the National Council.
3. A Connecticut Catholic official, Richard Joyce Smith, of the State Board of Public Education, suggested in *America,* November 10, 1956, that states should disregard constitutional prohibitions altogether and go ahead with payments to Catholic schools if they felt like it. The Protestant leader Dr. John C. Bennett of Union Theological Seminary made a much more tentative suggestion in his *Christians and the State,* Scribner, 1958, p. 242, that there might be local experiments deviating from national policy, but there is no reason to believe that he supports outright general grants to Catholic schools. This cannot be said of another Protestant leader, F. Ernest Johnson, who gave away

the Protestant case against such grants in a Fund for the Republic pamphlet, "Religion and the Schools," in 1959.

4. The elements of the Dutch system were described by Father E. F. Schroeder in *America,* April 23, 1949, with the frank comment that "the results obtained in this country of a mixed population will probably seem almost incredible to Americans." I have personally observed the Dutch situation. The RNS dispatch was dated January 20, 1955.

Index